More Praise for
The Unexpected Spy

"Walder has been able to accomplish more than most people do in a lifetime. . . . [A] tale of a woman whose mission was to help make America great."

—USC Annenberg Media

"A well-written, engaging memoir, a serious and candid inside view of two enigmatic and significant institutions from a woman's perspective."

—*Booklist*

"A compelling and well-written memoir that takes the reader on a journey from the CIA's 'Farm' and its 'black sites' to the FBI's training academy."

—Peter Bergen, author of *Manhunt: The Ten-Year Search for bin Laden from 9/11 to Abbottabad*

"Incredible book."

—Heather McDonald, *Juicy Scoop*

"Tracy Walder is an exceptionally gifted individual."

—*The Jerusalem Post*

"Riveting."

—Hearst Connecticut Media Group

"[Walder's] extraordinary commitment and expertise helped shatter the CIA's glass ceiling."

—Fox News

"Absorbing, if often frustrating, given the macho, male-dominant culture prevalent within the Bureau. Readers of memoirs, current events, and US history are all sure to enjoy *The Unexpected Spy*."

—Shelf Awareness

"Lively."

—*The American Jewish World*

"Walder's candid story will connect with readers curious about counterterrorism work and seeking an inspirational account of a woman seeking to change the balance of power in not only a male-dominated field but the world."

—*Library Journal*

"An engaging and thoughtful story of service that will inspire generations of young women to come . . . A glimpse into the rewards and risks of actualizing a dream in a male-dominated space."

—Lauren Bean Buitta, founder of Girl Security

THE
UNEXPECTED SPY

FROM THE CIA TO THE FBI,
MY SECRET LIFE TAKING DOWN SOME OF
THE WORLD'S MOST NOTORIOUS TERRORISTS

TRACY WALDER

with JESSICA ANYA BLAU

ST. MARTIN'S
GRIFFIN
NEW YORK

Published in the United States by St. Martin's Griffin, an imprint of St. Martin's Publishing Group

www.stmartins.com

Designed by Meryl Sussman Levavi

The Library of Congress has cataloged the hardcover edition as follows:

Names: Walder, Tracy, author. | Blau, Jessica Anya, author.
Title: The unexpected spy : from the CIA to the FBI, my secret life taking down some of the world's most notorious terrorists / Tracy Walder ; with Jessica Anya Blau.
Description: First edition. | New York : St. Martin's Press, 2020.
Identifiers: LCCN 2019036365 | ISBN 9781250230980 (hardcover) | ISBN 9781250230997 (ebook)
Subjects: LCSH: Walder, Tracy. | Intelligence service—United States. | United States. Central Intelligence Agency—Officials and employees—Biography. | United States. Federal Bureau of Investigation—Officials and employees—Biography. | Terrorism—Prevention—United States. | War on Terrorism, 2001–2009.
Classification: LCC JK468.I6 W348 2020 | DDC 363.325/16092 [B]—dc23
LC record available at https://lccn.loc.gov/2019036365

ISBN 978-1-250-23971-6 (trade paperback)

Our books may be purchased in bulk for promotional, educational, or business use. Please contact your local bookseller or the Macmillan Corporate and Premium Sales Department at 1-800-221-7945, extension 5442, or by email at MacmillanSpecialMarkets@macmillan.com.

First St. Martin's Griffin Edition: 2021

10 9 8 7 6 5 4 3 2 1

For my daughter, who already is my hero.

CONTENTS

AUTHOR'S NOTE

The Unexpected Spy is my account of my years as a counterterrorism staff operations officer in the CIA and a special agent at the FBI. Because this book is based on memory, it is fallible. Still, in consulting diaries, the internet, and other books about the operations I was involved in, I have made every effort to be accurate and true in my recounting.

Though the FBI agents I worked with were not undercover, I have changed all their names in an effort to protect their privacy.

The CIA, however, succeeds through clandestine operations. I have every intention to uphold the integrity of the agency and maintain the safety of all the people who worked there, who continue to work there, and of all the people who worked with the CIA during my time there. In that spirit, I have changed the names of the people I encountered as well as details of their lives so that they cannot be identified. I tried to remain true to the essence of their personalities, so that you, the reader, can understand what it was like to work closely with them. I have also removed the names of most of the countries and cities I visited while at the CIA. Within some chapters of this book, the nature of my CIA work is deliberately vague. My intention was to convey the work I did the best I could without giving away any classified information. My loyalty is to the

CIA, the people of the United States, and the safety of the people of the United States. Each sentence in this book was written with that in mind.

The Unexpected Spy was submitted to the CIA's Publications Review Board. The board approved the release of this book as long as certain passages or sentences that they deemed threats to national security were redacted. I have left those redactions in place (appearing as black lines on the page) and have tried to maintain the continuity of the narrative around them.

In short, there is much omitted in my story, but there is still so much to tell. From the attacks of September 11 through the invasion of Iraq, there was a heightened sense of urgency in the work I was doing. It is my wish to convey that urgency, to convey that story, while never revealing anything that could put our nation, and the women and men working on our behalf, at risk.

—TRACY WALDER

THE
UNEXPECTED SPY

ONE

WAR ZONE

After 9/11

It was the smallest thing, but I needed it to feel like myself, to feel human. I wanted to believe that the world hadn't changed completely.

"Mom," I said into the phone, "can you make me a root touch-up appointment at Salon Renee George in Reston, Virginia?"

"What?" my mother said. "Where are you calling from?"

I was standing on the other side of the world, in the middle of blown-out rubble, in 109-degree heat, armed, and with a charcoal pashmina draped around my shoulders. My mother had no idea where I was. No one did, other than those who were with me and the five people I worked with at Langley. But I'd spotted an Inmarsat phone—as large as a brick—in the room where I'd left my bulletproof vest. I'd snatched the Inmarsat and run outside to make the call. The phone was pressed to my ear. Sweat ran down my cheek. My back was to one of the armed guards two feet away, smoking an unfiltered cigarette. Beyond the heavily guarded borders of where I stood, people were being blown apart by improvised explosive devices (IEDs), museums were being looted, and men were holing up together in packs, trying to figure out the best way to kill the greatest number of people in one fell swoop.

My life felt upside down, and I needed just one thing to set me upright again, one thing to create a sense of normalcy. Even if that normalcy only extended to the ends of my hair.

Johnny ████████████████ came looking for me. The crunching of his boots on the gravel was the loudest sound around. I turned and gave him the one-minute signal.

"Mom, I have to go . . . just try and make the appointment for next month, I'll be there the twelfth, thirteenth, and fourteenth, and then I'll be back here. I love you!"

Those last three words always felt more emotional, more poignant, when I said them while standing in a war zone.

That morning had been like any other. I had gone to the kitchen of the abandoned building we used for offices, dining, and a makeshift bar, which we had named ██████████, and ate French fries. Other than black coffee, bottled water, and the cookie dough PowerBars I'd brought from the States, this was my only sustenance. Most people in this facility were suffering from dysentery. So far, the fries-and-bars diet had kept me safe.

After breakfast, I had picked out a perfect orange from the fruit bin, and then gone down the hall to the safe where I got my Glock and holster out of a lockbox and put on a bulletproof vest. Then I had trotted down the old, sloping marble steps and out of the decrepit building, through the dust to the single-wide trailer that was my home.

My trailer, number 4, was a plain white box inside and out. The only personal item I had was my pink reading lamp. Many nights, I was so tired that I never even turned it on. But when I wasn't tired, reading was the best way to empty my mind and escape the intensity of the day.

The trailer on my left belonged to a doctor, who regularly visited ██████████████ and was on call for any of the government employees.

The trailer on my right belonged to a guy in human resources. Beyond him was the resident psychologist, one of the few other women at this location. Like the medical doctor, her charge was ███████████ as well as employees. It must have been a tough job, as everyone's traumas were interconnected. Obviously, it would be worse to be a ███████████ than the person who is ███████████████████████████. But no one should ever think that the experience ███████████████████████████ is emotionally easy. It didn't bring about feelings of joy.

The gravel and dirt area around our four trailers was unadorned. But surrounding many of the other trailers, especially those inhabited by the Navy SEALS, were pink flamingos, blow-up pools, and lounge chairs. An ironic attempt to duplicate American trailer-park life.

The government-issued white sheets on everyone's bed were changed weekly by local men who had been thoroughly vetted. The guards who worked the entry gate and the people who worked in the kitchen were also local men. Because I could never leave the facility without hiding in some way, my only acquaintance with the people of the country I was now inhabiting was through these workers. I had to trust them with my life, and, I suppose, they were trusting us with their lives as well. A polite reserve was in place, however, and so I never felt like I knew any of them.

In my trailer, I sifted through the three pashminas I'd brought and pulled up the darkest one. Pink has always been my favorite color. In college, and even at the CIA in Langley, I often wore pink. Here, wearing pink felt as frivolous as wearing a feather boa. My essential uniform was cargo pants, long-sleeved Gap t-shirts, and combat boots. I still put on mascara every day. And every time I was stateside, I made sure to get highlights in my hair or touch up my roots. No matter how far away I went in the world, I needed to hold on to the sorority girl in me—I needed to believe that she, I, could survive all this.

I had draped the pashmina across my shoulders, over the vest, and then headed out. There was no time to work out in the gym trailer, but I popped my head in to say hey to anyone who might be there. It was filled, as usual, with the Navy SEAL guys. When I worked out with them, we'd argue about what to watch on TV. They usually wanted Fox News, while I preferred BBC or Al Jazeera. Though we often didn't agree politically, I had absolute faith that these guys would keep me safe and would save my life if needed. Also, they were good company— always willing to run through the halls and play fetch with the bomb-sniffing dogs and me. Our work was demanding and intense. Our surroundings were as stark as the surface of the moon. Sanity required a little reckless joy, some make-believe, and the whimsy of those ridiculous pink flamingos staked into the crumbling ground like big, plastic bouquets.

"Hey!" a SEAL named Kyle called. "Bike's waiting for you." Kyle pointed at the empty bike beside him.

"I've got a ███████████," I said. "I'll see you tonight."

"Beer! ███████ Seven!" Kyle said.

Here's the interesting thing about these macho, badass Navy SEAL guys, something that most people have a hard time believing: not one of them ever acted in a way that was sexist, sexually suggestive, or dismissive. Maybe in living together and witnessing firsthand what I and the two or three other women who were in and out were doing, they knew better than anyone that though we had different tasks and skills, we were undeniably equals. And when your life depends on the intelligence and efficiency of the people around you, respect takes on a whole new meaning.

Johnny ███████████████████████ would go with me to all my "meetings." He was tall, bulky, and somewhat soft-looking. The opposite of the Navy SEAL guys. I don't know where he was from—we never discussed that—but he had the calm, gentle politeness of a man from the Midwest. When he smiled, it was half hidden behind his Scandinavian-blond beard. And when he wasn't doing ███████████, he wore glasses—thick, black frames with Coke-bottle lenses that made him look like the nerd from a Lifetime channel movie. His voice, like the rest of him, was unremarkable, not intimidating. This should be noted not because Johnny was so unlike anyone else in the CIA, but because part of Johnny's job was ██████████████ ████████████████████████████████████ ██████████████████████████████████. Johnny, with his soft belly, nerdy glasses, and shy smile, followed protocol. And when he did, it was like he was an entirely different man.

"Ready?" Johnny leaned against the beat-up orange SUV we'd take to the other facility. He was always walking around with the Velcro sides of his bulletproof vest open. It was hot out, and even I found it hard to close myself in with more heat and weight. Sometimes the doctor, the psychologist, or another ██████████ joined us. That day it was just Johnny and me for the ride.

"Yup. Dino or Astro already come by?" Dino and Astro were the bomb-sniffing dogs. No one got in a car before the hounds had okayed it.

Johnny nodded in the direction of Dino and his handler, Bill, who were walking toward us. Bill was in sunglasses, a t-shirt, and shorts. Dino, a blond lab, wore only the maroon USC collar my dad had given me for the dogs. We weren't allowed to pet Dino while he was working, so I waited until he had circled the car before I leaned down and kissed his cheeks while scratching behind his velvety ears. The dogs, like carousing with the Navy SEAL guys, created necessary lightness.

Since women weren't allowed to drive here, Johnny, in his prescription sunglasses and a baseball cap, always took the wheel. And because the locations of where we worked and lived were both secret, I had to hide in the cargo bin whenever I left one of these two places. A blond American woman, even one with aviator glasses and a pashmina over her head, drew too much attention and created too much risk that we'd be followed.

"Let's do this," I said. I flipped open the back and climbed in. Once I was curled onto my side, the pashmina draped over my head, the gun digging into my hip, Johnny threw down the back gate and got in the driver's seat. The ride was bumpy—at the time there was only one paved road in this country—and the car was creaky. It was loud with the air-conditioning cranked up to the highest level, but sometimes we talked back and forth, shouting really. Usually, Johnny put a CD into the player and we listened to music: AC/DC or Guns N' Roses. Loud, chaotic stuff that pumped Johnny up—turning him from a pudgy nerd to an imposing force. It was the same kind of music to which the terrorists were subjected on a continuous basis. Electric guitars. Screaming voices. Mind-jangling noise.

I tuned out the music as best I could and ran through my notes in my head. I was going over what facts I knew for sure, ideas I was piecing together, and how I might get the single most important piece of information I hoped to obtain from the man I was about to meet.

I pulled down the edge of my pashmina and peeked out at the sky for a minute. It was a beautiful blue that day—as shiny and solid as a polished gemstone. I thought how strange it was that one sky could resemble any other sky in the world depending on the day, even when what was happening on the ground below was so drastically different. These trips in the cargo bin weren't my first. There was my twenty-first birthday, when I was still in college at the University of Southern California and living in the Delta Gamma house. A few sorority sisters had taken me out early in the evening for sushi and sake. I was the one who had driven us there, and when the doses of sake surpassed the doses of sushi, I handed my keys to a friend named Melissa.

"I gotta lie down," I had slurred as I staggered across the parking lot.

Melissa clicked unlock on my Acura, and I opened the hatch. A couple of friends tried to lead me into the backseat but I shook them off, repeating my need to lie down. Then I climbed into the cargo bin of the Acura. Melissa said happy birthday before she shut the hatch.

That entire ride, I had looked up out the slanted window and watched the sky. It was October 21, the sun had only just set, and there was an eerie orange-and-black gloaming. The sharply silhouetted treetops and telephone poles flickered by like an old-fashioned movie. I pulled my phone from my pocket and called my parents' house. My dad answered the landline.

"Dad, it's just so beautiful," I had said.

"What's so beautiful? Have you been drinking?" He laughed. I was legal, he knew I had planned to drink that day.

"The sky. It's the most beautiful sky I've ever seen."

"Where are you?"

"The trunk of the car." I spaced out for a couple minutes as I forgot I was on the phone. When I tuned in again, I realized my dad sounded concerned.

"*My* trunk," I said. "Melissa's driving and I had to lie down and then I looked up and there it was. We have the most beautiful sky in the world."

"It's the same sky all over the world," my dad said. "Just like it's the same world beneath our feet."

"Hmm." I may have hung up without saying goodbye.

□ □ □

Now here I was in the Middle East, entirely sober. That universal sky was still beautiful. But the world beneath the car couldn't have seemed any more different from Los Angeles, or Virginia, than it did just then.

Johnny shut off the music as we rolled to a stop at the gate. His window went down and he spoke with the armed guards. I couldn't quite hear what they were saying, but it had the cadence of friendly chitchat. Once we'd pulled past the gates, I sat up and draped the pashmina across my shoulders again. Johnny parked the car, got out, and flipped open the back. He reached his hand toward me and helped me out.

Other than a few armed guards standing by, this place was so desolate it looked recently abandoned. The setting was bleak, postapocalyptic, with crumbling concrete, piles of rubble, and not a living green plant in sight. The same hundred-plus degree heat beat down at the ████ as here, but this felt much hotter, like everything had been baked into a stunned silence. Everywhere you looked, all you saw was white, brown, or beige—different hues of sandpaper. And every surface was as dry as chalk. It sounded like shells crunching beneath our feet as we walked to the makeshift barracks—a former industrial building—where I would meet the terrorist I was to interview.

Johnny and I said hello to the guards, then went to a closet-sized room in the building where we tossed our bulletproof vests on the gritty cement floor. That was when I spotted the Inmarsat phone on a shelf. I picked it up and ran outside while shouting back to Johnny, "I gotta call my mom!"

□ □ □

Once I hung up the phone my focus was streamlined into a steel tunnel of thought that ran directly from me to Q, the man who held the answers to many of my questions. Others had spoken with him, but no one had yet obtained the key piece of information we were after. I was twenty-four, and can't tell you now why I thought I was capable of something as complicated as gaining the trust of a terrorist to the point where he'd open up and give me what others had failed to get. Maybe I was naïve. Maybe I was just determined. Or maybe I was driven by ever-present guilt.

I was at the CIA headquarters in Langley, Virginia, on September 11, 2001. As an operative in counterterrorism, I was on the team of people who were supposed to save America from men like Osama bin Laden, Khalid Sheikh Mohammed, and Mohammed Atef. I'd known their names when most others didn't. In fact, as a news junkie since high school, I'd been thinking about bin Laden, in particular, for years. So I'd expected more from myself. While America was focused on the disbanded Soviet Union and the drug wars in Central America, I was studying images of deserts in the Middle East. I watched and marked where terrorism was being grown and cultivated, new branches continuously sprouting like a well-pruned tree. I'd memorized the rocky, dry landscape. I'd memorized the faces of men who were hiding in reinforced, serpentine caves or sparsely furnished safe houses. I knew where they were. And I had thought I knew where they were going.

I should have seen it coming.

But I didn't.

And then came the invasion of Iraq. It was a war that hinged on the proof that Saddam Hussein was hoarding weapons of mass destruction. I belonged to the team of people assigned to find that proof. I didn't find it. None of us did. But the war began anyway. After that, all that was bad turned into all that was unthinkably awful. I knew I couldn't halt the downhill plummet. But, at the very least, I could stop the terrorists and terror plots that scrambled out of that war like cockroaches from a razed building.

I was young, fearless, and optimistic. My career in the CIA had started directly out of the University of Southern California when I was twenty-one. More specifically, I'd been recruited straight from the Delta Gamma sorority, where my long blond hair matched that of 90 percent of my sorority sisters'.

The first year, being an officer in the CIA was thrilling. The poli sci wonk in me thrived during the day, while the sorority girl inside me still had fun nights out with girlfriends or dating. But by the time I watched the sun come up on September 12, everything had changed. I felt the grief of a nation and the responsibility to make things better. And when America invaded Iraq, that responsibility only grew.

At times it felt like I was living in a hamster ball. I was running and running, rolling through countries where all I could see through my plastic shield was the terrorists I had to stop. Day by day, most of the real world, my stateside life, was slipping away from me as I rolled farther off into the distance.

Q would be the first terrorist I'd meet face to face. As Johnny and I walked to his living quarters, it didn't even occur to me to be nervous or scared. I had so much information in my head, and I had Johnny by my side. Also, according to the notes I'd read, Q—who had entered this place unwilling to even give his name—was now agreeable and talkative. Surely it hadn't been easy for him to turn from truculent to cooperative.

Let me say this now: I absolutely do not support torture as a means of information gathering. Also, after what I experienced, I do not believe that torture works. However, I do not agree with those who have vilified the CIA and its use of torture during this time when America was responding to the largest and most deadly terrorist attack on our soil while a "second wave" of terror was in the works. Imagine the pressure of being responsible for the lives of more than 300 million people. Imagine what you might do if you had high-ranking al-Qaeda members in your hands. In the context of that moment in history, and with the additional information that bin Laden had most certainly met with Pakistani nuclear scientists and was acquiring plans for the development of nuclear weapons, getting the high-level detainees to talk was a life-or-death task. Remember, the people who were detained in war zones were men who were not only willing to die but who wanted to die so that they would be crowned martyrs for their cause. Enhanced Interrogation Technique (IET, or torture) was what the CIA, with full disclosure to and approval from Congress and the Bush administration, believed would be the most effective way to get information from known terrorists. And it wasn't a first resort; it was a last resort. Of the hundred men held in war zones over eight years, only 30 were subjected to EIT. The point wasn't to hurt them. The point was to save lives. And not just American lives. Human lives. I, and just about everyone else I knew in the CIA, wanted the whole world to be safe. No exceptions.

□ □ □

I entered Q's dark room just inside the doorway. As had been trained in me since childhood, I smiled. This is how I've always greeted people, and it didn't occur to me to stop that smile for a terrorist.

"Can I offer you tea?" Q asked. Like my smile, his question was a formality ingrained in him. Criminal or not, he was doing the polite thing in offering me tea, even though he had no way to procure or serve tea. Though it seemed like he'd lived decades already after all he'd done, Q wasn't much older than I. Maybe this was our first point of connection: each of us still carried the culture of our childhood into the room.

I politely declined the tea and then held up the orange I had brought for him from the cafeteria.

"Let's go in the other room where it's easier to talk." It sounded so genteel and formal, like we were in the Four Seasons in D.C. and were going to move over to a meeting room with monochromatic furniture and a modern, square chandelier. In actuality, we were in the former garage of a half-destroyed building and were moving to what had probably been a large storage closet.

Q and I sat at a small metal table across from each other; there was a light above us, but it was far from a chandelier. I handed him the orange and he nodded thanks. I asked the most important question I had come to ask, and he put his hand to his newly grown beard and ran his fingers like he was playing a keyboard. He may have been compliant, he may have been polite, but he wasn't yet ready to give me the central piece of information I needed.

That simple gesture reminded me that I was everything Q hated; I belonged to every group he wished to kill. I could feel my childhood self vibrating inside me, the girl who occasionally went to synagogue.

My family belonged to Temple Beth Am, where you had to be buzzed in, and then walk past several uniformed and armed security guards. Orange County, California, felt so safe, so sunny, I couldn't imagine who would want to come to temple to do something mean or dangerous to Tracy Schandler, her parents, her brother, her grandpa Jack, or her grandmother Geraldine. I'd known of bank robberies, and carjackings, and road rage on the knotted freeways of Los Angeles. But Beth Am seemed outside all that. Separate from it. It appeared to be as calm and safe as our house. But now here I was, not that many years later, and the reason for Tobias, the Beth Am guard who reached out and bumped fists with me every time I passed him, was sitting across from me peeling a fat orange I had picked out especially for him.

Still, I remained unafraid. Yes, I was a Jewish American woman, but I was free and currently wielding more power than Q. And though I was slight compared to his grizzled form, I also had the force of Johnny behind me.

I flashed a smile as Q jammed his shoehorn-sized thumbs into the center of the peeled orange and split it open, releasing a thin spray of juice onto the table. Q offered half the orange to me.

"It's all for you." I relaxed into a moment of silence as I prepared for my next move. I would do this right. I knew how to proceed. I needed to create trust; a relationship. I had to find a point of connection between this man, who absolutely wanted me dead, and myself, who absolutely wanted him locked away for life.

"Do you miss your mother?" I asked. "Because I really miss mine."

□ □ □

Over the next couple weeks I spent several hours a day with Q at that table, Johnny looming somewhere behind me. At each meeting, I brought Q a fresh, plump piece of fruit, selected especially for him. He wasn't starved or hungry, but he loved fruit. And, if only for a few minutes, it gave him something to do with his hands and created a point of focus other than the young, blond American sitting across from him.

Sometimes it felt like my brain was a sparking electrical panel as I tried to piece together the stories Q told me of loving parents and a swooping rush of religious devotion, alongside the brutal, violent killings of Westerners and Muslims whose poor luck had put them in the places where he had rained terror. It was like a book I'd had as a kid. Other than the cover, the book was cut in half so you could match different top pages with bottom pages: a giraffe head with a hippopotamus body, an ape head with a curled-kitten body. Q was two mismatched pages: a cunning, hateful murderer and a man who loved his people, his country, and his religion.

What I learned about Q was this: he had been poor, uneducated, and displaced by war in his country. Al-Qaeda provided him food, a home, medical care, education, a community that in its best form represented what he'd had as a young child, and a purpose. It was easy to see the appeal of the al-Qaeda "family." But I didn't get the appeal of the jihadi lifestyle. I asked Q, more than once, to try to help me understand why—beyond the religious rhetoric—he had chosen to live and die as a jihadi. Q explained: society had maligned him, al-Qaeda had lifted him up. He owed them everything. Including his life.

It may have been my open, youthful curiosity. It may have been my lack of fear when faced with his answers. And maybe it was just luck. But, eventually, after a cornucopia of fruit and hours of seemingly casual conversation, Q gave me exactly the information I had come for.

And another pod of terrorists were stopped before they could kill.

TWO

THE SORORITY LIFE

Los Angeles, California
1978–2000

I was my parents' first child, born two years after America's bi-centennial. It was a time when the country felt confident, secure. Both world wars, the Korean War, and the Vietnam War were behind us, and everything was forward looking. Kids no longer practiced bomb scare positions, ducking under their desks with their hands over their heads as if that could save them from a nuclear mushroom cloud. The Cuban Missile Crisis seemed far behind us, and the craze to build a bomb shelter in one's back-yard, as President Kennedy had suggested in 1961, had mostly passed. Every home had a television (usually color), with ABC, CBS, NBC, and PBS. In the Los Angeles area, where I lived, there was Metromedia Television, Channel 11. You couldn't watch a show on Channel 11 without being interrupted by a used-car ad with Cal Worthington and "his dog, Spot," who was either a tiger or a monkey, depending on the year. Cal and Spot ran along his enormous lot lined with hundreds of low, flat cars—like boats—each with a giant silver antenna. A rumbling Johnny Cash–like voice sang "Go see Cal, go see Cal, go see Cal . . ." These were the last years of cars and California housing being affordable to anyone with a salaried job.

My father was a psychology professor at Chapman University. My mother, who eventually worked at a bank, was a stay-at-home mom then. My parents started our family in a tidy ranch home with a two-car garage and an actual white picket fence in a sunny mid-century development in Van Nuys. White sidewalks framed each street, fruit trees grew in the yards, and every few houses there was a basketball hoop hanging over a garage door. (When I was six or seven, we moved down the coast to Orange County. The yards were a little wider, our house was a little bigger. It was the slightly grander version of what we'd just left.)

In Van Nuys, everything seemed perfect, in place, moving along as my parents expected and hoped. Then, around the time I was five months old, my mother realized I wasn't doing the things the neighbors' babies were doing. I didn't sit up. I didn't try to crawl. I didn't even grab at things. I smiled and cooed, but my head and body flopped around like a doll's. Or, as my mother once said, a "limp fish."

After numerous appointments, my flaccid little body being carted from one specialist to the next, I was diagnosed with hypotonia, otherwise known as floppy baby syndrome. There was no internet then and not even much to be found in books at the library. All the information my parents got was strictly from the specialists they visited. And the information they got was, to my mother especially, terrifying.

I might be brain damaged.

I'd never walk.

I'd need to be in a special school.

College was out of the question.

Don't expect her to be a ballerina, one particular doctor muttered. As if being a ballerina was the single great hope for a little girl with a big, then-toothless smile. There was no physical therapy, no therapy at all for kids with hypotonia. Parents were just supposed to accept it, throw the kid over their shoulder like a bag of dog kibble, and expect nothing.

Not my mother. On the floor of the den, she'd put her hands

behind each of my feet so I'd have something against which to gain purchase. And from there I crawled. Then she held my hands, stood me up, and worked on my putting one foot in front of the other.

At age two, later than most kids, I walked across the pale tan wall-to-wall carpet in the den. Once I'd started walking, I couldn't stop. I didn't know I wasn't supposed to be able to do the things I did. Something inside me seemed determined and intent. I was like an engine that wouldn't shut down.

At two and a half, I was in a dance class showing just as much talent as the other wobbling, diaper-wearing kids. In elementary school and junior high I continued with dance classes: modern, jazz, and ballet. Through all four years of high school I was on the elite dance team, practicing three hours a day and then competing every Saturday in routines that incorporated ballet, jazz, and modern. I loved the training and the intense work it involved. And I tolerated the showy public performances as something to get through simply so I could stay on the team and return to practice the next day.

In college, at the University of Southern California, I took dance classes on campus and at private studios in Los Angeles. I studied everything but tap and clogging.

But that doctor was right. I wasn't going to be a ballerina. I had other things on my mind. Far more pressing things than whether or not I could nail a triple pirouette.

□ □ □

I joined Delta Gamma my freshman year at USC. If you haven't been in a sorority then let me explain a little. Greek life is both what you imagine and what you likely haven't imagined. Yes, there are parties, and people are expected to wear the right clothes and have hair that looks a certain way. It's a bit like a country club with members holding fast to an idea of themselves as "one of these people," but with a lot of alcohol and maybe some marijuana thrown in. I did drink at times, but I have never tried pot, or any other drug, to this day. A minority, an outlier, I know.

Many people I've spoken with abhor the Greek system, so I feel compelled to point out its values. You have to maintain a good GPA to stay in, so it keeps students on track (and women in sororities have a higher average GPA than the non-Greek population). At a large school like USC, where it's easy to feel isolated and cut off, a sorority (maybe not a fraternity, I can't speak for them) can provide a community. A place where you feel a sense of belonging. Where you feel safe. For an introvert like me, someone who is shy and has never been socially comfortable, the sorority gave me a place to hide. Rather than using it as a calling card, or defining myself as a Delta Gamma, I used it as camouflage. The sorority was a place where I wouldn't stand out as . . . as anything: the blond with shiny white teeth, the girl on the purple bike, the nut reading *Newsweek* instead of *People*. In the DG house I felt relatively unnoticed. And for me, to be unnoticed was a gift.

From third grade to ninth grade I was noticed every school day in exactly the wrong way. I was bullied. Always by girls. The fact that by age eleven I had grown to my full height of five feet seven inches didn't help. Before the braces went on, there was a gap in my teeth that kids found comical. The girls called me fat because I didn't have that gymnast's thinness that was popular at the time. And I suffered years of severe acne that even a tube of Retin-A couldn't wipe out. The most common nickname they used for me was *Zidiot*, zit + idiot. According to the in crowd, everything about me was "wrong."

The girls on the high school dance team were nice enough, though I was never an insider. After so much bullying, it was hard to trust people outside my family. Also, the world in my head never quite matched my surroundings. While dance-team girls fretted about boys, I fretted about Nelson Mandela and if he could be sworn in as South Africa's first black president without being assassinated. When kids in class talked about *Pulp Fiction*, the radical new movie out, my mind drifted to the Oklahoma City bomber and the fact that many American government buildings were vulnerable and unfortified.

I wish the person I am now could go back in time and talk to that girl who was taunted daily just for walking down a hallway. Though maybe my advice would be to do exactly what I did: ignore them, shore up, focus on what you want to do, who you want to be and not what other people want from you. Even in twelfth grade, when I was inexplicably chosen to be one of four Homecoming princesses, I didn't suddenly feel like I was an "insider" in my high school. It was terrifying to sit on a float, wave to a crowd as if I were Elizabeth II, and wear a tiara. I was awkward. And unsettled. Engaged in a performance I didn't want to take part in, though I was honestly grateful that I was being appreciated for something . . . kindness, maybe? My skills on the dance team?

My childhood was a continuous rerun of how my "floppy baby" syndrome played out. Once again, other people's expectations had nothing to do with who I really was. Or what I was capable of.

Until Delta Gamma. It was in a sorority that I finally blended into the crowd without feeling like a complete outsider. It was also there that I came out, in a sense, as my true self.

I ran for the position of vice president of social standards in Delta Gamma. And I won. It was a position that let me take action rather than bitch about things I didn't like within the sorority. I was a history major, a poli sci nerd, who wanted systems to run smoothly and people to do and act as their highest selves. This all seemed to sit well with the Delta Gamma sisters. They accepted me exactly as I was.

The morning in 1997 when Peter Bergen spoke with CNN about his interview with Osama bin Laden, I was working out alone on the elliptical in the gym/TV room of the Delta Gamma house. I was riveted. Bergen laid it all out quite simply. Bin Laden, a millionaire, had gone to fight alongside U.S. troops in Afghanistan after the Soviet Union had invaded that country. There, he secured his position as a leader of Islamic extremists who rejected the U.S. presence in all Arab countries. The interview was filmed in an undisclosed location in Afghanistan—one of the few countries that openly welcomed bin Laden within its borders. Bin Laden looked calm, serene almost, as he explained in his dulcet, feathery voice the jihad he had declared against American Jews, the United States, and any people of the United States who were in Arab countries. This was likely the first time the American public had heard the word jihad. As the interview came to an end, Bergen asked bin Laden, "What are your future plans?"

Bin Laden, with a sly but gentle smile on his face, answered, "You'll see them and hear about them in the media. God willing."

I was chilled. And outraged. Bin Laden's face, that smug little grin, and every word he said felt like a fire in my head. I wanted to take action, but I wasn't sure where, or how. I no more wanted to accept a jihad against the people of the United States, and particularly against the men and women of the armed forces who were then in the Middle East, than I'd accept excessive partying in the Delta Gamma house.

As much as I wanted to, I couldn't run for vice president of social standards of the world. But I also couldn't stand by and let this happen. I decided to read and follow the news as closely as possible so that I could learn everything about current affairs and foreign affairs. My plan was this: I'd become a teacher. I'd educate young people so that they could understand what was happening in the world and their, our, place in it all. And, hopefully, together we could effect change through policy, politics . . . op-ed pieces in the *New York Times*!

I felt secure in this plan. Certain of my path.

Then, in the spring of my junior year, I took a bike ride across campus. And everything changed.

It was another of those ideal Southern California days: sun so bright it looked like the sky had been bleached clean. I left the sorority house on my purple Huffy bike wearing a pink t-shirt, jeans, and flip-flops and rode through the roar of students. That day, like many, I was struck by that TV-goodlookingness of the students at USC. It was as if they were all extras on a Hollywood film set.

At Trousdale Parkway, the main pedestrian thoroughfare on campus, tables were set up in two long rows for a career fair. My roommate, Melissa, and I had typed up our resumes the night before. I had five copies in my backpack and just hoped that some private school, where I wouldn't yet need a higher degree, would be there, recruiting. Many tables had bowls of candy displayed, as if the recruiters were witches luring in greedy children. Here and there were colorful, bobbing balloons tied to chairs. Mobs of students crowded around the dot-com tables—most people worshiped Steve Jobs, Steve Wozniak, and Bill Gates. Every boy I knew wanted to be one of them. On foot now, I walked my bike through the shoulder-to-shoulder throngs, glancing left and right, looking for someone who needed a teacher.

And then I saw a quiet table with a cardboard placard that said Central Intelligence Agency. The only person there was the recruiter, a middle-aged Asian man in a polo shirt and khakis. He looked so lonely, I almost felt bad for him.

"Hi." I smiled, as I usually did on instinct, and then I awkwardly reached into my backpack and handed him my resume.

"Hi. I'm Mike Smith." He glanced down at the single sheet of paper, and then said, "And you're Tracy Schandler."

"That's me." I shrugged.

Mike Smith perused my resume. Then he peered into my face and said, "So, Tracy Schandler, do you want to be in the CIA?"

"Yes," I said. "Yes, I do." Until the moment he asked, it never occurred to me that I could be in the CIA. I was a floppy baby! A girl who had been teased relentlessly about the gap in her teeth, the width of her hips, and the flush of acne across her cheeks. I'd never touched a gun or even thought about shooting one. But the simple fact that Mike Smith held my resume in his hand as if I were a viable candidate made me see that my internal self—someone whose favorite class was on the history of Islam; someone who had memorized the map of the Middle East as a way of trying to understand the relationships between countries, religions, and tribes; someone who would rather work with Peter Bergen than Bill Gates—might one day be my external self. I'd be able to effect change and to have an impact on terrorism, a worldwide threat I thought about every single day.

Better yet, I'd be undercover. Invisible. Even more than I was in the Delta Gamma house.

□ □ □

Each pair of roommates in the sorority house picked a coordinated color scheme for their room. There was a lot of sorbet yellow, powder blue, bone white, lime green, and every shade of pink. If it hadn't been for Melissa, I would have picked pink for our room, too. In defiance of our forest green and maroon decorating agreement, I'd brought in a pink leather beanbag chair from home. It was comfortable, and I preferred to sit there when I studied rather than on the stiff plastic chair at the desk.

Two weeks after the career fair, I was nestled in that beanbag when the phone rang. This was the time of landlines, and each room in the sorority house had its own phone and phone number. Melissa, who was studying at the desk beside me, picked up. I kept on with my reading, a yellow highlighter pen in my hand.

"Traaaaacy, it's the CIA—" Melissa had a teasing smile as she handed me the phone, adding, "yeah, right!" She figured it was one of the frat boys playing a game. I hadn't told her, or anyone else, that I'd left my resume with the CIA. Already, even the act of applying for a job there was clandestine.

I snatched the receiver from Melissa and pressed the phone to my ear.

"Hello?" I shifted away from Melissa, who leaned her head in toward me to find out who was really on the phone. The beanbag chair let out a crunching Styrofoam sound, almost drowning out the voice of Mike Smith on the line.

My heart thumped like a rabbit kicking in my chest. Melissa inched closer, but I didn't want to move in the noisy chair. "Hi, Mr. Smith!" I smiled even though he couldn't see me.

"We like your resume, and we want to interview you for a position."

I got up from the chair as quietly as I could, leaned over the desk where Melissa sat, and wrote down the letters: C. I. A. Mr. Smith said he was mailing me a letter. The information for the first step in the interview process would be detailed in that letter.

When I hung up the phone, I was still smiling.

"I thought you wanted to be a history teacher." Melissa tilted her head and smiled to let me know she still believed it was a frat boy on the other end of the phone.

"I did," I said. And then I thought, *but making history would be way better than teaching it.*

□ □ □

I've never had good luck with cars. My first car, an ancient Oldsmobile—like something out of *Starsky and Hutch*—caught on fire when I drove it to the Homecoming game the year I was a reluctant Homecoming princess. I always thought the fire was karma for my disinterest in being a princess when so many other girls really, really wanted the position. My next car, a used Honda Accord, was stolen over winter break my freshman year in college, when I was working at a sporting-goods store. Three girls in a gang stole it. Before they could get too far, they sailed it into the air—like Chitty Chitty Bang Bang—straight off an overpass. I always wondered if they were nervous, distracted, or just driving too fast. They ended up in the hospital, and the car ended up in the junkyard; it'd been totaled from the hard, nose-first landing. My next car was a hatchback Acura that had been purchased with the insurance money from the Accord. I drove that Acura to my first CIA interview, which took place the summer before my senior year, while I was living in my parents' home in Orange County.

I wore a black suit with a pink blouse and toe-pinching black pumps. It was the only suit I owned so I was careful with it, wiping dirt from the driver's seat before I sat down. As soon as I hit the freeway, however, I was overcome with nausea. This wasn't nerves; I rarely got nervous or scared. And it wasn't a hangover—I'd never drunk enough to throw up. It was just a bug. Or food poisoning. Whatever it was, it planned to shoot out of me soon. I careened off the freeway, cranked up the parking brake, opened the door, and vomited on the road. Then I leaned back in the seat and waited a few minutes before round two came up. Once that was done, I drove to the hotel near the Los Angeles airport where the interview was being held.

It cost ten dollars for the garage, a lot of money for me at the time. There was a spot alongside the curb across the street, so I parked there, then staggered into the lobby and followed the signs to the conference room.

Around 40 applicants, the women in some version of the suit I wore, the men in jackets and ties, were told to sit at a very long Formica table. In turn, each person gave his or her name and said what school they went to. I could barely hear what was being said as my focus was on my stomach, on not throwing up.

After the introductions, we waited at the table until we were sent, individually, to one of the hotel's suites. My first thought when I walked in the suite was that the man interviewing me had no taste in glasses. He wore big lenses the shape of television sets; the kind of spectacles associated with kidnappers or lone wolf deviants hiding out in their mothers' basements. My second thought was that I needed to find a place to vomit should the urge arise. I sat in the chair in front of the desk where Mr. Glasses sat, then reached out and pulled the black, plastic trash can toward myself.

"I'm sorry," I said. "I need this nearby because I think I have the flu."

"Oh. Well. Okay." Mr. Glasses scooted his chair back another ten inches, creating a larger air barrier between us. In front of him was a paper I'd written for my modern Chinese history class, in which I explained why I believed communism worked in China. In the weeks before the interview, I had been asked to send in a writing sample that showed both my skills as a writer and my knowledge of world affairs. Instead of writing something new, I had sent in that paper.

"So, you're a communist," Mr. Glasses said.

"I'm a staunch capitalist." I eyed the trash can and pulled it a little closer.

"But you said you supported communism in China." He took his pointer finger and pushed the giant glasses further up the bridge of his nose.

"I don't support all of the government's actions in China. I do think, however, that in the world's most populous country, communism manages the needs of a great many people in a way that capitalism just can't. I mean, any system that feeds 1.25 billion people is working on some level, don't you think?"

He didn't answer, and so I continued, "If you were to remove that system, you might end up with something like the famine of the 1960s. That thing wiped out a whole chunk of the Chinese population." The word *chunk* caught in my throat. I glanced toward the trash can and willed myself not to vomit.

Mr. Glasses slid his specs up again and paused. Then he leaned back in his chair and started throwing questions at me like darts—all of them regarding China and communism. I stuck to my beliefs and answered the best I could, but it was hard to think straight as I simultaneously focused on holding in the churning soup in my gut.

When I was finally released, I hurried out of the hotel without even saying goodbye to the other interviewees who were gathered in the lobby exchanging phone numbers. I rushed across the street and then stood on the sidewalk looking at the open curb.

I'd been towed.

□ □ □

Later that summer, I received another call from Mike Smith. In spite of my illness and ill-perceived communist tendencies, I'd made a good impression on Mr. Glasses. Mike Smith said I'd be moving on to the next step: a polygraph test, a physical, and a psychological examination. All these tests were administered in Virginia, not far from the CIA headquarters in Langley.

I asked my mother to come with me to Virginia. I was only twenty years old, still had a year left of college, and hadn't yet traveled without my parents. For the duration of the flight, my mother fretted over how we'd locate the rental car agency and, if we actually found it, how we'd manage our way from D.C. to Virginia. I was an excellent map reader, I reminded her, and airports were loaded with people who could direct us to the rental agency. She also worried about the fact that I had a fake ID, which she had in fact paid for as a Hanukkah gift my first year in Delta Gamma. Though I wasn't a big drinker, carrying a working ID was standard operating procedure in every sorority house.

Before we landed at Dulles Airport, my mother held out her delicate hand with her perfectly manicured red nails and said,

"I think you should give me the fake ID." The ownership of this ID was the only thing that marred my perfect record. Once I'd handed it over, the vice president of social standards at Delta Gamma was clean.

The interviewees were housed in two different chain motels. A CIA bus picked us up early the first morning, stopping at one hotel and then the next. We were driven to an unmarked low-rise building that was as nondescript as the parking lot and the thin trees that surrounded it. I couldn't help but wonder if the people eating in the nearby McDonald's realized there were spies all around.

On day one we took a long "logic" test that felt more like a personal questionnaire. It was impossible to figure out what the right answer to any question might be, impossible to know exactly what kind of person they were looking for. I decided not to second-guess, or guess at all, and just to respond to the questions honestly. After the tests were turned in, there was much chatter among the applicants about what people had and hadn't revealed.

I stood in a circle of five people, everyone nervously divulging their answers.

"Did you say you preferred a bath or shower?" a girl asked me. She had intense blue eyes and blinked continuously as she spoke.

"Shower," I said. "I hate baths."

"I think that was wrong!" she said.

"How is it wrong that I hate baths?" I asked.

"I hate baths, too," a guy said. "But I said I preferred them anyway."

"Baths is definitely the right answer!" the woman said. "They want to know if you're mellow, like, relaxed, right?"

"Totally," the guy said.

No one discussed the details of the medical exam. We each had to pee in a cup, and blood was drawn. We were weighed, measured, listened to with stethoscopes. Nothing we all hadn't done before.

Day two was much more intense. It was the day of my first "lifestyle" polygraph test.

The man administering the test seemed old to me, though he was likely only in his forties. He wore a white button-down and khakis. His hands were big and gnarled, and the lines in his face were so deeply etched he looked like he'd been carved from a giant block of wood. His lips never parted for a smile.

We were in a small, white room with a table, a computer, and a one-way mirror. Without speaking to me, the wooden man hooked me up to wires on my fingertips, heart, and abdomen. The blood pressure cuff he tried to put on me was too big for my arm, so he left the room and returned with a child's cuff, which worked.

Like I had in the written test, I answered honestly. These questions were less abstract. I was asked if I'd done illegal drugs, if I drank alcohol, if my friends thought I was an honest person, and if I thought I was an honest person. There were questions about my sex life as well, but my experiences were so limited (the shy girl who stays home worrying about bin Laden is not often pursued) that my first couple of answers precluded follow-up questions.

After three hours of divulging what appeared to be a milky clean past, I was told that I hadn't passed. Nor had I failed. The results of my polygraph, according to the wooden man, were inconclusive. I was to come back the next day and take the test once more.

That night, I was so worried about the polygraph that I couldn't sleep. My mother, who felt my feelings and then magnified them in the funhouse mirror inside herself, also couldn't sleep. When I tossed and turned in my motel bed, she tossed and turned twice in hers. For half the night, I watched the crack in the curtains that frequently lit up like an alien presence from the headlights of passing cars. Was there a truth about myself that I didn't know? Had I thought I was telling the truth but was actually lying about something that only my subconscious understood? Once I'd imagined myself as a spy, I didn't want to be anything else. I was getting closer and closer to this dream, but everything would end soon if I couldn't prove I wasn't lying.

"I can't think of anything I'm hiding," I whispered around four in the morning. I had spent the evening mentally shuffling through each year of my life. I revisited everything from my first kiss at age sixteen in the family room of Alison B.'s house to the time I watched my friend Kelley smoke a cigarette. I hadn't even tried the cigarette. I had just watched.

"I can't think of anything either," my mother whispered back. There was little in my life I hadn't told her.

The next morning, the wooden man and I were stationed in the same room. He hooked me up to the wires and blood pressure cuff. Then he sat on a chair in front of me, his forearms resting on his thighs, and he said, "Tracy, what aren't you telling us? What are you hiding?"

"I don't know . . . I've searched my memory."

"There's something, though," he said. "There's something you're hiding. Your test wouldn't be so inconclusive if you weren't hiding anything."

"I can't think of anything . . ." There was the fake ID I had given to my mother on the plane, but that didn't seem worth mentioning. This was, after all, an organization that operated under fake IDs.

"Are you sure you haven't done any drugs?" he asked. "It's okay if you have. Most people have tried something at least once in college."

"I've never been interested," I said.

"You weren't even curious about pot?"

"Nope." In truth, I had been mildly curious after watching a few girls in the sorority laugh to the point of crying after smoking pot. But I was afraid of the "munchies," which every-one claimed followed. After so many bullying years when I had been called fat, pillaging a can of Pringles or a bag of Fritos was something I actively avoided. And, at twenty, I was still im-mersed in the culture and tyranny of thinness that particularly dominated places like sororities, if not all of Southern California, at the time. Still, I loved to eat candy and always had something with me in my purse. That morning, after having skipped the free pastries at the motel, I was hungry. With the wires attached to my body, I reached into my black tote bag and pulled out a box of Hot Tamales, my favorite candy.

"Hot Tamales?" I held the box out toward the wooden man. He shook his head no, and then watched as I poured some out in my hand and ate them.

"And no strange sexual encounters?"

"God, no!" I palmed another handful of Hot Tamales. "Un-less you count that really bad kiss from Tommy Greenspan in eleventh grade. His tongue went up my nostril." I had forgotten about that kiss until my middle-of-the-night ruminations.

"You never harmed any animals? Cut the whiskers off the family cat?"

"No. We're dog people. And I love my dog."

We did the test again. It took hours. And then the wooden man gave me one last chance to confess.

"Tracy," he said. "There's something you're not telling us. You can say it. Just tell me."

An image popped in my head. A face. And suddenly I thought I knew what I'd been unconsciously hiding.

"Okay," I said. "But please don't call the police."

"Trust me," the wooden man said.

"My mother's cleaning lady, Rosa, is an illegal immigrant." My eyes blinked hard as I looked into the wooden man's face. His lips twitched a little. Not a smile, but a tilt up.

"That really doesn't concern us." He stood and left the room.

I glanced up at the mirrored wall where I assumed a person (if not a team of people) was watching me. And then I shut my eyes and fell quickly and deeply asleep, still wired and upright.

It was a sleep that eliminated any awareness of time, so I don't know how long it was before the wooden man returned to the room and woke me.

"Congratulations," he said. "You passed your polygraph."

The final leg of the three days of interviewing was a visit with a psychiatrist. After revealing everything I could possibly dig up from every layer of consciousness for the polygraph test, the psych exam felt minimally invasive.

□ □ □

Sorority sisters are required to return to the house in early August in order to get ready for Rush Week. This is the time when sororities and fraternities recruit new members over five days of parties along with traditional rituals, which for the girls include a lot of singing, cheering, and chanting. I have never been one to shirk my responsibilities, so I participated fully as required. But as someone who doesn't like to be seen, it was hard to stand on the rolling front lawn and sing to passersby, or to do the more complicated door chant, for which we planned to spend two days rehearsing. Here's how the door chant works: girls wanting to join Delta Gamma would open the great red door of the spectacular Federal style house and find the doorway filled from top to bottom with smiling, shout-singing faces. When done right, it looks like a cartoon cannibal's stack of heads. To properly achieve this, sorority sisters stood on ladders, chairs, and each other's shoulders. I didn't worry about my safety, but I did always try to find a place where I wouldn't stand out, where I would be an anonymous head on which no one would focus.

It was in the middle of this rehearsal week, just before lunch, when some girls started talking about a shooting that had taken place in Los Angeles at a community center. I ran upstairs to the den and put on the news. A few girls filtered into the room; we filled the couches and chairs as we heard about what had unfolded.

A man named Buford O. Furrow, Jr. (the name alone deserves a paragraph or two, but I'll ignore it), had driven from Tacoma, Washington, to Los Angeles with the purpose of "killing Jews." He found that he couldn't get close to the big institutions, like the Simon Wiesenthal Center's Museum of Tolerance, but he was able to walk right into the lobby of a Jewish community center in Granada Hills. There, with a submachine gun, he opened fire on a crowd that included many children. Seventy bullet casings were found on the floor. Many people, including three young kids, were shot.

We were aghast. Horrified. Shootings like these are so common now that it's hard to remember how shocking they used to be. How they unnerved us deep into our hearts and souls. How we sat around the TV for hours on the rare times these horrors did unfold. And how we thought about the tragedy for more than just a few seconds or an hour. If you were like me, it was just about the only thing you thought about for months.

In the TV room that afternoon, I had one of the most engaging conversations I'd ever had with my sorority sisters. We talked about anti-Semitism, racism, terrorism, and guns. There was a pulsing in my limbs, and my heart pounded steadily. I could have sat in that room through the night, trying to find ways to work through the muck that was weighing down the country. More than ever, I wanted to be part of the solution to these worldwide and domestic problems, but I couldn't bring myself to admit this aloud. Other than my roommate and my parents, I had only told the people whose names I'd written down as references that I had applied to the CIA. And I'd asked all of them, four sorority sisters, to not let others know I was applying. It seemed too . . . outlandish, in a way. And I envisioned people asking themselves, *Why does SHE think she could be a spy?*

The conversation escalated, not to an argument, but toward solutions—one person, working off the ideas of another. We were discussing politics now, action, writing to members of Congress, when a redheaded girl named Alicia looked at her watch and screamed, "Oh my god, it's time to practice the door chant!"

That was it. We filed out and never picked up the thread again.

My body was at the door chant rehearsal, while my mind remained at the Jewish community center. Claire, the Rush chair, was frantically trying to get everyone in place so that the doorway wouldn't have an inch of background light shining through. At our first run-through, the girls at the top of the doorway—perched on ladders—were continually looking down, probably afraid of tumbling and cracking open their heads on the marble landing.

"Look up!" Claire shouted. "UP! UP! UP!" I wasn't one of the problem heads, as I had hidden myself behind the group of overflow girls who filled the window beside the door. We were the side act, as the doorway was where all the action was.

The next day, I was still thinking about the community center—puzzling through the possible ways to deal with domestic terrorism as opposed to forces outside our borders—when it was time for another door chant practice. I went to the entrance hall and stood behind the mass at the window, while other girls teetered on their footstools and ladders. We started the chant. *D-E-L-T-A, Delta! D-E-L-T-A, G-A-double-M-A, Gamma!* . . .

Claire shouted, "LOOK UP!"

I looked over at the ladder girls to see if they were following Claire's orders. And then I burst out laughing, just as they did.

Taped above the transom window was a *Playgirl* magazine cen-
terfold from the mid-1970s. The model was a man with exuber-
antly curly hair in every place a male body can have hair. His
penis—slung across his thigh like a sleeping lap animal—was
enormous. It was a single moment when I momentarily forgot
about terrorism in any form.

Two days later, the guy with the lap penis was still posted
above the door when a man from the CIA arrived unannounced.
He said he was there to interview the four references I had given
on my application, and he hoped they were all home or could
be summoned home quickly. My eyes flitted back and forth between the CIA agent and the penis. I willed him not to turn his
head to see what I was looking at.

"Would you like to talk to them in the parlor? Or maybe the
library?" I was smiling too big for the moment.

"No. I need to see your bedroom. I'll speak to your references there." He was over six feet tall, older than everyone else
I'd met in the agency, and had a military buzz cut. Everything
about him was contained, controlled. He even spoke with the
minimum number of words.

"Of course." I pushed my finger on the buzzer button of
the wall-mounted intercom system. Boys, men, weren't allowed
above the first floor in our house. If someone did need to go up
there for any reason, it had to be announced.

"Gentleman caller coming up," I said into the speaker. Gentleman caller was what any guy was called. Girls were summoned to meet their dates or friends with the words, "There's a
gentleman caller for . . ."

I was in jeans and a t-shirt that day, but most girls were
in shorts and tank tops or sweatpants—a staple of any college
wardrobe. The agent said he'd find his way to my room, and
then asked that I stay downstairs while he conducted the interviews. Melissa was in our room doing homework on her bed, so

I assumed he'd start by talking to her. I tried to imagine where he might sit. There was no way he'd drop into the beanbag chair, and I couldn't fathom him on a bed. And how could he fold his stiff, lanky body into the flimsy desk chair?

While he was upstairs, I nervously waited in the parlor, picking at a loose thread in the hem of my jeans. I hoped that I hadn't done anything that my sorority sisters would find unbecoming for a spy and a representative of the United States. Would the fact that I hadn't flung myself enthusiastically into the door chant work against me? And what about the penis? Would the agent see it on his way down the stairs, out the door? My stomach clenched as I waited for those interviews to be over so that I could . . . well, I wanted to interrogate my friends and find out every word they'd said. But I knew that wasn't right. I knew I'd have to temper my curiosity.

The agent left without looking up toward the transom window. Maybe he was excellent at his job and actually had seen the lap penis without letting on that he had. Melissa and my three other friends gave me minimal feedback, though I did hear that he'd sat on the desk chair and they'd sat on the beds. Basically, I was told that they each had confirmed facts I'd given about myself, and then were asked if there was someone else he should interview. In this way, the vetting process was expanded past my sorority all the way to my mother's friends. When I asked my mother what her friends had said, the only thing she could report was that Pat, her best friend, had offered him coffee in her favorite golden retriever mug. Mom wasn't sure if he had drunk the coffee or not.

I knew there was no dirt on me: I'd never stolen anything, smoked anything, or betrayed anyone. But the *me* who wanted to be in the CIA—the person I was when I lay in bed at night thinking about security checks in Gaza and where a person might hide in Afghanistan—was as closeted as Bruce Jenner before *he* became *she*. How could people take me or my desires seriously if I'd never revealed that side of myself to anyone but Mike Smith, the recruiter?

□ □ □

A girl named Tammy was sorting mail into the boxes under the grand staircase of the Delta Gamma house. It was the end of November, and I had just come in from a run and was lingering in the entrance hall waiting to see if there were letters for me.

"Who the *FUCK* is getting mail from the CIA?!" Tammy shouted. She looked at the name, then jerked her head toward me with raised eyebrows. In her mind, I was probably the least likely spy in the house.

I snatched the letter and dashed upstairs to my room.

The sweat on my legs suctioned against the pink leather as I settled into the beanbag chair. I ripped open the envelope. My stomach tumbled, and I wanted to scream. Instead, I just smiled and bit my lip.

Tracy Schandler—the floppy baby who had been ridiculed for years, whose Bat Mitzvah party theme was the solar system, who had never left the country without her parents, who was a devoted history major at the University of Southern California, who was vice president of social standards at Delta Gamma— was going to be in the CIA.

THREE

THE TURNING POINT

**Langley, Virginia
September 11, 2001**

It was 6:45 a.m. when I pulled my silver Acura into the car dealership–sized CIA lot and then cruised through the gaps between cars. The lot would be full in a couple of hours, but I always came in early enough to park only a short hike's distance from the new CIA building with the pretty blue-green glass windows.

I'd been listening to Sting's *Brand New Day* CD continuously the past few weeks. "Desert Rose" was my favorite song, and I often hit the replay button and listened to that alone for the drive into work. The opening of the song—the music and a plaintive ululating voice—sounded more Middle Eastern than Western. And, of course, the desert I saw in my mind as I belted out the words along with Sting was the Registan in Afghanistan. It was a place that was becoming more familiar to me than the fenced front yard of the house I grew up in.

For the past year I'd been in the mapping department, reading satellite images sent mostly from the Middle East. At my desk, in my cubicle on the second floor, I'd stare at the screen with the geolocators typed in white on the lower-right corner, and then write out what I was seeing. It was like I'd learned to read another language; or maybe I was more like a radiologist looking at a sonogram and seeing a full-fledged baby where everyone else only saw Rorschach blots. You could throw any photo my way, and within 30 seconds I could tell you from only the fuzzy shape of a head who was standing there and what he was standing next to. Closing my eyes at night, yearning desperately for a couple hours of sleep, I would see the high-lighted, craggy wedges of mountains, the shadowy gray nooks of rocky crevices, caves, valleys. And the square and rectangu-lar outlines of seemingly lonely outposts—safe houses, ware-houses, factories, and training camps where unbeknownst to most of America, al-Qaeda was rapidly building its forces. I'd assembled binder after binder filled with images and informa-tion about all the known terrorists, their locations, and their ac-tivities.

And then, a week ago, I'd been approved for a higher secu-rity clearance, as I'd been moved into what was then a deeply classified operation within the CIA, the ███████ Program. The work would demand intense concentration over long hours, so each team—and I was in the first team created—would only work in the ███████ ███████ for four months. At this point, I had friends at work, pals I'd go to lunch with or go out with on the weekends, and even a boyfriend in the agency, an oper-ative who reminded me of a living G.I. Joe. But I couldn't tell any of them about the ████████████████. I couldn't even tell my boss, though he was the only one in my division who knew I was leaving for another department. I hadn't changed offices yet, so for the past few days I'd been straddling the two worlds, reporting to two different bosses and sitting in the same cubicle where I'd been all year.

The song ended, and I cut the engine. I took my flip phone out of my purse and opened the glovebox. My flexible Velcro back brace was jammed in there. A few months earlier, I'd had increasing pain up my spine that made every breath feel like it was directing a team of knives to make sliver-thin cuts down the length of my body. I ignored the pain the best I could until the day I could barely stand but forced myself in to work anyway. I ended up on the floor unable to move. A trip to the hospital revealed bony overgrowths on my vertebrae, pressing in on my spinal nerves. The only solution was surgery, where they had shaved off the overgrowths, creating space and relieving the pressure. After a month of recovery, I felt fine but still kept the brace nearby in case I was stuck in traffic and found it hard to sit, trapped in the car.

I shoved my phone into the glovebox, beneath the brace. Cell phones were confiscated by security if you tried to enter the building with one. Before I got out of the car, I flipped down the visor and looked at myself. I liked my outfit that day. It was new. Fresh. A blue button-down with a blue pencil skirt, both from J. Crew. On my feet were nude peep-toe pumps that pinched my toes but seemed worth it for the overall look. I took my pink lipstick from my purse and reapplied it. The meeting I'd had with the ███████ ███████ team just a few days ago was running in my head. There had been the seven of us who had been selected for the program and our immediate supervisor. At twenty-two, I was the youngest person on the team. I was also the only woman. The men had a confidence that made them seem much older than me; most of them were in their thirties, though some hadn't quite hit thirty yet. Our supervisor was a tall, thin Hispanic man who wore a long tie that he tucked into the top of his pants. We all called each other by our first names, and I'd called my boss in mapping by his first name. But this boss seemed stern, mature, and I wasn't sure if I should call him by his first name or not. So I didn't use any name, though in my head I called him by his first name, Anton.

Anton explained that we'd be watching the terrorists and the training camps from a place I called The Vault. ████████
██
██
██

██
██
██
██
██
██
██
██
██
██
██

████████████ After learning all we needed to know about the program, I had asked, "So, what are the chances we will need to use this?"

Anton had said, "Slim. Unless they attack us." He had gone on to explain that if we ever were to ████████████████████, that action would never be taken without thorough analysis, insight, intel, and a final approval from Tommy Franks, the general in charge of huge swaths of the globe: parts of North Africa, Central Asia, and the Middle East.

In other words, *no one was taking this lightly.* And our job, to accurately and correctly identify who and what we were seeing *before* anything was ever fired off, felt all the more important.

I flipped up the visor and then threw the lipstick back into my crowded purse. It took a minute to fish out my ID, which hung from a blue-and-gold lanyard. I hung the ID from my neck, got out of the car, clicked the lock, and wobbled in those peep-toes toward the entrance. Before entering the building, I looked up toward the sky. It was a perfect day: bright, sunny, clear. The air smelled as pure as fresh-cut grass. I kept my face in the warm, beating sun for one last moment. Once I was at my cubicle, I'd have to say goodbye to the sun and close the blinds at my window so I could better see the maps on my screen.

The guards were always nice and said hello as I scanned my

ID. I went down the escalator and crossed out of the new building into the food court, where I headed straight to Starbucks.

The CIA food court is similar to a mall food court, only smaller. There are no restaurants, only food stands with tables and chairs in the center of the great room. The people who work at the food stands go through a stringent vetting process. They're not allowed to say they work at the CIA food court. And they're not allowed to ask questions, not even a name, of their customers. This was a problem for Starbucks employees who wanted to put names on the cups. What they didn't understand was that, for undercover operatives, even if you're giving a false name, you feel vulnerable. Who knows how a fake name—let's say you use your grandmother's maiden name—could be traced back to you? Even a random number could be linked to your true identity. So there were no names, not even aliases. And conversation never revolved around work. I always smiled and chatted with the Starbucks workers. That day a woman helped me and we both remarked on how beautiful it was outside and how we wished we could work outdoors.

I said goodbye and then walked away with my usual venti dark roast with no room for milk and sugar. It was 7:00 a.m. now, and I needed that coffee to get me through to lunch, when I might get another cup of coffee with the daily salad that I brought to my desk and ate robotically as I continued to analyze images.

With my coffee and my purse, I headed up another escalator into the original CIA building. From there, I got in an elevator with a man whose face looked ten years younger than his gray hair implied. *Stress*, I thought. This job, and the pressure of feeling responsible for the lives of an entire nation, chipped away at all signs of youth. In one year, I'd seen colleagues age as though they were in a time-lapse movie. I hadn't slept through the night in 12 months and had shadow bags under my eyes that were so pronounced, I felt like I was emptying out CoverGirl concealer sticks like they were packs of gum. The gray-haired man pushed the button for the seventh floor. I pushed three. Now I knew why he was so gray. The seventh floor was almost mythical. It was where George Tenet, then the director of the CIA, had his office. The closer you were in the ranks to Tenet, the closer you were to the seventh floor, if not on it. If you were ever going to run into President Bush, or Vice President Cheney, or anyone in the administration, it would be on the seventh floor. Even though I'd been moved into a position of high priority and even higher security clearance, I still saw myself as a rookie, a novice. Someone who could only watch someone push that button for the seventh floor and not someone who'd be going there herself. I had yet to meet any of the seventh-floor people, though their names were on emails, memos, and notices. When my friend Lindsay attended a meeting on the seventh floor with Tenet, she ran straight to my desk afterward just to tell me what it had been like to sit in a room with him. Things felt more important, bigger, when Tenet was directly involved.

The elevator stopped at the third floor, and the gray-haired man nodded at me.

"Bye." I smiled and lifted my hand in an embarrassing half-wave before I stepped out.

Of the 15 people in my division, about a third were at their desks already. I chatted with a few of them as I headed toward my cubicle in the far corner, next to the windows. Before I closed the blinds, I turned my head toward the sun. One last moment to appreciate that perfect day.

I sipped my coffee as my computer started up. When the images came in, I was so focused, I was almost in a dream state. All the photos were of training camps, though for the past couple of weeks people seemed to be clearing out of the camps. I counted heads. I cross-referenced images to make sure I wasn't counting the same people twice. All men. Some of them easily identifiable to me. Everyone youngish and upright. Where were they now, if they weren't in the camps? We knew their plans involved nonspecific attacks in the United States. Hopefully this dearth of armed boys didn't mean they were here, in the United States, under aliases or names that we just hadn't found yet, renting cars and trucks, building bombs, driving through tunnels . . . no wonder I couldn't sleep at night.

By 8:30 a.m., most—if not all—of the people in my division were at their desks working. My friend Randy stopped by to chat for a moment. He had an idea that we should start color-coding folders, reorganizing them by rank in al-Qaeda. As he spoke, I couldn't help but think, *I'm not going to be here, Randy. I'll be in The Vault. But I can't tell you, or anyone else, that The Vault even exists.* Until then, my secret life as a CIA agent hadn't felt so secret. It was too hard to maintain friendships outside of the agency, as the inability to reveal what you did for 50 hours a week created a wall that prevented real intimacy. The result of that was that all my friends were in the agency. They knew I worked in mapping, and I was free to discuss my day with them. But now that I was being moved, I felt the strange tickle of distraction created by a secret. G.I. Joe had even asked if I was having an affair. I'd told him I'd never have an affair (I'd just break up with him if I met someone more compelling), but that I was involved in something new and I couldn't reveal to him what it was. This didn't appear to sit well with G.I. Joe, and immediately I could feel that part of his pleasure in our relationship depended on his seniority and experience being far beyond my single year in.

There were two phones on my desk: a black one that led to the outside world, which I used to call my mother every day, and a beige one that was secure within the CIA. At 8:50 the secure phone on my desk rang. It was Jeff, a guy who had started in the agency around the same time as I did, and one of my pals.

"Go to CNN," he said. "A plane just hit the north tower of the World Trade Center."

"Oh, shit," I said, and I held the phone between my shoulder and ear while I pulled up CNN on the closed-circuit TV that ran through my computer.

There had been chatter about al-Qaeda's plan to hijack planes, there had been chatter about plans to blow up buildings. But no one in the CIA had detailed information about when or where. It was all conjecture—words, phrases, and movements gathered here and there with some of the smartest people I've ever met trying to piece it all together into a cohesive narrative. Also, no one knew if al-Qaeda had the organizational skills to pull off something like flying a plane into a building. Certainly, there had not been nearly enough information to shut down any of the 15,000-plus airports in the United States or cancel the 87,000 flights that crisscrossed the nation each day. Just as there hadn't been enough information to close off every tunnel in the country to an unknown car, driven by an unknown driver, that might have had unknown explosives.

Now, I know that much of what the 9/11 Commission later presented was a failure on the part of the CIA to communicate with the FBI. But from where I sat, this is what I know to be true: every person I came in contact with, every person I worked with, every person to whom I sent or received information was working toward the same goal—to keep America safe and to shut down the terrorist operations of al-Qaeda. There were thousands of people in the CIA who were working toward that same goal. The snafu between the CIA and the FBI might be where the blame lies in hindsight, but to narrow the tragedy to a single error is to oversimplify a complex battle between those who wanted to destroy the Western world and those who wanted to save lives. Additionally, one cannot ignore the sleepless and devoted hours put in by every operative and analyst I saw. And, more importantly, one cannot ignore the documented fact that George Tenet went to the Bush administration several times to explain that an attack was being planned *on American soil* and told them that we needed to be proactive in defending our country. The administration didn't seem able to wrap their minds or imagination around the extent, breadth, and financial resources of al-Qaeda. The locus of their "worry" was more on the disbanded Soviet Union and the drug cartels in Central America. The administration refused to approve action other than that in which we were already engaged.

Jeff and I stayed on the phone together, mostly in silence, as we each watched from our desks. We were both stunned. Groups of people were gathered around desks, computers, TV screens. There wasn't much noise, but there was talk, commentary. My mind was racing over the images I'd been studying: had I missed anything, were there any airplane mock-ups I hadn't seen, was there something I should have caught that I didn't? And were all those people who had been missing from the camps the past few days currently sitting on American airplanes?

At 9:03 a.m., American Airlines flight 175 hit the south tower. The entire floor went eerily silent. I don't think I took a breath for at least a minute, and I doubt anyone else did either. Again, I thought back to the images I'd seen lately. *How many people were missing from the camps? How many more planes might hit?*

"I'll talk to you later," I finally said to Jeff, and we hung up. I went to the binders, leafed through the images I'd seen over the last week, and tried to compare them to images from two or six or eight weeks earlier. My brain felt frozen, stuck in a rerun of *What did I miss?* I closed the binders and joined the others in my area who were gathered around a TV in a conference room. The office doors to all the supervisors on that floor were now shut.

It was 9:37 a.m. when American Airlines flight 77 crashed into the south side of the Pentagon. That plane might as well have crashed into the south side of my body. I wanted to crumple, collapse in on myself like a foot-smashed soda can. The pain, the guilt, the sense that my failures were resulting in lives lost had taken over my body and erased all other thoughts.

A woman named April, whom another friend had once described as "the skinniest, whitest person I've ever met," clapped her hands and smiled. "Here we go!" she said. It was misplaced excitement, like finally being deployed to war after all you'd done was train. No one really wants to go and shoot people, but if you've been prepping for it, you do feel the thrill of knowing that you'll finally be executing the maneuvers in which you'd been trained. My guess is that April, who was also tracking terrorist training camps, was excited that the hours and hours of work she'd been doing weren't for naught. Still, that clap of the hands has haunted me ever since.

By 10:00 a.m., everyone in the CIA had been emailed that we were on lockdown and should shelter in place. No one went under a desk with their hands over their heads. We continued to watch TV, talk, speculate. Every person I spoke with—every single one—went through all the work he or she had been doing up to that day and tried to figure out if they'd missed something. Or misjudged something. Or misread something.

By 11:00 a.m., notices went out that said everyone was to evacuate the building, except those of us in counterterrorism. G.I. Joe called me to suggest we leave together.

"I have to stay." I scanned the room. No one near me was leaving.

"But we've been evacuated."

"Everyone in counterterrorism has to stay," I said. He sighed, mumbled goodbye, and abruptly hung up.

By 11:30 a.m., all the buildings were emptied, except the pockets of counterterrorism operatives and analysts on various floors and the bigwigs on the seventh floor. On my floor, all the private office doors remained closed, and groups of us remained huddled together in front of the TVs, methodically unraveling all we knew as we tried to puzzle together what had just happened.

The food court was closed. There was no salad to be had,

no more Starbucks. But all of that was the farthest thing from my mind as the next few hours progressed. I wasn't scared and I wasn't panicked. I was simply determined to identify every terrorist involved in this attack so I could cross-reference them with any photos or groups I had from training camps. I wanted their names. And I wanted the names and locations of all their known associates. Mostly, though, I wanted to know exactly where Osama bin Laden was. Though it hadn't been confirmed in the media yet, I—and everyone else in the antiterrorism units—knew he was behind this atrocious attack.

At 2:00 p.m., my boss from mapping instructed us to go home. As people went to their desks to gather their things, I approached him and asked if I should go see Anton, the supervisor of my new department. My boss tilted his head for a second and smiled. He couldn't have known exactly what we were doing—no one but Tenet and those chosen for the program knew. But the fact that I had asked that question made him realize that I now had a security clearance higher than his. He was a supportive man, however, and I could tell that this pleased him.

"Yes," he said. "Go there. That's where you're needed."

Anton was in a SCIF (the agency's name for a secure room or space) in the new CIA building, where The Vault also was located.

He had a line of sweat across his forehead, but he didn't look panicked. A woman was sitting at a table with him. They had papers, charts, and a white board laid flat on the table.

"What should I do?" I asked.

"I don't know what the fuck any of us should do," Anton said, and I could see he was feeling the onus of this attack even more than I. "I didn't think we'd have to use the ▮▮▮▮ so soon."

"Yeah," I said. "I was hoping we'd never have to use them."

"It's gonna be intense," Anton said. "Go home. Eat. Sleep. And meet me here at 6:30 tomorrow morning. We'll have a schedule figured out by then."

"I don't think I'll be able to sleep," I said. "Haven't quite mastered that one yet."

"Yeah." Anton looked down at the objects scattered across the table. There was a pile of black beepers. He flipped a few over, found one that had my name on it, and handed it to me. "Wear this at all times you're not in the building, not in the room."

By *the room*, he meant The Vault. "Oh, okay." I put the beeper in my purse because I wasn't sure how or where to wear it. At the time beepers seemed exclusive to drug dealers and doctors. I'd never even touched one before.

"And do try to sleep tonight," he said. "Because from today forward, you're on. It's you and the rest of team who've got to stop this crazy shit."

It felt as if a lead bowling ball had dropped into my stomach. I understood then, probably for the first time, just how serious, how integral, how impactful, my new position was.

□ □ □

The parking lot was virtually empty. It appeared larger than usual when seen as an expansive field of blacktop. I looked up toward the sky again, my face to the sun. How odd that the whole country could change in an instant and yet the sun still sat in the sky, shining as if this were the most beautiful day on Earth.

I got in the car, took my cell phone from the glovebox, and tried to call my mother. Nothing was going through. After several attempts, I threw the phone on the seat, started up the engine, and pushed the CD back into the player.

With Sting singing "Desert Rose" again, I left Langley and tried to head toward my apartment in Alexandria, Virginia. Twenty minutes later, when I hit the George Washington Parkway, the traffic was dead-stopped. It looked like the CIA parking lot, midday. I rested my foot on the brake, leaned back in my seat, and turned up the music. Sting was singing "The End of the Game." It's a haunting, eerie song with lyrics that mention the western sky, the sun, and a cliche that didn't feel so much like a cliche on September 11: *What did not kill me, just made me tougher . . .*

It was clear that it would be hours before I could make it to my apartment in Alexandria. Rather than sitting in traffic, I pulled off at the next exit and headed to my friend Jenny's house. She was a CIA analyst, good with numbers, statistics, and other mathematical abstractions.

Jenny pulled into the parking lot of her apartment complex just as I did. I could see her punching off her radio as I shut down Sting. We got out of our cars, walked toward each other, and hugged. Neither of us spoke.

"Shit," she finally said.

"I know," I said. She was on a different floor of the CIA, and we hadn't seen each other or talked all day.

I followed Jenny into her apartment. She turned on the TV before she even took off her shoes. I sat on the small couch and kicked off my peep-toe pumps. How could I ever wear those shoes again, or look at them even, without thinking of this day?

We stayed on that couch, in front of CNN, for hours. There were few other people I could have been with, for who else could understand the bolts of guilt that ran through me every time the news mentioned that it was believed to be (though not yet confirmed) al-Qaeda fighters, under the leadership of bin Laden, who had flown those jets? Jenny and I both knew that confirmation of these facts would be coming shortly.

Jenny didn't even get off the couch to order Chinese food, she just pulled out her cell phone and dialed the restaurant across the street. It was a number she'd memorized, she told me, after only two weeks in the CIA. I don't remember who paid for the food, but I do remember that it was a time when you could scarcely care about who paid for the food. Our nation was under attack. At this point the score was bin Laden 1, America 0. Little else seemed to matter.

Around midnight I drove to my apartment in Alexandria. I should have put Sting back in the CD player, but my mind wouldn't let go, and, instead, I listened to the news on the radio. As they talked about terrorists, I saw shadows in my mind, images from the satellite photos of grainy figures assembled in the training camps.

When I got home, I peeled off my clothes and let them drop to the floor. Then I pulled on pajama bottoms and a tank top, got into bed, and turned on the TV.

"Sleep," I commanded myself, then turned down the volume with the hope that the humming drone of voices would let me drift off.

Sleep never came. At 5:00 a.m., I got out of bed, showered, and dressed. I wore pants with a belt, just so I could thread it through that beeper. I wasn't sure how the thing worked, or what I was to do when it did beep. But I figured Anton would go over it that day.

Before 6:30 a.m., I was with my colleagues in the ████████████████████. Every one of us had shown up early. I felt wide awake. Alert. Focused.

I was ready to even the score.

FOUR

THE VAULT

Langley, Virginia
September 2001–January 2002

I never made it up to the seventh floor of the CIA headquarters. I didn't need to. Because the seventh floor came to me.

It was midnight, my third night in The Vault, when I first met George Tenet, the director of the CIA. I wasn't used to the 11:30 p.m. shift yet and was feeling a little dazed in spite of the thermos of coffee I was chugging. There were three people working in the tiny room, lit blue by the screens on the wall at which we were all staring. Unlike most countries in the Middle East, which are usually eight hours ahead of the United States, the one I was watching then was eight and a half hours ahead. A small thing, I know, but that 30-minute tilt only seemed to magnify how off-kilter this place was.

Tenet stepped into the dark room, said hello to everyone, and then stepped out again. My heart raced, and I took a few sips of coffee. He was back within seconds, rolling in a chair from the adjoining room where we had meetings, or ate, or just took a break with the lights on.

"Tracy, right?" he asked, and he pushed that chair next to mine, sat down, lifted his feet, and crossed them on the table.

"Yeah!" I smiled and moved my thermos to make more room for his giant wingtips. There was no way I was going to call him *George*, though that's how my boss, Anton, referred to him.

"How are you tonight, sir?" Brayden, my colleague, asked. Brayden had gone to a boarding school where he wore a tie every day and then Georgetown, where he got straight As studying foreign policy. I thought I was straight, but Brayden made me look like a feral woman. I bet he'd never even gotten a parking ticket.

"Good, good," Tenet said. There was an unlit cigar in his mouth, and it bobbed up and down when he spoke. The room was always a little bit chilly, probably to keep the equipment cool, and I was in a light blue fleece. Tenet had on a bomber jacket. I didn't know it then, but he was often in that bomber jacket and usually had a dry cigar hanging from his mouth.

"What are you looking at there?" Tenet brought his feet down, half-stood, sat again, and moved the chair forward.

I handed him the binder that had a file on Muhammad B., someone I felt I knew intimately. He was in bin Laden's inner circle, having grown up with him in Saudi Arabia. Unlike most of al-Qaeda, which then was young, undereducated, disadvantaged boys, Muhammad B. came from a family with money, and had gone to college in the United States.

"A training camp. I'm working toward being certain that that guy in the center front is Muhammad B."

"He's been in and out, sir," Brayden said. "When he walks, others walk behind."

The third person working in the room, an Air Force guy named Bill, glanced toward us and then back to the screen. He was friendly, as the Air Force liaisons always were. But he kept to himself, mostly, and never wanted to go to breakfast with me or anyone else when the shift was over.

"Any sign of bin Laden?" Tenet asked.

"No, sir," Brayden answered.

"I saw three people following a guy in white robes yesterday . . . or, last night, you know, last night here, yesterday there, well, actually, today there—"

Tenet laughed, and I immediately relaxed.

"Yeah, I know what you're saying, go on," Tenet said.

"Well, he looked too short," I said. "The guy in the white robe."

"So not the madman we're after?" Bin Laden had been identified as somewhere between six-three and six-five. For a Middle Easterner, that's like being a human high-rise.

"No, sir," Brayden said.

"Yeah," I said. "Of the three guys near him, two were taller and the other was the same height, so there's just no way. These boys don't eat well enough to grow so much."

"Yup," Tenet said. "It's no damn basketball team, that's for sure."

We were quiet as we continued to watch the screens. I sipped my coffee.

After a few minutes, Tenet asked, "What d'you got in there?"

"Black coffee," I said. "Dark roast."

"Keep you awake?"

"Yeah," I said. "Or maybe it has a paradoxical effect on me. I feel calm when I drink it."

"I get that." Tenet nodded. Then he looked to Brayden and asked, "What about you?"

"I don't drink coffee, sir," he said. "I've trained my body to be on full alert without it."

Tenet smiled, leaned forward, and gave Brayden a little pat on the shoulder. He stayed another few minutes, and then said he had to get home to his very patient wife and his sleeping son.

At seven the next morning, 30 minutes before my shift would end, Tenet showed up in the room again, with a single Starbucks black coffee and two bottles of water.

"There's a box of doughnuts out there for all of you." He nodded toward the other room, gave the water to the men, and handed me the Starbucks. "I ordered a dozen but I ate two in the car on the way over here." He smiled, and I laughed nervously.

"Ten doughnuts is plenty for the three of us." Brayden nodded without even the smallest grin. "And thank you for the water."

It was only a few days later, around 6:30 in the morning, when President Bush came into The Vault. I'd been working that night with a guy named Phillip, who'd grown up in Lincoln, Nebraska. He was maybe the first person I'd ever met from Nebraska. Phillip was a little more relaxed than Brayden, and he noticed the smallest things that could make a difference—a hat that had to have originated in Jordan, for example. Phillip's sharp eye made him one of my favorite people to be paired with. We were identifying places, camps, chemical labs that might be eliminated on our shift. It was a focus, a task that I felt from my toes to my hair. I never took off my shoes, I never kicked my feet up onto the desk, and I rarely slouched in my seat. But I was slouching at the end of that shift, when President Bush walked into The Vault.

"How y'all doin' this morning?" he asked, and I immediately sat up straight.

Phillip and an Air Force guy, Timmy, both stood. I wasn't sure if I should stand or not, but since they had already, I did, too.

Timmy stuck out his hand and shook Bush's hand.

"What's your name, son?" Bush asked, and Timmy told him.

He moved on to Phillip, who gave him his full name and then added, "from Lincoln, Nebraska."

"You don't say," Bush said. "Cornhuskers! One of the best teams in college football."

"Go 'huskers!" Phillip said, and his face flushed red.

"And you are?" Bush put his hand toward me and I shook it.

"Tracy Schandler." I smiled and nodded my head.

"Well, thank you Timmy, Phillip from Nebraska, and Tracy Schandler for your hard work. Now y'all get back to it and don't mind me, I'm just gonna stand here and watch for a minute." Bush crossed his arms and squinted at the screens. Every now and then he'd ask a question or say something. The longer he stood there, the more comfortable I felt. He was one of those people who puts everyone around him at ease. It was like he was thinking about and aware of how other people felt.

It seemed that at least one person from the seventh floor, the administration, or Congress visited The Vault every day. The country was still shocked by the events of September 11. The rubble of the towers was months from being cleared out. And the work we were doing was both active and visible. People wanted to witness the response to the attacks—they wanted to know for sure that something was being done.

The reaction was often the same. The visitor would watch the ▮▮▮▮▮▮▮▮▮ and then say, "It's like playing a video game, isn't it?" Though most of our visitors weren't of the generation who played video games, they all had kids or grandkids who did and so had seen plenty of video game action.

That video game action felt nothing like a game on October 20, the night before my twenty-third birthday and the very first time the ▮▮▮▮▮▮▮▮▮▮▮▮▮▮▮▮. We had just confirmed the location of Mullah Omar's compound in Afghanistan. Mullah Omar was the founder of the Taliban, the supreme leader of a murderous troupe, and one of bin Laden's protectors. The men and women on the ground, around two hundred of them, established that Mullah Omar himself was not in the compound but many of his Taliban leaders were. If we took out the compound, it would not only eliminate much of Mullah Omar's leadership, but it would be a show of strength and power. To the terrorists, it might even be a show of magic, in a sense, as no one outside of those in the ██████████████ knew how immense our capabilities were. ████████████████████████

██
██
██
██
██
██
██████████████████████████████

I watched the rising cloud of dust and rubble bloom and then dissipate. And then I continued to watch as soldiers on the ground entered the destroyed shell of the compound. I didn't tell anyone that my birthday was approaching within minutes. It seemed silly just then to mention it, but I thought about it: the simple fact that I was alive. And that I wished to live for many more years to come, hopefully in a safer world.

██
██
██
██
██
██████████████████████████████████ We must have seemed like vengeful gods.

G.I. Joe broke up with me only a few weeks into my rotation in The Vault. No matter how much he pestered me, I wouldn't tell him what I was doing on these night shifts. The experience pushed me away from ever again getting in too deep with any agency men. Though others had more manageable egos, none of them lasted long enough to be mentioned in these pages.

The entirety of my social life while I worked in the The Vault consisted of going to the Silver Diner in McLean, Virginia, with whomever I'd covered the night shift with and a few other people from Langley who were also on night shifts. We'd grab a booth and order up like we hadn't eaten in days. Often I was the only woman, but that never seemed to matter to anyone. And it only mattered to me in that I believe any operation of any kind—including running a diner—could always be improved by bringing in different kinds of people and different perspectives. That said, there were women in the CIA, just not where I was working right then.

The guys always ordered things with bacon on the side: pancakes and bacon, eggs and bacon, huevos rancheros and bacon. Once I saw someone order fried chicken with a side of bacon. I usually ordered whole wheat toast and egg whites, a fruit bowl, and sometimes a half grapefruit on the side because I feared that my odd hours would lead to odd illnesses like scurvy.

When I got home to my apartment, the plan was to work out in the gym and watch anything that wasn't the news so that mentally I could leave work for a few hours. Sometimes I made it to the gym. Usually, I put on pajama bottoms and a tank top, lay in bed, and waited for sleep to overcome me. My bedroom was so sunny, just the cracks of light on the edges of the roller shades made it bright enough to read. If I didn't fall right asleep, I'd get up and gather a bunch of charcoal-colored bath towels from the bathroom. I'd throw them up toward the window shades in my bedroom, trying to hook them over the edges so they'd block the light. They never failed to fall down, and I'd spend the first 20 minutes of attempted sleep getting up and down as I'd re-fling those towels until they were hooked well enough to stay.

Often I'd stay asleep for three hours. If I was lucky, I'd sleep for four. When I got up, I tended to the business of daily life: grocery shopping for one, touching up my roots when they looked too brown, calling my mother, and cleaning the apartment. I'd try to nab another hour or two of sleep if I could from 4:00 to 6:00 p.m., while most people were starting their commute home from work. Whether I'd slept again or not, I prepared dinner for myself each night. I liked to cook, so I'd actually make a real, grown-up-human meal—something like roasted chicken, sautéed asparagus, and Israeli couscous. I'd eat in front of the TV, watching the most shallow, materialistic, consumer-obsessed reality show I could find. Turned out that once I was living the news—thinking, dreaming, working, and creating it—I just couldn't bear to watch it on TV.

Every day, things seemed to be intensifying in The Vault. National Security Advisor Condoleezza Rice, in nifty pantsuits, came in regularly. She never spoke to me, or anyone else in the room, other than to ask a simple question, something like, "What are you looking at?" Once she was in The Vault when the Muslim call to prayer played out in the room. We had programmed one of the computers to sound the call—a man singing—whenever it sounded in the place we were watching. The rule was that no one would be attacked while praying.

Rice looked at me, her brow crimped into worry lines. "What's that?"

"The *adhan*," I said. "The call to prayer." I had loved the mystical, plangent, almost-haunting sound of it from the first time I heard it. Most people working in The Vault enjoyed the adhan. Even if you're not going to pray, it does make you stop and think or reflect.

"Does someone in here pray?" Rice asked.

"I do, ma'am," Matthew, an Air Force guy, said.

"You're Muslim?" Rice asked.

"Christian," he said. "I just pray when it sounds."

A few minutes later, the *iqama* sounded from the computer.

"Now what?" Rice asked.

"The first one was calling everyone to the mosque," I said. "And this one says that it's actually time to pray."

She had no further questions, but I could see her eyes were trained on Matthew to see if he was praying.

Vice President Dick Cheney came in The Vault a few times, though nothing memorable ever happened when he was around. Secretary of Defense Donald Rumsfeld never came in on my shift. Maybe he only worked regular hours and so was never around early enough or late enough to be there when I was. Secretary of State Colin Powell came in regularly. He was very serious. Upright. He stared intensely at the screens without even seeming to blink. President Bush continued to drop in on us. He was always kind and cracked jokes, even as the tension mounted. His mood, his energy, and his support bolstered everyone in that room. I have voted Democrat in every election since my eighteenth birthday. But if Bush had been running during the three months I was in The Vault, I would have voted for him.

Of course Director Tenet showed up regularly, with that cigar in his mouth and the bomber jacket straining at his bulky shoulders. Just a quick visit from Tenet, who remembered everyone's name, always made you feel like you were on the right team and fighting for the greater good.

By mid-November the war in Afghanistan was on and Kabul had fallen. All of us in the group were working six days a week and wearing those beepers whenever we weren't in The Vault. My beeper only went off once. A guy named Andy was vomiting on every break. He had a fever. I had to rush over to Langley and get my eyes in that room before Andy was allowed to go home and just *be sick*.

Right before the third week of November, schedules were shifted, and I was asked to work on Thanksgiving Day. My family was in California, so I wouldn't be seeing them anyway, as there was no time to fly home, even for 24 hours.

That day, I focused as hard as ever on the screens, never allowing my attention to waver. But each time I took a break, I felt great pangs of sadness. I had just turned twenty-three, and I had never spent my favorite holiday away from my parents and my brother. Instead of sitting down with the people I loved and eating a good, long meal, I was in a tiny, windowless room with a member of the Air Force whose name I can no longer remember, and Brayden, the straightest man in the CIA.

I felt lonely. And sad. And I was hungry because I had refused to pack a lunch, since I knew that eating that lunch would only remind me that I wasn't eating Thanksgiving dinner.

And then George Tenet stepped into the room.

"How you doing? Tracy? Brayden?" He didn't know the Air Force guy's name and just nodded at him.

"Fine, sir," Brayden said.

"Anything I should know here?" Tenet pointed to the screens. "Anything new?"

"Looks like more people are showing up—" I pointed toward the screen on the left where there were mountains. It was night there, cold and barren in a place with the lovely rhythmic name Tora Bora. No one was outside, but we'd seen a few guys arrive on foot earlier.

"Yup, let them keep showing up. 'Cause we sure as hell are gonna show up, too." Tenet pointed at the screens. "Listen, I really appreciate what you all are doing here. I'm honestly thankful for you three sitting in this dark room while everyone else is off eating."

"I'm happy to be here, sir," Brayden said, and I just nodded.

"The whole country's staring at a TV screen right now, watching a football game and eating pie with whipped cream, while you three are looking at that damn place until your eyes must hurt."

"My eyes are pretty used to it by now," I said. They were. It was amazing how long I could follow even minimal movement: an hour straight with just one guy walking out to pee in the rocks.

"Well, I stole some food off my own table and stuck it out

there in the other room for all of you. There should be plenty for the bunch of you. Maybe even leftovers, too."

"Thank you, sir," Brayden said.

The Air Force guy and I thanked him, too. At this point I was so hungry, I wanted to run out of that room and start eating. But I played it calm, casual. I didn't go fix myself a plate until Tenet was gone.

The food was amazing. I never asked if he made it or his wife made it, or some other person came to his house and made it. But it tasted homemade, and there was a rumor going around The Vault that his wife was a great cook. That meal didn't just feed me; it made me feel like it was okay to be away from my family for one holiday. The work was important, and these people—even the guy whose name I can't remember—were my family for the time being. And when the head of this makeshift family showed he cared enough to leave his own house just so that we would have a proper Thanksgiving meal, I was glad to be a part of it.

□ □ □

In the first week of December, CIA agents on the ground in Afghanistan were able to confirm bin Laden's presence in the caves of Tora Bora. The caves had been formed from streams that had eroded the soft limestone rock of the White Mountains. In the eighties, the Americans, the Afghan rebel force (Mujahadeen), and bin Laden and his team fought side by side against the Russians, who had invaded Afghanistan. These caves were put to use as a fortress then. They'd been tunneled and built out, with meeting rooms, bunk rooms, and ammunition storage rooms. Some of the build-out had been done with American dollars. But much of it, including a road carved straight through the White Mountains, had been financed by the bin Laden family business. This was before bin Laden wanted to kill Americans. In fact, he'd even praised them back then. Once he'd turned into the terrorist he was, his family and his country of residence—Saudi Arabia—disowned him and wanted nothing to do with him.

The caves held great meaning for bin Laden, who liked to model himself after the Prophet Mohammed, who had taken refuge in a cave. Even bin Laden's rejection of material luxuries was done in the spirit of Mohammed. This would have been admirable if his mission hadn't been to kill all Westerners, particularly "Jews, Christians, and their agents." In fact, it had been somewhere near the caves of Tora Bora where Peter Bergen conducted the first American interview with bin Laden, which brought him to my attention in 1997. It was also in these caves, in 1996, that bin Laden agreed to meet with Khalid Sheikh Mohammed, the uncle of Ramzi Yousef, the man who had bombed the World Trade Center in 1993. During this meeting, ideas were brought forth that eventually percolated into the attacks of September 11.

Now, in 2001, Tora Bora was a terrorist clubhouse, with bin Laden as the scoutmaster. His troops were snuggled in close to him, along with stores of American Stinger missiles, which had been left behind from the Soviet invasion. I imagine bin Laden as happy then, in his element, camping out with his boy-pack and waiting for his followers to kill so they could earn his warped idea of scout badges.

It was Ramadan, the monthlong daylight fast practiced by millions of Muslims worldwide. Ramadan is said to be a period of swelling religious feelings and frequent praying; a time to reflect on one's devotion and piety. It is also a communal time, with large meals taken together once the sun has gone down, or before the sun has come up. In a war, however, it would be a time when Muslim soldiers would be weaker during the day as they refused both water and food. Bin Laden was devout in his word (certainly not in his practice, as the Quran states that

Muslims should not commit murder or suicide) and insisted his men be his kind of devout as well. His army would be fasting in Tora Bora, and this could give us an edge.

The plan was to take out Osama bin Laden by taking out the caves. The problem was, it was difficult to get to Tora Bora, especially in the snowy winter, and especially when one wasn't used to the terrain or the thin air at an altitude of 14,000 feet. There were no paved roads, only the unpaved one plowed out years ago. And there was very little cover in the rocky, snow-covered slopes leading up to Tora Bora. Anyone approaching would be an easy target to those in the caves looking down.

As I'd spent more than 50 hours that week visually and mentally flying over Tora Bora, I knew the terrain way better than I knew D.C. or Virginia. It was clear to me, and to everyone else in The Vault, that an aerial bombing would be the best way to flush al-Qaeda out of the caves. Once they'd been flushed out, however, they'd have to be captured. To enclose and nab this ragtag, armed mob would take manpower. We needed to create a wall around them, a lasso, so that none of bin Laden's guerrillas could escape to Pakistan, only 20 miles away. It was like a giant game of hide-and-seek, with Pakistan as the home base that the terrorists could run to, tag, and call, "Free!"

Tenet explained the situation to General Franks, President Bush, Secretary of Defense Rumsfeld, and others. He explained it again, stressing the fact that CIA agents on the ground had confirmed that America's most wanted man was there. As Tenet was making our case, the *New York Times* and other newspapers got ahold of the information that we knew bin Laden was there. Within a matter of days, this news was published and now *bin Laden knew we had found him*. Time was running out.

And yet the manpower to create the lasso wasn't granted.

I could speculate as to why the thousands of soldiers in the area weren't handed over when needed, but from where I sat it really would be speculation. I do know this: Bush, Cheney, and Rumsfeld were preparing for the invasion of Iraq. Much of their energy was directed toward connecting Saddam Hussein with weapons of mass destruction. Also, there were tensions between the CIA and the administration because the threats that we knew were real and poised to launch were not being taken as seriously as the threats that they were searching for.

Still, even without the requested troops, General Franks, under the command of George W. Bush, okayed the attack, as this was the first time since September 11 that bin Laden's presence had been pinpointed.

□ □ □

On December 3, 2001, anyone who had an office on the seventh floor of the CIA was in The Vault. That unlit cigar was in George Tenet's mouth, and he was wearing his bomber jacket, but he was almost unrecognizable in his seriousness and focus.

The president and some senators were also moving in and out of the room. That day, The Vault felt like it was the beating heart of the war, the muscle pumping to keep the system going.

The temperature in Tora Bora fell well below zero at night; daytime wasn't much warmer. A light snow was falling. In my mind's eye I could see bin Laden and his truculent crew deep in their limestone bunks, burrowing like prairie dogs. Prairie dogs who would soon have to pop out of their holes.

There were around 100 newspeople covering the war in the area of Tora Bora. There were only five dozen American troops fighting that battle. Risking their lives alongside them were a few special forces troops from Great Britain and Germany. Soldiers from the Afghan military and German special forces—though not many—were in charge of securing the escape routes along the border to Pakistan. With so few people guarding the borders, trying to hold the terrorists in Afghanistan was like trying to hold water in a colander. Yeah, there are places where the water can't get out, but there are so many holes that it's going to get out anyway. Still, we were going to try to flush out and capture as many backward-murderous boy scouts as possible before they could make it to those holes.

From the start of the battle, those of us in The Vault were in continuous conversation with the Air Force. The missiles they were using were nicknamed Daisy Cutters. It's a delicate name for a high-precision, laser-guided missile that can cut straight through stone. The Air Force needed our eyes to plant those missiles in the right places.

The work was so intense, the missile drops and explosions so continuous, that members of the team took 30-minute shifts: 30 on, 30 off. Even during those free minutes, when I sat with others in the adjoining room, there was near silence. I could feel tension like a chain-mail suit pushing straight through my skin to my bones. When I shut my eyes, I saw the missile drops all over again: the flash of a red fireball in the center, which dies and then rises again in the shape of billowing dust balls that dissipate like an aerosol spray. I don't think I can say that I understood what it would be like to be a soldier on that day, for my life at that particular moment wasn't in danger. But I did understand part of what it might feel like to be a soldier in general: the immense responsibility in making lightning-quick life-and-death decisions while trying to act for the greatest good of the greatest number of people. And there was also the feeling of being an integral part of a larger unit. It was apparent right then that each individual was important, but also that each individual wasn't really an individual; rather, she or he was part of a bigger machine in which every piece needed to work perfectly for the whole to properly do its job. I was at once immensely important and utterly insignificant.

Each time I stepped back into that room, I took a deep breath, shoring up for what was to come. I wanted to do my part exactly right, so the Air Force and the few men on the ground could do their parts exactly right.

For 56 hours straight the Air Force dropped its missiles. By the end of those 56 hours, we knew—though it wouldn't be confirmed for another few days—that Osama bin Laden had eluded us. Once we acknowledged that he was gone, it felt like the room was a sinkhole and we were all dropping straight down through mud. People barely spoke. Directions were given with single words. The group heartbeat behind this attack felt like a group heartbreak. It kept thumping, but it was a painful, grieving thump.

There are many reasons, from many different angles, given about why we didn't capture bin Laden in Tora Bora. I think that in the end, it had to do with manpower. To attack during Ramadan seemed wise, as bin Laden's soldiers would be weakened. What no one took into account, though, was that the Afghan forces who were helping us were also practicing Muslims. Many of them, if not all, left their posts after sunset to break the fast with their families. This left even more holes in the already flimsy wall of people who guarded the border. Even so, 220 of bin Laden's men were killed in the battle, and we captured 52 others as well.

What we didn't realize at the time was that al-Qaeda was turning into a starfish: cut off one arm, and another grows back. Or maybe it was more alien and sinister than that: cut off one arm, two grow back. No matter how many people we took out in one way or another, nothing would actually die. Al-Qaeda was, is, an ideology, a belief system, a life choice. Each arm we eliminated did take something away, but it also fed the growing mythos on which al-Qaeda thrived and continues to thrive.

FIVE

POISON SCHOOL

United States and Western Europe
2001, 2002

Before the fourth month of my tour of duty in The Vault was over, I applied for, and was accepted into, the position of staff operations officer in the Weapons of Mass Destruction office of the Counterterrorism Center (CTC). This new position would keep me in Counterterrorism and would entail a lot of traveling. I'd get to engage firsthand with the people I was trying to bring down.

I was in charge of Europe and North Africa, which thrilled me, as that was where all the action was. I've always liked being in the eye of the storm, the quiet, hidden center of it all, rather than with the crowds outside observing.

Before I could get to work on any of that, I had to go to poison school for two weeks to learn as much as the boys and men in al-Qaeda knew about how to make and disperse poisons.

Unfortunately, poison school operated from 9 to 6 in a building far from CIA headquarters. This meant I had to drive during rush-hour traffic. Also, with no food court in the training building, I had to pack a lunch. I realize this is what most American men and women do every single day; I'm not saying I should have it better than anyone else. But part of the appeal of the CIA, and part of what I'd enjoyed in the ██████████████████, was living a life off the regular grid, being part of a different universe in a way. Anyone who works a night shift anywhere knows what I'm talking about here.

Fortunately, there's lots of great music in the world, so I listened to CDs during the drive, usually Sting, or Train, or the Dave Matthews Band.

There were 13 of us in poison school, all from different branches of defense and intelligence. My friend Virginia was also from the CIA and also joining Counterterrorism. Virginia was an overachiever, a world-class swimmer who spoke three languages, one from each of her foreign-born parents (Turkish and Chinese) and English, of course. We sat together every day; both of us were eager, enthusiastic students.

The poison courses were taught in a plain, white-walled classroom with long tables and blue plastic chairs. I wanted it to look more lab-like than it did; instead, the entire building reminded me of any American middle school: functional and with little aesthetic value. Our courses were taught by a woman named Jean who wore khaki pants and a polo shirt just about every day. She was no-nonsense, humorless, and a leading expert in the field. Jean had come from a government agency where they developed the most lethal pathogens in the world in order to figure out how to undo the damage that would be inflicted on civilians were the wrong people to create these poisons. It was a futuristic death center with biohazard suits, goggles, and gloves, and where no one, so far, had ever died. Jean's assistant, Gary, was a slim man who silently did the grunt work for all of us: setting up labs, handing out petri dishes, helping us with gloves and masks.

During the initial hour of training Gary gave each of us pages from an al-Qaeda manual on creating WMDs. Jean told us that before the end of this course we would have memorized the entire document, something that proved to be true. The wording and tone in the manual wasn't dry corporate-speak. It was high-drama, end-of-the-world stuff; the crazed rhetoric of any extremist organization: the alt-right or the KKK.

By the end of that first day, I knew three things for sure: 1. Making bio-weapons was relatively easy and could be done with very little money. 2. If these guys who lived and died with a wish to kill Westerners could learn this stuff, then I would have to master it all beyond what they knew. 3. It wasn't going to be enough for me to sit in Langley and acquire information, I had to eventually get out to the places where both the poisons and the plots to poison were being developed and shut them down.

There were no tests, quizzes, or grades in poison school. But everyone seemed enthusiastic and appeared to be doing A+ work as we dove into the chemistry of it all. I found it fascinating, sometimes comical, disgusting, and compelling. I can never look at raw meat now without thinking about how if it sat on a plate in the sun and spoiled, eventually there would be enough ingredients for the botulinum bacteria. From the botulinum one can create eight different types of neurotoxins that can be deadly even in microscopic amounts. At their lowest dose, they can merely cause paralysis.

There was a working assignment at poison school. Each of us, our minds freshly sparking from what we knew after memorizing the manual, had to try to make what the boys in al-Qaeda were making but on an even smaller budget than what they likely had. We used gloves, masks, and a high-tech laboratory. Also, we had the security of a supervisor to make sure nothing we created left the confines of a test tube. It was reassuring to discover firsthand that nothing they did was smarter or more difficult than something we could do. And in knowing exactly how they did what they did, we also came to understand how to *undo* what they were doing.

Upon graduating from poison school, we were each given

a certificate that I have saved to this day, not as much for the record of achievement as for the memory of a fun and engaging two weeks.

□ □ □

The CTC Weapons of Mass Destruction office (WMD) was on a lower floor of the CIA headquarters. With this new position, I returned to my routine of driving into work right after the sun was up, procuring a Starbucks dark, bold coffee from the food court, and getting to my desk early. Still, I had a hard time beating Graham Andersson in. No matter what time I showed up, he was already there, striding along the cubicles or sitting in his office with the door open, available to whomever might need him.

Graham's official title was chief of the WMD office. He was tall and looked like a Viking. Everything about him—the way he dressed, the way he worded his emails, the way he stood still and upright when he spoke—exuded competence and intelligence.

Victor was the assistant chief of WMD. He had thick hair that swooped back from his head like he'd just walked in from a windstorm. He was always impeccably dressed, with a hand-kerchief in his suit pocket.

Sally usually arrived to work at the same time as I. She was the head of my division within WMD. Sally was a mother, around forty, and was enviably fit. She never joked around or chatted the way other people did, or the way George Tenet did every time I saw him. But I trusted her. We all did. We had a few moments to speak alone in the mornings, before my other two colleagues arrived, and this time proved valuable for me. Sally would check in on what I was doing, give me advice when needed, and praise the advances I was making in tracking WMDs. Often, Sally would tell me that I was the "future of the agency." The reason I point this out isn't to broadcast that I was the *future of the agency*. Rather, it's to say that a little bit of faith and support from the right person can change your perspective. Even though I was always performing at the highest level, and I knew that, I still often felt like the floppy baby, or the girl with acne and funky teeth who was bullied in school. So when Sally told me that my work was outstanding and that I was an important and integral part of the team, it changed how I saw myself. I know we're supposed to find our confidence from within. But really, my sense of who I was in the context of the agency took root in how Sally saw me.

Next into the office was usually Ben. He was in charge of Asia. Ben was tall, slim, a former Marine who had recently married. His clothes were always stylish, current; the guy looked like an Italian movie star. I suspected that his wife picked out his outfits, as he didn't have the fussy personality of someone so well dressed. He was kind and thoughtful from the first day we met. The more we worked together, the funnier and more fun he got. This was also true for the third person in our Poison Trio, and the last one to arrive each morning, David.

David was in charge of Russia. He wore a black trench coat into the office, no matter the weather. Until I really knew him, I thought he looked like a serial killer with that coat, his sharp balding hairline, and an equally sharp goatee. Once he took the coat off and relaxed, the guy was as sweet as a stuffed animal. One who spoke Russian and could track down terrorists like a hound dog on a fox. Every morning, David took a newspaper from the stacks of world papers at the front desk on our floor and hid in the bathroom with it, on the toilet, I presumed, for what always felt like a long time. Because of this, I had a hard time ever touching the papers he returned.

David, Ben, and I were the Three Musketeers. Or maybe we were another version of Charlie's Angels (if I can be a Musketeer, they can be Angels).

Each morning, once everyone had settled in, Graham came into our area, and the three of us, along with Sally and usually

Victor, too, stood around one cubicle or another and had a meeting. We took turns telling the group what we'd found, whom we'd followed, and where our leads were taking us. In this way we triangulated our targets—each of us following training camps and watching how the people from within those camps spread out to other areas. We had all the collected data on the terrorists at our fingertips: photos from mapping, intel from agents on the ground and from other agencies around the world. Cables—which are like impenetrable, untraceable emails—were routinely sent between agencies, tracking any particular terrorist's movement in a route that might start in the Middle East and then go to North Africa before landing in Western Europe. As much as was possible we tried to find where these guys went, who they met there, what they did there. The goal was to figure out where they were going next and what their plan was for that destination. We knew for sure they wanted to kill Westerners and Jews—al-Qaeda openly stated that and even printed it as their goal in their handbook. The only questions were when, where, and how.

Trying to save the Western world from being poisoned is intense stuff. When you look at a series of pictures of a particular terrorist, then look at more photos of his chemical lab in his dingy little bathroom in Yemen, and then see that he's bought a plane ticket to London, it's hard not to feel a burning intensity, a yearning almost, to put a stop to it. And the only way I was able to live with that kind of ongoing intensity was to create lightness, silliness even, in my daily life. In this way, David and Ben continually kept me afloat.

We'd each decorated our cubicles in ways that matched our personalities. I had a crystal-blinged pink calculator, tape dispenser, and computer mouse, all of which I still use today. On the inside wall of my cubicle was a poster of a smiling American soldier holding a tin cup. Above his helmeted head it said, *How about a nice cup of Shut the Fuck Up.* On the bottom of the poster it said, *Think before you say something stupid.* This was a reminder to me as much as to anyone else. As I was being called on to speak every morning at our standing meetings with Graham, I always wanted to be precise, correct, and relevant. In other words, I only wanted to speak if I actually had something to say, and I felt that if I didn't have something to say I wasn't doing my job right.

In his cubicle, David had a nightlight in the form of Jesus' face, made of glowing plastic. I can't tell you if David was a believer or nonbeliever; but I can tell you that he found the idea of a nightlight in His image sort of fun. Amusing! Ben's cubicle, like Ben himself, appeared to have been decorated by his wife. There were tasteful silver-framed pictures of the two of them, and a matching, dark-wood stapler and tape-dispenser set.

I kept snacks in the top drawer of my desk, fuel to keep me going when I didn't want to stop what I was doing, even to pee. When I did get up and use the bathroom, however, David and Ben raided my drawer, throwing down Cheez-Its or York Peppermint Patties as if the two of them hadn't eaten for days. Their goal was to consume as much of my food as possible before I returned to my desk. I wouldn't discover the looting until the next time I'd open the drawer to find the bag or box completely gone. Usually with just the empty wrappers left behind.

Oh, there was another poster, a fake magazine cover, which I hung on the inside wall of my cubicle. This one, mocking a foreign city in a clever and funny way, wasn't tacked up until after I'd had a disagreement with an intelligence agent in that country about a person of interest I'll call POI. My sources who were in contact with POI had seen that he was working on acquiring the necessary elements to make a nuclear bomb. Once he was into bombing, he was passed on to my friend Virginia. I wanted to keep my eyes on POI, however, just to see this through and make sure he was stopped before he'd created anything deadly. It was a Sunday when Virginia and I, both there in the office,

discovered that POI would be flying to a certain world capital that day. A cable was immediately sent out to the intelligence agency in the country where he'd land. The cable had his
name, a photo, the facts about his bombing ambitions, his flight
number, and what time he was supposed to land so that they
could meet him and keep an eye on him. The response from the
agency came back right away. In English, it said, "Regrets. We
don't do the work on Sunday." This wouldn't be the last time
I had to deal with people who wouldn't work on Sunday. But
it was my first time, and so it came as a shock to me. As I lost
sleep, worked any day or night, burned my eyes out on computer images, all to protect civilization from chemical warfare,
the very people I was trying to save didn't want to make the
effort on a Sunday. I know there are many cultural differences
between America and the rest of the world. I know that we are
one of a handful of countries that don't think twice about working through the weekend if necessary. But even if you remove
my American bias, I can't help but think that when human lives
are at risk, that lovely commitment to rest, church, and family
should be put aside for a few hours. I respect all people from
all cultures. All good people, that is. But the loss of POI, when
he could have been put on the radar that day, infuriated me
enough to post that fake cover. The fictional magazine, which
I'd found online, was called Soldier of Surrender, The Official
Magazine of the ------ Military. On the cover were headlines for
articles like "Surrendering Made Easy! Five Great Exercises to
Keep Your Arms Up Longer!" I respect the men and women of
that particular country. But that day, I was angry enough to let
my feelings be known through my cubicle wall art.

□ □ □

By the fall of 2002, we—the Poison Trio—had created a web of
information that flowed in to us from various posts: CIA operatives overseas; the embedded people, called "sources," from

whom overseas operatives got information; sources that we ourselves had in other countries; spies from foreign agencies and their sources; CIA operatives who had debriefed detained terrorists; along with the intelligence collected from overheard phone calls, intercepted emails, and confiscated computers. We were the eye of the web, hoarding it all at our cubicles, sorting it, and making connections until we had unpuzzled a poison network that spread from Pakistan to Afghanistan, the UK, Spain, France, Italy, Africa, and Russia. Starbucks was starting its worldwide expansion around the same time, and I wondered who would proliferate farther: the guys trying to kill us, or the people trying to keep us alert by putting paper cups of coffee in our hands.

This poison network was led by a man named Abu Musab al-Zarqawi. Zarqawi was a former pimp and video store worker. He'd also been a mama's boy who adored his mother as much as she adored him. He'd dropped out of high school, was barely articulate or literate, had multiple tattoos (which is against Muslim law), and was in and out of jail or prison starting at age twelve, when he cut a neighborhood boy in a street fight. His attraction to perverse torture started in his youth, as one of his methods to humiliate those beneath him was to dominate and sexually abuse boys younger than himself. This was and remains a practice that is common in terrorist groups. The men of al-Qaeda don't classify this as homosexuality—it is all about power and domination. What they view as homosexuality is forbidden by al-Qaeda, and known homosexuals are tortured or, as has been witnessed, thrown from buildings to their death.

It was Zarqawi's mother who pushed him toward the Quran as a way of saving her favorite child. It seems she may have pushed too far, as this street thug took religion to a whole new level, one that does not exist in true Islam. He worked on memorizing the Quran and even trained himself to speak differently so he sounded less thuggish and more like a person who had the intelligence to be a leader. In the relentless heat of the Middle East, Zarqawi wore long sleeves to hide his tattoos. Eventually he took a knife and sliced them off his skin, so they were replaced with raised, folding white scars, like worms crawling up his arms. Even with Zarqawi's newfound devotion and elocution, Osama bin Laden found him too crude. They fought together in the eighties alongside the United States during the Soviet occupation of Afghanistan. But after that, though bin Laden financed many of Zarqawi's endeavors, the two men rarely interacted and almost never resided in the same country.

By 1993, Zarqawi was locked up in the Al-Jafr prison in Jordan. Six years later, when the new crown prince of Jordan pardoned 2,000 prisoners, Zarqawi was mistakenly freed. He didn't go far, though, as he returned the next day to preach to those who remained incarcerated. Prison had provided Zarqawi with hordes of young, angry, frustrated men who easily flocked to his perverse ideology. Zarqawi had gone into Al-Jafr as a ruffian. He came out a guru of mass murder.

Only someone as perversely sinister as Zarqawi could scheme to engage in chemical warfare. Imagine the mind of someone who wants to spread a lethal mist of ricin powder into the air so that it is inhaled by entire crowds—everyone inside a theater, for example—mothers, fathers, children, grandparents; people of every nationality and faith, including possibly Muslims. At first the victims feel nothing. But within a few hours they'll have difficulty breathing as fluid builds up in their lungs. Soon, their blood pressure will drop and their hearts might fail. Many will suffer seizures. At this point, the old, frail, and physically impaired will be dead. Those who survive might only survive for another week until they die of shock and multiple organ failure. It's chilling to think that an entire organization has made mass murder like this its goal.

At the start of that winter, the Poison Trio had honed in on a single terror plot that had us all worrying about civilians in a European city. When I couldn't sleep at night, my mind conjured up images of cuddly babies napping peacefully in prams; teenagers playing soccer against an ancient wall; and archetypical happy people drinking red wine and playing cards, all murdered by a few fanatics who couldn't imagine a coexistence of beliefs.

Though we were certain about what we'd uncovered, we faced a problem similar to what had gone down earlier in the year in London when the police arrested a team of radicalized Muslims who appeared to be planning to release ricin into the underground subway system there. Raids on their flats and a warehouse found false passports, recipes for ricin, and *all the ingredients* to make the deadly poison. But as none of the ingredients are illegal, it turned out to be a hard case to prosecute.

We, too, could see the intentions of the terrorists we were tracking, but they hadn't yet done anything illegal. We had photos of the men hanging around and observing a crowded public space for hours at a time. We had copies of receipts for purchases of the ingredients to make weapons of mass destruction. And we knew they had been actively recruited and trained by al-Qaeda. In short, we had everything except a definitive statement that said, "We're going to poison a massive number of people." Our hope was that a face-to-face visit with the agency in the country where the plot was to be executed would help stress the importance of what we'd found and compel them to do whatever was necessary to make an arrest.

Graham had decided that Ben and I would go with him to Europe to present our findings. This was the beginning of months of travel. I couldn't have known it then, but this first trip would turn out to be the most civilized, the calmest, and the least dangerous of all. It was a dignified start to my pursuit of WMDs and the misguided ideologues who create them.

██

██████████████████████████████████ Graham, Ben,

and I took a car service to Dulles Airport. In the car, Graham handed me the package of documents of the evidence we'd gathered of this pending attack. None of this information was to leave my side: I was to hang on to it as if it were chained to me, including when we went through security.

I was already nervous about my ███████ responsibilities when we approached the airport. Then, as we marched side by side toward the security line, my thoughts went to my belly button. Virginia and I, on our last day off together, had gone to Dupont Circle in D.C. and had our navels pierced. This was the era of Britney Spears with her pierced belly button, and at twenty-three, Britney was not much younger than me. In the spirit of Britney, I got a silver bar with a pink rhinestone running horizontally along my navel. Virginia, being much more reasonable that day, had a simple silver bar. I suddenly feared that this belly-bar would be revealed while I was being hand-searched and Graham would lose all respect for me. I had worked so hard with Ben and David to uncover this plot, I had devoted my life to it for the past several months, and the idea that all that effort would be diminished by an impulsive act on a day off made me feel a little ill. I trusted that Ben would laugh it off. This was a guy who once covered my desk and chair with David's post-bathroom newspaper. But Graham, a man I admired, respected, and, in a sense, *wanted to be*, had only seen my serious side. To suddenly flash a silly pink rhinestone on my midriff seemed like a dangerous act considering the dedication I had to my job.

I saw a sign for the restroom and stopped.

"I'm going to run in there before security," I said, the ███████ clasped firmly in my hands.

"You can't put it down," Ben teased, "even when you wipe."

Graham smiled. "That's true," he said.

"Got it." I left my rolling bag with them, and rushed into the ladies' room.

In the locked stall, I wedged the ███████ under my right armpit. Holding it in place, so that I could only move my right arm the way an animated T. rex moves its tiny arms, I quickly unfastened the belly bar and placed it on top of the metal box that holds discarded feminine napkins.

"So long, Britney," I whispered.

I removed the packet from my armpit and then, with it safely in my hands, I exited the stall, leaving the jewelry behind.

Only seconds after the flight took off, both Graham and Ben conked out. I was too scared of losing the ███████ to sleep, though I did doze off and on with my arms crossed over the ███████, which rested against my belly. I was used to operating on very little sleep, however, and was fully ready to save the world, or at least save the people who would be unlucky enough to find themselves in the terrorists' target zone.

☐ ☐ ☐

As we approached the headquarters of the local secret service agency, I wanted to stop the cab, jump out, and take a picture. ███████████████████████████████████████ ███████████████████████████████████████ ███████████████████████████████████████ ███████████████████████████████████████ ███████ I glanced toward Graham, and he was reading through papers. Ben's eyes were closed, though he wasn't sleeping. He might have been going over things in his head. I knew I'd have to play the part of tourist and get a picture of this spectacular place later.

Graham was not someone who had to get credit for everything or anything his team did. He was happy to let others take the spotlight and the glory. So it was entirely like him to suggest that, at the opening meeting, I present all that we had discovered about the plot. He wanted me to take the credit. Of course, Graham had no way of knowing that I am an introvert and am always more comfortable when I'm invisible rather than when I'm seen. But I couldn't say no. And I knew that in order to do my job right, I had to get over my fear of public speaking, get over my fear of being the center of attention, and just do what had been asked of me. I decided that I would pretend I was speaking in the morning meeting in the office, something that had initially terrified me but to which I had quickly acclimated.

The room in which we all met looked out over a river and toward a spectacular government building on the other side. The exterior didn't betray the interior: modern and clean, with all sorts of screens, buttons, and panels on the walls. This was a little sexier than the CIA offices at Langley; it reminded me of a set from a James Bond movie. The group of 25 or so people sat around a massive table. Everyone had notebooks and pens, though I knew there was a microphone somewhere in the room that was recording everything that was being said.

When Graham indicated it was my turn to speak, I felt breathless for a second. I looked around the table, and then inhaled deeply to gather courage. The group waited for me with polite, thin smiles. They were impeccable in their pin-striped suits with pocket handkerchiefs and cuff links. There was only one other woman present, and her hair, skin, and eyes seemed to be a single color, making her a beige blur in the room.

The information I'd been carrying in the ▮▮▮▮ had been removed and was now sitting in front of me in a stack. I knew it all so well that I didn't have to look down. All I had to do was speak. Something I'd done since before I even walked! I pictured myself standing by my cubicle with my team—I fixated on that image when everything poured out of me. It was as if my brain were operating outside my fear, relaying the information with a demanding accuracy and specificity. When I was done, there was silence for a moment. And then the questions began. They were taking me seriously. They were taking my words seriously. We were accomplishing something.

Over the week, Graham made several presentations, and Ben made one, too. We took many meetings with smaller groups of people, each of whom worked in a specialized area. They seemed as determined as we were to shut down the ████████ masters living in their capital.

Every night, the three of us were taken to a different elegant, expensive restaurant where there was a lot of wine poured and several courses served. I'm not a very picky eater, but even in the nicest restaurants the food was . . . well, it was often bland and tasteless to the point of being inedible. I'd cut things into bits, spread them out, and push them around my plate to make it look as if I was enjoying this meal, compliments of our hosts.

After all the talk, the food, and the wine, Graham and Ben always went to their rooms to sleep in preparation for the next day of meetings. It was my first time in this city, however, and I didn't know if I'd ever be back, so I usually took off walking around, mostly just looking, as things closed down fairly early.

One night, when I had skipped dinner, I walked from the hotel to an area that used to be inhabited by Jews. It was where, my mother had told me, her father's family had lived. My maternal grandfather, Jack Davis, was my biggest champion, supporting me and cheering me on in all I did with great enthusiasm. I've come to realize that everyone needs at least one person like this in their life. We need an audience of some sort, an admirer who fully, openly, and unabashedly adores us and is always happy for us. For me, it was my grandpa. No one was more proud of the various certificates and medals I was awarded in school, and eventually in the CIA, than he. Often it seemed like the only point in getting a certificate or award was so that I could take it home and show my grandpa.

But as proud as he was of me, I was also proud of him. Jack Davis fought in the Second World War, eventually opened a travel agency in Newport Beach, California, and was kind and helpful to everyone. Oh, everyone except the one boyfriend I brought home to meet him. That was a side of my grandpa that I'd never seen before, but one that only reinforced the idea that he irrationally believed I was better than everyone else.

Grandpa Jack's old neighborhood had clearly gone through many incarnations—originally it had been where the tanneries, breweries, and slaughterhouses had been. A famous serial murderer had also lived there; I looked for his house but never found it. I did see the homes of three of his five victims. Yeah. Five. I wondered what the people of his era would think of the thousands of murders committed by members of al-Qaeda. Terrorists were out-serial-killing even the most notorious serial killers by far.

The streets were narrow, with crowded, cobblestone streets. Most of the residents were immigrants. The area was fascinating to me but not a place that attracted a lot of tourists.

I paused in front of a tilting row house, glancing in the illuminated windows, trying to imagine what kind of house my grandfather's family had lived in, when a cab pulled over. The window went down, and the cabby called to me. I approached his window. He had a broad forehead, pale eyes, and an Eastern European accent.

"A girl like you cannot walk here alone at night!" he said.

"I'll be fine." I started to walk away.

"It's not safe!" he yelled out the window. When I kept walking, he threw up his hands and drove away. Because of September 11, my time in The Vault, and then my immediate immersion in the search for WMDs, I hadn't gone to "The Farm" yet, the place where CIA operatives learn to crash cars, survive being taken hostage, and handle firearms. My work was so intensive that I would do The Farm training in bits and pieces over the coming months. It was no matter to me at the time. I certainly didn't need a gun to walk where I was. I did feel powerful, and I did feel safe. I knew where the terrorists lived, and they weren't in this area.

Later that night, around 11, on my way back to the hotel, another cab pulled over. This time I was standing at the edge of the river, finally getting a photo of the beautiful high-tech building where we'd been having our meetings.

"You shouldn't be out here alone," the cabby said.

"I'm fine," I said.

"America! Don't be silly. Get in my cab and I'll take you to your hotel for free." When he smiled, I could see the silver nubs that replaced some of his teeth.

"Honestly," I said, "I'm happy where I am." By my guess, I was safer on the street than in a free ride in a cab.

□ □ □

Not long after we returned from this trip, the local law enforcement raided half a dozen safe houses and arrested all the men whose names we'd passed along to them. A few more people were arrested two days later. They were charged with possessing articles for the preparation, instigation, and commission of terrorist acts. As news of the planned attack emerged, a liquor company canceled its ad campaign that was to include billboards that would waft the smell of almonds. Ricin is odorless. But cyanide smells like almonds. Scented public ads were a clever idea that I knew would never again be possible to execute.

We were now fully in the new age of terror.

SIX

MR. TOAD'S WILD RIDE

Africa
September 2002

It was like I was at Disneyland on Mr. Toad's Wild Ride—the attraction where you're carted around in a fast-moving vehicle that comes a hairbreadth away from hitting something (a brick wall, etc.) or being hit (by a train, etc.). Victor, the assistant chief of WMD, and I were being driven from an airport in an African capital to a hotel in the middle of the hillside city. Every moment presented new possible disasters as we darted around moving objects—people, cars, dogs, children—and they leapt to safety away from us.

Victor, with his perfectly coiffed helmet of thick hair, sat in the front seat, as instructed by our driver. I was just behind him in the back. I'd packed a pashmina to throw over my head but couldn't get to it as our bags had been whisked away at the airport by another member of the country's intelligence service.

"Too many guns," our driver had said when he rushed us to the car. "They see Americans, blond lady, and . . ." He lifted his hand and did a pointer-finger blow to his temple.

I couldn't see the speedometer, but we were going far too fast for the poorly paved and sometimes cobblestone streets that wound up and down and often turned in hairpin curves. The car must have been from the eighties and surely didn't have any airbags. The windows had cranks to roll them, but the crank on my side was missing, as was the inside paneling of the door. I wasn't worried about dying so much as I was about my back if we were thrown into a sudden stop. And there were many sudden stops, as the people of the town seemed to walk in thick crowds directly into traffic. But we never stopped for long, and never when we were supposed to, as our driver rejected all traffic signals. He found a way around every stop and more than once pulled right up onto the sidewalk, forcing the crowds to part like the Red Sea as he barreled through.

The sparkling blue sea was on one side or the other—depending which way we were turned. It popped into view whenever there was a gap between the crumbling buildings of the city, and again when we were high enough to see over the rooftops. Other than the few mosques I saw, the place looked more European than Arab. There were small wrought-iron balconies, or balconettes, off every window. Most of the buildings were a dirty shade of white. It was as if a decorator had swooped in, looked at the sea, and declared, "Blue and white, those are our colors!" Some of the roofs were red tile, though many weren't. I wondered if they had all started out with tile, but none had been replaced over the years. There was a layer of black, sooty grit everywhere and a crumbling, sagging, distressed look. Ripped awnings waved in the breeze; chunks of masonry were missing, like bits of a body blown off; air conditioners precariously balanced out of windows. Most of the signs were in two languages, and when our driver and the men who removed our bags had spoken, I had heard a mixture of the two: trilling, fluid words punctuating and blending into the throatier Arabic. I was trying to learn words and phrases when I could, but still, English was—and remains—my only language.

Our car stopped short and I slammed into the back of Victor's seat. He turned, looked at me, and then pointed at a seatbelt beside me. I picked it up and waved it at him. There was a band but no buckle.

Then we were off again, weaving through the crowds. Two women in jeans, long half-dress tops, and hijabs held hands as they jumped out of the way.

"They are going to university," the driver said, as if he hadn't been only inches away from maiming or killing them. "In my country our women are educated. Intelligent!"

For a few meters we had two side wheels on the sidewalk of a street so narrow it was a wonder the entire car would fit. A ripple of people pulled their bodies back against the storefronts as we passed. We wound up and down past the numerous staircases that striped this vertical city and finally landed—with no bodies in our wake—at a hotel that looked as welcoming as a half-blown-up munitions storehouse.

This country ███████████████████████████████
███
████████████. There were no official numbers for how many people had been killed, but it was certainly over a hundred thousand. The conflict was essentially between the government and various extremist Islamic groups that rejected the secularism of the past few generations. It was a turbulent and violent war, with bands of extremists raiding and killing entire villages in nighttime massacres. Journalists, Westerners, feminists, diplomats, anyone who worked for the government, and children were also hunted down and killed. The brutality seemed to have no bounds.

██
██
██
██
██
██
██
██
██

███████████████████████████████████

███████████████████████████████████

████████████████████████ Osama bin Laden, and particularly Abu Musab al-Zarqawi, his head of chemical warfare, knew exactly what the ravages of this war had left behind: hundreds of thousands of poor, disillusioned, disenfranchised, angry, frustrated, uneducated, and often orphaned young men. In other words, prime potential al-Qaeda recruits. And recruit they did. Rather successfully, too.

Following September 11, 2001, most of the intelligence agencies of the world—most of the world, in fact—had been looking at the Middle East as a terrorist training ground. Of the 19 men involved in the 9/11 attack, 15 were citizens of Saudi Arabia, 2 were from the United Arab Emirates, 1 was Lebanese, and 1 was Egyptian. Bin Laden was from Saudi Arabia, though his family was originally from Yemen. But the intel was pointing more and more to Africa. And the men from this country, in particular, were dominating the chemical warfare scene. Like all African countries that had once been colonized by European countries, many of these people shared languages with Europe and had easier access to Europe than most Middle Easterners.

□ □ □

Our driver informed us that his agency had already checked us into the hotel. He then handed us each our room keys, which were actual keys hanging from a plastic diamond-shaped key ring. We walked past the front desk—which looked about as sturdy as a homemade lemonade stand—and then to a stairway with filthy once-white walls that curved out of sight.

"Second floor," he said.

"We're probably the first Westerners this hotel has seen in over ten years," Victor said as we climbed the stairs.

"Looks more like we're the first of any kind of people this hotel has seen in over ten years," I said.

We walked down a dark corridor. The lights blinked, signaling a power outage. Our rooms were across the hall from each other. We each put our keys in the keyholes, which seemed large enough to spy through. Victor was jiggling his key. He stopped and turned toward me.

"Ninety minutes to shower and nap and then meet in the lobby," he said.

"Okay," I said, though I knew I wouldn't nap. I never did. To nap meant I wouldn't sleep at night, and I needed that night sleep.

The room was small but bright. The curtains were open, and light flooded in, illuminating my bag on the bed. It was unzipped and open. The clothes I had ironed and either folded or rolled were now exclusively folded. And organized, too. Pants in one stack, tops in another. On top of the bag was what I took as a gift: a colored-sand picture of two Bedouins on camels crossing the desert. I ran my fingers over it, feeling the nubby surface, and then propped it up on the dresser. It really was lovely, and I was happy to have it.

Next, I went through my neatly folded clothes, feeling around in the collars and checking the pockets to make sure I hadn't forgotten something. It was like doing a breast exam, tiny palpations with my fingers. But no, there was nothing I'd left behind. I'd been exceedingly cautious, as I didn't want anything on me that might reveal my real address or details about my life in Virginia. Not even a gym membership card, or a receipt for granola from Whole Foods. The less information anyone had about me, the safer I was.

This was my first trip traveling under my alias ID. A couple weeks before my flight I'd gone to the CIA's Office of Technical Services, ██

██

██

██

. I repacked my suitcase and moved it to the luggage stand in the closet. I refused to nap, but I did want to lie down for a moment, so I yanked down the thin, faded bedspread and lay on the bed. I wanted to laugh, but didn't. The ceiling looked like it had been hacked out with an ax. I could see pipes, beams, wiring, essentially the guts of the hotel. I don't know why I didn't suspect there was a camera or microphone up there. Maybe I was just too tired to think it through. I was fairly sure, though not certain, that the reason they had gone through my luggage was simply to make sure I was who I had said I was. Which, of course, I wasn't.

I talked to myself quietly as I went through what I knew and what I wanted to know about YY, an African man I'd recently tracked from his family village in Africa to Europe. He had a terrifying nickname, which revealed his desires and intentions.

The equivalent would be if Jeffrey Dahmer had called himself *Boy Rape-Murderer.* The intel I was gathering from the CIA operatives on the ground in Europe had led me to believe that YY was manufacturing chemical weapons in an apartment in a European capital. Not only that, but he appeared to be the head of an al-Qaeda arm in that country and was recruiting new members every week. His fishing hole was the displaced and virtually homeless population of boys and men from his homeland. People who felt that they had no rightful place on any continent and were loyal to extremist Islam above all else.

Several European countries at that time weren't taking terrorism even half as seriously as they take it now. And no matter how I approached them (pal-like, sternly, matter-of-factly), I was having no success in getting them as worked up about these guys as I was. I sent cables to different agencies, informing them of YY's presence in Europe while detailing his power and influence with the untethered boys in the city where he was residing.

In spite of the intense racism against Africans in much of Europe, the Europeans like to think of themselves as more open-minded than the "racist Americans." Or they pretended to be more open-minded as they responded to my cables as if I were asking to do a root canal on each of their agents. The usual response was, *Show me that this really needs to be taken seriously.*

The more Europe threw up blockades to my progress in tracking ▆▆▆▆▆, the more determined I became to declare myself ▆▆▆▆▆▆▆▆▆▆▆▆▆. It occurred to me that if I couldn't get Europe to work with me in tracking African terrorists, maybe I could get the Africans to help. ▆▆▆▆▆▆▆▆▆▆▆▆▆▆
▆▆▆▆▆▆▆▆▆▆▆▆▆▆▆▆▆▆▆▆▆▆▆▆
▆▆▆▆▆▆▆▆▆▆▆▆▆▆ Lucky me, though, a new CIA station had recently opened, giving Victor and me a home base from which we could work. Also, we could create liaisons with the local operatives; something that would help

both our nations. Or help the whole world, really. After all, the greatest number of casualties from al-Qaeda's quest to rid the Arab world of Westerners was, and remains, Muslims themselves. Only a small percentage of al-Qaeda's casualties were, and are, Westerners.

After organizing everything in my mind, I got up to shower. When I flicked on the bathroom light, darting scratches of black cockroaches fled into gaps behind the sink and in the floorboards. That moment was my first in dealing with real-life, running-for-cover roaches. They weren't as awful as I'd imagined. And they seemed appropriate in this hotel that appeared to be a tremor away from total collapse.

A couple hours after we'd checked in, I threw a pashmina over my head, and Victor and I took a cab to the new CIA office. I'd recently been communicating in cables with the head of this station, Patty, and already respected and liked her. Cable communication can be like internet dating, though. Who you meet electronically might not be who you meet in person. Fortunately, this was not the case. Patty was an impressive woman.

██

██

██

████████████████████████████ Her office was almost as run-down as the hotel. There was mold on the ceiling and growing down the walls in the shapes of continents. Every window had a small air-conditioning unit jammed into place, with thick, brownish, rubbery-looking glue lines around it.

Victor and I updated her on the chart we'd made, which showed the leaders of each of al-Qaeda's poison cells. We went over what information we'd discuss with the local intelligence operatives. When the business part of our meeting was done, Patty and I covered our heads with shawls, and the three of us went outside, where her driver was waiting with a car.

Surrounded by the dusty ruins of this city, Patty's home

was startlingly lovely. It reminded me of a hammam, with Arabic-style vaulted ceilings decorated with intricate geometric patterns. Everything was a muted green, muddy red, and rusty brown. The floors were tiled with the same colors and patterns.

She had a larger staff in her house than in her office. Cocktails and appetizers were set out in the living room, where we sat and talked. When I got up to use the bathroom, she directed me, "It's down the hall, past the panic room, and then to your left."

I assumed the metal bulletproof door led to the impenetrable panic room—the place where Patty would hole up, like a jewel in a safe, if there ever was a home invasion.

□ □ □

That night, Victor and I dined with five men from the country's intelligence community in a restaurant that looked like a cement bunker. The men were friendly, almost jovial. The ravages of war and poverty were written on their faces with missing teeth, craggy scars, and hairlines that seemed to be receding prematurely. I had less than half a glass of wine, and I don't think Victor drank much at all. We were still on guard, trying to assess if these really were people we could trust. Without a team based here, assets other than these foreign intelligence workers would be almost impossible to acquire. In other words, we needed them, but we couldn't use them unless we trusted them to have the same goals as us.

Over the evening, it became apparent that these men were highly motivated to help us. After what they'd gone through in the war, they were outraged, incensed, and impatient to capture the same people we wanted and all their known associates. Their country had been destroyed by Islamic extremists over many years. Americans had one day of being attacked, on September 11. Imagine thousands of days of that and you can see how these guys, and most of their compatriots, would be furious.

Enraged. Determined. Eventually, Victor and I both came to understand that not only did they want to catch every terrorist who stepped on their soil, they wanted to kill them.

There was a wedding going on in a room next to the one where we were eating. I wanted to peer in for a moment—see what the bride was wearing and if they were dancing to the music and on-beat clapping I'd been hearing. Victor was an excellent traveling companion, as he was just as curious as I. When we were leaving, he nodded toward the doorway and the two of us stood there for a moment, looking in. The couple was dressed in elaborate traditional wedding clothes. The bride's veil was both a hijab and an ornately jeweled crown. The groom's embroidered shirt had a Nehru collar and fell to his knees. It was a boisterous affair with lots of noise, singing, and dancing. There was the joyfulness of any great wedding, in any country.

The next day, by the time Victor and I arrived at the local intelligence headquarters, I was used to the postwar ravages of this country and thought nothing could surprise me. Yet I was completely taken aback when we took a meeting with five agents at a square table in a ground-floor room with an open door and open windows. There were no air conditioners glued into place as at the local CIA office, just a breeze passing through the room.

I had never once given information, or asked for information, in a space with an open door or window. It was unheard of in the CIA. But there we were, with no choice but to talk and hope that no one was standing beneath those windows, or outside that doorway, listening in or recording us.

The conversation that had started at dinner intensified at the office. The agents were willing to go to any length to help us nab the men who had destroyed their homeland. If anything, we had to talk them down—convince them that it was worth keeping these men alive. Each terrorist we got would lead us to two or three more, and so on. If they killed one, that was the end of the line. Whether or not the terrorist would be a loss to humankind was debatable, but each death would absolutely be a loss to information gathering.

These men did have several embedded assets on the ground. And they were willing to let us use them, too. That is, we could ask them questions or for specific intel or contacts, and they would find us the answers through their embedded assets. We, in turn, could provide them with names and bits of other information about the people they despised. All the information we held was in my head, memorized. Each time I threw out the name and last-known location of a member of ██████, it was like throwing bloody chum to sharks. The men became even more ravenous to capture these guys, and I couldn't have been more thrilled.

When there was a brief moment of working out logistics, when I wouldn't miss any life-or-death information, I stood to excuse myself so I could use the bathroom. Our hosts had graciously offered us traditional coffee in glass espresso-sized cups during the meeting. It's considered an insult to refuse it, and so I had been drinking it throughout our talks: glass after glass of thick, milky, gritty, sweet coffee. By late afternoon, I had to pee so badly, my teeth were hurting.

One of the men from the table got up to escort me to the toilet. We walked down a dark, grubby hall, and then he opened a door and pointed into what looked like a broom closet. There was no sink. There was no toilet. There was only a large white bucket with a bare unlit lightbulb hanging above it. The man reached up and screwed the bulb in tighter to light it.

"It is all we have." He shrugged apologetically before leaving me to do my business.

If I could have held it, I would have. Instead, I dropped my Banana Republic pants to the dusty floor, and did a squat over that bucket. I never looked in. I didn't want to see what it already held. There was no toilet paper, of course. I drip-dried for as long as my thighs could hold the hover, then pulled up my pants and hurried out of there.

Back at the table in the meeting room, I looked at the plate of fig cookies on the table. I'd only had one, to be polite. But surely whoever had put them there hadn't washed their hands after using the bucket. And how were they making the coffee? Bottled water and an electric kettle poured over a press was my guess.

"Where's the restroom?" Victor whispered in my ear.

"Bucket," I whispered.

"What?"

"No restroom. Just a bucket."

Victor nodded and adjusted himself in his seat. He'd hold it, of course. Men, as far as I've seen, all seem to be related to dromedaries.

□ □ □

Over the following few days, as we met with the African intelligence officers, I grew more and more confident that this would be an excellent working relationship. Of course, as with all relationships, there was much to balance among honesty, openness, and a certain amount of manipulation and subterfuge. These guys wanted the names of every single terrorist connected to the al-Qaeda network chart we'd made. But we had to pretend that we didn't have the names or the whereabouts of everyone.

██████████████████████████████████
██████████████████████████████████
██████████████████████████████████
██████████████████████████████████
██████████████████████████████████
██████████████████████████████████
██████████████████████████████████
██████████████████████████████████

████████████████████████████████████

████████████████████████████████████

████████████████ Loyalty in the intelligence world resembles loyalty in love, marriage, and friendship. It's impossible to be entirely faithful when more than two parties are involved.

□ □ □

On our last night in Africa, Victor and I went to dinner with the men whom I now considered our teammates. Unlike every place else I'd seen, this restaurant didn't look like it had survived a bombing. Our hosts insisted on ordering the house specialty for us. There aren't too many things I won't eat, so I wasn't worried about what might show up on my plate. I was taken aback, however, when the waiter rolled out our meal. On the wheeled table, like a body on a skirted hospital gurney, was the largest fish I'd ever seen outside of a sporting show on television. It was the length of a kitchen island. As wide as my hips. The sound of it being violently gutted—the spine yanked out with a sucking, slushing sound—made my stomach roll and tumble like the sea. It was then that I decided I'd bring cases of Power-Bars whenever I traveled. I didn't have time for food poisoning. I didn't have time to be sick. I'd seen people get sent back to the States for what appeared to be incurable dysentery. I was never going to be one of those people.

□ □ □

I'd heard officers at the CIA refer to Air France as Air Chance. When I returned from Africa, I found out why. My luggage didn't return to Dulles when I did. At the lost luggage office where I went to do the paperwork, the Air France employees insisted that when my bag was found it must be sent to me—the "me" on my passport and luggage tags—rather than held at the airport to be picked up. ████████████████████████

████████████████████████████████████

██████████████████████████████████ After much bargaining and negotiating, more difficult than anything I'd gone through with the foreign intelligence officers, Air Chance agreed to send the luggage to "my best friend, Tracy Schandler," with whom I said I was staying for a while. Thankfully, this worked.

Not long after I'd returned, I went into the office on Saturday to catch up on some work. While there, I was cabled a lead from a source abroad. My source had specific information on a notorious terrorist who was now trying to make a name for himself in the chemical warfare world. He was currently on a plane flying from a country that was protecting him to a country that wouldn't protect him. After hours of flying and a layover, he would be landing Sunday morning. If I could get local operatives to tail him once he'd disembarked, it might be like following a bee back to the hive.

Immediately, I started sending cables to my contacts at the intelligence agency in the city where he was headed. I sent one after another, each with information of who this man was, what he'd done, and what I had surmised he was planning to do soon in a Western country. I checked my inbox every few minutes, waiting for a reply. By the time two hours had passed I was feeling like a desperate internet dater, just hoping anyone would respond to me. (If this had been a dating site, I would have scared away all semi-sane suitors with my relentlessness.)

The day wore on and I continued to cable. With each missive, I added more information, including the man's heinous crimes against women and children.

Finally, a simply worded one-line cable dinged in from an intelligence operative of the country where he'd soon be. No one works on Sunday, she said. And so this man, whose motives I knew so well, would get in a cab and virtually disappear into the landscape. Another terrorist to keep me awake at night.

SEVEN

ONE WORLD

Europe
Winter 2002

There was a meeting of many Western intelligence services, and our team was invited. The purpose of the meeting was to share information, discuss problems, and come up with solutions. Everyone working together with the same goal: shut down terrorists and stop terror plots before they're executed. We were in the post-9/11, pre–Iraq invasion era when al-Qaeda was ramping things up and the United States was determined to stop them no matter where in the world they planned to attack.

Three of us from the CTC/WMD teams went. The most senior CIA invitee was Victor. I liked traveling with Victor, with his huge head of hair and sharp suits. He made each person feel important, as if we all were integral parts of a puzzle in which every piece held equal value. Bernard was the third person traveling with us, though he would be arriving a day later, as he had a newborn baby at home. In his thirties, Bernard dressed as if he were playing a dad on a sitcom: every day a sweater over a button-down shirt, his small belly puffing out. I'm sure the people Bernard encountered at dinner parties or Lamaze class could never imagine that this soft-spoken, cardigan-wearing man was a razor-sharp analyst in the nukes department. I, of course, was there to speak for the WMD group. On many trips we were cross-represented like that: an analyst (Bernard), an operative (me), and a boss (Victor).

I had three goals for this visit: 1. To impart the invaluable information I had to the proper people, people who would utilize this information in the right way. 2. To gather as much information from the foreign agencies as possible. 3. To create productive alliances with intelligence officers from other countries.

The men and women who would be present at these meetings would be the heads of each intelligence agency along with those who were most effective on the ground. Either way, these were resources who could help. I was still struggling to forge relationships with operatives from a few European countries. Unfortunately, the closer we drew to the invasion of Iraq, the harder this was proving to be. Americans, and America, weren't adored by Europeans at the time. In our dogged and relentless tracking of terrorists, terrorist cells, and WMDs, along with our presence in Afghanistan, it appeared we were perceived as bullies. Even though we were trying to save the whole wide world. No exceptions.

Still, I was one woman. One Californian. One former sorority girl who was utterly determined to be seen as the individual resource I was rather than the government I represented. I was hopeful that because the "top" members of the intelligence communities would be there, I'd have more success in finding someone who would put world safety above politics.

We arrived the day before the meetings started. Our only obligation was to have dinner at the home of an associate in the city we were in. In the cab on the way to her apartment, my head was whipping from side to side as I looked out the windows. There were sparkling lights everywhere. It was as if the snowy world outside my window was in a constant glittering shimmer. The sun had set hours ago, while I had been in the hotel unpacking my bags. Darkness, coupled with below-zero temperatures, usually makes me want to hunker down in bed and watch reality TV. That's clearly not how the people of this country feel. The streets had plenty of bustling activity. There were open shops and restaurants that looked crowded and full of energy as we swooshed past them in the cab. Bicyclists were on the street, too, not one of them wearing a helmet.

I pointed out the window to a helmetless bike rider passing the cab. Victor, who had spent a lot of time there, said, "They don't worry here. About anything."

"Not even al-Qaeda?" I had recently tracked one of Zarqawi's most devoted followers to a city near here. In fact, many terrorists were relocating to Europe for the same reason you or I would go: generous health care, good public transportation, a baguette for less than a euro. Also, there was the internet. It had been banned by Taliban rule and Sharia law in some places in the Middle East. Plotting a poison attack and finding followers is much easier when you can meet up in a chat room rather than in a gritty, cold cave that might take days to get to.

"No, they're not worried about al-Qaeda. Look—" Victor pointed out the window where three prams were lined up outside a cafe. "They leave their babies outside."

"In this weather?!" It took years before my mother would let me walk to 7-Eleven alone. And that was in the dry sunshine of Southern California.

"In this weather, in any weather. They're bundled up. Kids nap outside, too. Always. Really. No matter what the weather." Victor shrugged and smiled.

"And no one gets kidnapped?"

"The only thing that gets stolen here are bikes," Victor said.

It occurred to me then that fear is often a choice. There *are* kidnappings and bike crashes and suicide bombers. And you can spend your life trying to avoid them all. Or you can live exactly as you please and enjoy each moment—drinking a beer while your kid naps outside, feeling the snow in your hair as you

pedal down the road, taking an American Airlines flight to anywhere interesting and exciting. I'd always had a certain fearless-
ness anyway, but now I was thinking of it as *European*. I would
adopt it as my outlook when I traveled, ate new foods, took in
all the world has to offer, without fear. And, in the meantime, I'd
try to get rid of the people who wanted to poison and kill us all.

I slid out of the cab while Victor paid. It had been cold in
Langley that winter, so I was adequately prepared with my
long, hooded down jacket. Black, of course, because I wanted it
to go with everything. I'd recently splurged on a pair of warm
leather gloves, and I hadn't left the house that winter without
the cashmere scarf my parents had given me for Hanukkah.

Victor paused in front of the building. It looked stately and
elegant, and I wondered what it would be like to live in a place
like that, in a country like this. Then Victor put his hand on my
puffy down shoulder and said, "She knows nothing about our
operations." I wanted to laugh. I knew the work was important,
and I felt confident that I was doing a good job, but it seemed
almost comical to me that at twenty-three years old, I'd outrank
someone who had been doing this longer than I.

"So do we just talk about . . . the darkness?" My friendships
in the mid-Atlantic still hadn't branched out past the CIA. I
rarely had conversations where I couldn't mention my work.

Victor smiled. "Follow my lead and you'll be fine."

The apartment was beautiful, tasteful, elegant, with an-
tiques that were approachable and touchable. When I sat in an
armchair, I felt like I had been tucked into a nest. There were lit
candles on the mantel and the table, and a fire burning in the
fireplace. The associate herself was every bit as elegant as the
apartment. I dealt with men so often at work, and even more
so when I interacted with other agencies in Europe and Africa,
that it felt special to see a woman abroad in a position of power.
I hadn't thought much about representation until then—I'd
been busy working, doing, thinking, trying to learn as much as

I could. But this, seeing a woman, made me realize how impactful it is for anyone of any group to see a version of themselves represented. It makes you feel included. It makes you feel like there are possibilities beyond what you already know.

The dinner conversation could have gone on without me, but I was very happy to sit and listen. I did learn about the local customs, local foods, and how the people in that country lived in a very relaxed, no-pressure way. It was as if the place was populated by surfery Californians. But instead of riding waves, they rode bikes.

□ □ □

The following morning, Victor and I took a cab to that country's intelligence headquarters. Just as I had on my last trip, I wanted to jump out of the cab and take a picture. ▮▮▮▮▮▮▮▮▮▮▮ ▮▮▮▮▮▮▮▮▮▮▮▮▮▮▮▮▮▮▮▮▮▮▮▮▮▮▮▮▮▮▮▮▮▮▮▮▮▮ ▮▮▮▮▮▮▮▮▮▮▮▮▮▮▮▮▮▮▮▮▮▮▮▮▮▮▮▮▮▮▮▮▮▮▮▮▮▮ ▮▮▮▮▮▮▮▮▮▮▮▮▮▮▮▮▮▮▮▮▮▮▮▮▮▮▮▮▮▮▮▮▮▮▮▮▮▮ ▮▮▮▮▮▮▮▮▮▮▮▮▮▮▮▮▮▮▮▮▮▮ Our purpose there was simply to meet other operatives and let them know we were in town. It's an unwritten rule in the intelligence community that when you're in another country, you announce yourself as a way of saying, "Hey, I'm not spying on *you* while I'm here." I'd had many meetings in Langley with operatives from other countries who were letting us know they were in the States. The only time someone wasn't expected to announce her- or himself was when traveling under an alias.

I was looking forward to talking to people from the intelligence community of this country. Unlike many other Europeans, these euro-Californians didn't appear to be actively hating *me* because of Bush's planned invasion of Iraq. Also, they understood the enormity of the chemical terrorism threats. They were willing to work on a Sunday.

After getting to know the locals, Victor and I spent the day separately, gathering and analyzing information from various sources. Because terror cells are like pulse points on an entire circulatory system, it takes a broader point of view, and lots of different perspectives, to really hone in on what you're seeing. In short, we were trying to make our web of information bigger than al-Qaeda's web of terror. We needed to encircle and contain them.

At the end of the day, Victor and I met up again to cross-reference our discoveries. Together, we were able to zero in on YY, and track his movements. He was someone we wanted to watch more closely—meaning we wanted eyes on him in every place he landed. YY was a bigger threat than many others, for he had passion and charisma, and was handsome and articulate. He even wrote for an al-Qaeda newsletter, broadcasting his murderous ambitions. With his charm and public-facing position, YY was attracting followers and exploiting their vulnerabilities to draw them into his extremist army. In the fold of YY, these unmoored boys and men had purpose, a community, and what they were tricked into believing was a spiritual calling. YY was becoming a top priority for us. We needed to anticipate where he'd go next, who was going with him, and what they planned to do there. In this way, we could stop YY before he and his crew were able to execute any of their plans to kill, as he frequently stated, *Westerners and Jews.*

□ □ □

Bernard arrived early that evening, in time to attend a dinner to which we'd been invited. Victor mentioned that we'd be the only ones at the dinner who weren't from Europe. At the time, that seemed like no big deal.

Again, as the cab pulled up, I wanted to take pictures. The hotel where the dinner was being held was so elegant that it made a romantic out of me. Victor, Bernard, and I stood on the sidewalk for a moment, staring at the massive stone edifice with three flags blowing from upright poles high on the roof. There were four wreaths across the front of the hotel, three or four floors up. Each was the size of the ten-foot window over which it hung. It was exactly the kind of thing I never saw growing up in Southern California.

Bernard pulled the lapels of his overcoat tighter and said, "I've gotta bring my wife here."

"When your baby's bigger," Victor said, and he started walking into the hotel. It would be a while before I'd think about things like spouses or babies, but the idea did seem sort of nice when seen through Bernard.

The inside of the hotel was luxurious: candlelight everywhere, plum-colored bouquets on tables and counters, plush velvet chairs. Victor was perfectly dressed for the setting in a dark gray suit with a lavender tie and a lavender handkerchief in his pocket. Bernard was in the same suit he'd been wearing on his flight. I was in a slim black pantsuit with a red blouse. I had taken the time to curl my hair and had put on bright red lipstick that perfectly matched my nail polish. I don't particularly like the attention of strangers, and I hate to be the focus of any group, but I love clothes, makeup, and dressing up. Since my time in the sorority, I have fully rejected the idea of anyone—any man, woman, or institution—telling me I have to dress a certain way to play a role I've been assigned through the expectations of others. So even as an intelligence officer working mostly with men, I wanted to be taken seriously while exercising the right to curl my hair into long ringlets, *because I like my hair that way.*

Of the many people in the room, I was one of only five women. Each of them was at least a couple decades older than I. I made a note of where they were so I could find them and meet them later. I tried to make eye contact with one woman who walked by me on the way to her table, but she looked past me as if I wasn't there.

Victor, Bernard, and I were seated at different tables. I was with seven men. Three were already seated and the rest of us approached around the same time. English was the common language used by everyone at each of the tables that night. Well, except mine.

The man on my left, Patrick, had short red hair, teeth that looked like they'd been blown around in a hurricane, an easy smile, and a friendly way about him. Instead of the usual gray, blue, and black worn by most men, Patrick was in a dark green suit. We shook hands, introduced ourselves, and then I turned to the man on my right, whose lips were so tight they created a straight Charlie Brown–looking line of a mouth. He had blue eyes, dark brown hair, and wore a suit so slim and fitted it looked as if he had been sewn into it.

"I'm Tracy," I said, and stuck out my hand. He looked down at my painted nails for a second before lifting his dangling wrist and offering me what felt like a damp piece of Wonder Bread.

"John . . ." he started. The rest of what he said sounded to me like foreign-movie dialogue. But without the subtitles.

Everyone at this dinner spoke English. But John refused to speak English to *me*, the only American at the table. To the Northern European beside him, he spoke English. To the Eastern and the Southern European men, he spoke English. To the hundred-year-old-looking man from a country where they speak John's native language, he spoke English. But to me: Non! Nein! Nej! John appeared to be angry at America. And he let that be known by answering me in a long series of incomprehensible (to me) sentences each time I turned to him. Even when I just asked him to pass the salt.

I'd learned long ago, when I was being bullied in school, that you can't make someone like you. And when you try, when you open your arms and ask to be liked, they swoop into that empty space and attempt to destroy you further. Working to make people like you reduces your power. Ignoring them reduces their power. *Salt* was the last word I spoke to John.

Thankfully, Patrick was happy to engage in conversation with me. He was smart, interesting, and offered valuable insights for me when we were discussing bin Laden and the attacks of September 11.

After much back and forth, he said, "Tracy, I feel bad for your people, really I do. No one ever wants anything like that to happen to America."

"Maybe—" I joked, nodding toward my right.

"Even him." He grinned. "But you have to look at it from the European perspective. The Irish were embroiled in what was basically a civil war for over thirty years—"

"The Troubles," I said.

"Yes, the Troubles. They lost more people during the Troubles than you lost on September 11, and no one besides the mothers, brothers, fathers, and children of the dead seem to give two fecks—"

"Two fecks?" I asked.

"Two fecks," he said, and I realized he was saying *two fucks*.

"You think no one cared?" I asked.

"I think individuals cared, of course. I'm sure you as an intelligent woman cared. But that doesn't mean you—or America—jumped up and tried to do anything about it. But since the Twin Towers went down, everyone in America acts like the world should drop to their knees weeping and then stand and take up arms to defend America."

I'd barely eaten my dinner. John had rattled me a bit and now this. I'd lived in the States my whole life. Most of my travel so far had been for the CIA. I did know about the Troubles. I knew about troubles and civil wars and uprisings and insurgencies and invasions and displacements on every continent for as long as *Homo sapiens* has existed. I had been a history major! But Patrick was right. I was a typical American in so many ways. In all I knew, in all I'd learned, I'd always filtered this knowledge through my love and loyalty to my own country.

This conversation with Patrick set me off on an effort toward more global thinking. It led me to believe that to be the best CIA agent I could be, and the best defender of the United States, I'd have to shift my perspective slightly so that I wasn't standing with my feet stuck in American soil like two Kansas cornstalks. Rather, I'd need to float above it all and look at the globe with all its interconnected parts so I could see more clearly how an American Navy ship anchored in the Gulf of Aden might feel like an occupation to someone on the shore of Yemen, which might send a ripple of reactionary fear to a group of displaced refugee boys being supported by al-Qaeda in a madrassa in Afghanistan. You can see where this is going. Global thinking, I began to believe, would allow me to better serve the needs of the greatest number of people. And, also, it would help me understand the point of view of my fellow operatives from Europe and Africa. There was likely no hope for me and Mister What's-His-Name. Still, there were other operatives from other countries. Surely I could find another person, besides Patrick, with whom I might be able to speak civilly.

After dinner, Victor convinced Bernard and me to go to a local amusement park. Like most kids who grow up in Southern California, Disneyland was part of my life, a familiar, seasonal joy. So I never say no to an amusement park.

This one was prettier than I imagined. More park than amusement. There were over a thousand Christmas trees covered in twinkling lights. In fact, the whole place was lit up: every building, ride, bush, and tree outlined with glittery lights, like a three-dimensional scene from a Lite-Brite toy. Or like the Main Street Electric Parade at Disney, where every float was lit the way the gardens were. The three of us walked around for a bit before Bernard decided to take a cab back to the hotel. He was worried about our presentation the next morning and wanted to get some sleep. Victor and I split up as he wanted to grab a drink in one of the many restaurants, and I preferred to continue walking through what felt like a magical wonderland.

Holiday shops had been set up along the walks, and behind them was what looked to be an illuminated mosque. It was like an Arabian Christmas village (there is a very small Orthodox Christian minority in some Arab countries, so it's not totally off base!). I'd already grown to love Islamic designs and architecture: the Hershey kiss–shaped building tops, the pointed arches in doorways, the complex patterned tilework. It is a highly mathematical aesthetic that I find deeply appealing. I admired the lit mosque for a good long time. Its presence in the park seemed wonderfully fitting for my life at the time: a Jewish American intelligence officer hunting Islamic extremists, wandering through a Christmas market with illuminated minarets in the background in Europe.

When the cold began biting through my down jacket, I went to one of the warming stations, which looked to me to be a giant trash can with a fire burning in it. I scooted in with the crowd, then saw Victor on the other side of the fire. We laughed when we spotted each other. Victor and I walked around a bit more, taking in all the sights until the park closed at midnight.

By the time I was brushing my teeth in the hotel room, it was after 1:00 a.m. The next morning we were to give our presentation, but I knew the material as well as I'd ever known anything in my life. Better even. I could have given you the date of birth and exact geo-coordinates for X and YY before I could have given you my mailing address in Virginia. Sleep, or lack of it, wasn't going to change that.

□ □ □

Early in the morning, a page led the three of us down a long, empty corridor to the room where we were to make our presentation. No one spoke. I was going over what I would say and assumed Bernard and Victor were doing the same.

We were all three in suits. Victor, who was one of the sharpest dressers at the agency, looked especially crisp that day, with a stiff pocket handkerchief and gold knot cuff links on his glowing white shirt.

We entered the conference room near the stage. I looked up at the stadium seating, at all the faces staring down at us. I felt shaky, outnumbered, like an outsider in the worst sense. I stood out. And not in a way that they—the crowd—would think was good. I was certain that what I had to offer was as valuable as what anyone else in the spy world had to offer. But after the dinner in the hotel last night, I was acutely aware of the three strikes against me. They were big strikes, too. Glowing red neon Xs on my forehead. 1. I was young. 2. I was American. 3. I was female.

Victor barely glanced at the crowd, they weren't intimidating to him. He confidently held his head high, and walked to the stage with Bernard and me following. Victor introduced himself and then told the group about the progress the CIA was making and the reliability of our sources. Next he introduced me with flowery praise, citing my work in bringing down two WMD plots and the fact that I had identified and charted the key leaders for each poison cell around the globe. Victor stepped aside and I approached the podium. My hands were shaking, so I pushed them into the slanted top of the podium. I had to get over my fear, my "otherness," quickly if I wanted to do my job right. I closed my eyes, for just a second, then opened them and let my vision go out of focus, eliminating the audience as I spoke. Within seconds I forgot that I was of a category that everyone seemed to dismiss. I forgot my fear. I forgot how much Americans were resented just then. And I said what I needed to say with the immense power of all my hard work and the work of the Poison Trio behind me. For a few moments, I felt unstoppable.

□ □ □

Several days after our presentations, Victor, Bernard, and I had dinner at a charming restaurant not far from the hotel. Like just about everything in this city, the small brick building was outlined in tiny white lights. We sat by the window, and I held the menu close to the lit candle on the table to better read it. From what I'd seen so far, these people ate a lot of pork, which was something I'd never eaten in my life. This was a point of commonality for me and the terrorists I was tracking. I was feeling slightly self-conscious about my no-pork diet and was hoping there'd be something else offered on the menu.

There was a fish dish with a complicated name. Victor translated it for me—it sounded like the title of a love song—I laughed and decided that *that* was what I'd have. Victor and Bernard ordered pork.

As soon as the waitress walked away with our orders, we started talking. And we didn't stop. For over three hours, we cross-referenced and built up our collective intelligence. We uncovered and filled in holes for one another until we had clearly mapped an entire system with names, cities, and intentions. The only thing that made this more thrilling, more glorious than usual, was the fact that I was getting this information along with one of the best meals I'd ever had abroad. You'd think it would be hard to have these two experiences simultaneously: unraveling terrorist cells while biting into steamed whitefish, along with breaded and fried whitefish, on buttered toast with shrimp, cucumber, caviar, and lemon. But it wasn't hard at all. Instead, it was a joyful confluence of new, fresh tastes along with new, fresh intelligence that almost made me want to push back my chair and applaud.

The morning we were to fly back to Langley, I set my alarm for 4:30 a.m., got up, showered, and put on warm running clothes. By 5:00 a.m., I was on the dark street in the below-zero temperature, with a hotel map in my hand and a mental route in my mind. My breath chugged out little white clouds and the cold zapped my nose like little electric shocks.

Just as I was about to turn back, I came across a statue of a winged woman with claws for feet, perched on the edge of a rock. I stopped to look at her, my hands on my knees, panting as the wind blew tears from my eyes that quickly froze on my cheeks. I had read about this statue before and knew that she had suffered multiple attacks and abuses over the years. Everything from being declawed, to being decapitated (twice!), to being decorated with a hijab and spray-painted a new color.

I examined her face. She looked a little sad, or anxious. Though maybe that look was determination: the courage to persist.

It didn't occur to me until later, when I was on the flight home, that the statue represented a version of me. She was one girl—woman—on whom some people projected their beliefs, ideas, anger, conceptions, and misconceptions. But she was impervious to it all; she appeared steadfast in spite of the bullying she'd endured. And no matter what people did to me—dismiss me because of my nationality or gender, refuse to speak to me at dinner, ignore my requests to arrest someone—I would carry on. I would endure it all. In fact, I'd do better than endure it. I'd move forward and push it behind me, rendering all those people, all those obstacles, all those judgmental words, utterly irrelevant. I'd show up in countries where America, Americans, and Jews were hated. I'd show up in countries where armies of terrorists wanted to kill Westerners.

I'd wear red lipstick, curl my hair, and stand firmly on the rock of my convictions.

EIGHT

CRASH AND BANG

Undisclosed Location, USA
March 2003

It was like camp. But maybe more fun. And with far fewer campers: ten guys and two women. Oh, and the only singing that happened was when I was alone in my car, listening to the scratchy radio that barely got a signal at the remote location where the CIA trained operatives in everything from firearms to surveillance.

I did bring a blow dryer, mascara, and lipstick, but I didn't bring a curling iron or any nice clothes. Just jeans, t-shirts, hoodies, and sweatpants. This would be my first stay at what is commonly called The Farm. Because of the urgency and intensity of my work following the September 11 attacks, I wasn't doing things in the agency's usual order. Rather than the normal three-month residency at The Farm, I'd be dropped in a week here and a week there, accumulating the skills I needed when there were breaks in my work schedule.

It took a while to get to The Farm from my apartment in Virginia. The entrance was guarded by a gate and a guard with a machine gun strapped across his chest. Gravel crunched and popped under the tires as I drove into the facility. The dense woods and towering trees created a dark and shadowy canopy.

I parked the car outside the main building and walked inside. An efficient woman in a small office gave me my room number in the dorm and a map of The Farm. Everything was so spread out that to get from one building to the next, you had to drive.

The dorm was much more spartan than the one in which I had lived at USC the year before I moved into the Delta Gamma house, but at least here I had my own bathroom. There was a toilet, a plastic-molded shower, and a dingy little sink with a mirror that was chipped in the corner. I stood in the bathroom, glanced at myself in the mirror, and shrugged. This was a rare moment, maybe the first since my freshman year in college, when I had nothing to do. As was my habit, I had arrived early, the first person to show up for the weeklong course called Crash and Bang.

Classes wouldn't officially be starting until the next day. That afternoon I hung out in my box of a room, with its cot, dresser, and pocked tiled ceiling, and unpacked the few things I had brought. Then I changed my clothes so I could go for a run.

The air was cool and felt good on my cheeks as I ran down a dirt road through the woods. I took a turn, ran for a while, and then stopped. The trees all looked alike, and the vines and shrubs growing on the damp, loamy ground all looked alike. It would be easy to get lost. I looked back to where I'd turned, marked it in my memory, and then kept running. The runner's high set in, and I started to float above myself, envisioning a map of the woods, me a moving dot along the path. I was my own drone, tracking myself, so I could see myself safely back to the dorm.

It wasn't easy to sleep with the scratching sound of rats scurrying between the walls and behind the ceiling tiles. I startled awake several times, just waiting for a square of the ceiling to come sailing down on me, being ridden by a rat as if on a surfboard. When the twelve of us met in the mess hall for breakfast, talk of the rats dominated the conversation. I felt like one of the lucky ones, as there weren't any rat droppings in the corners of my room.

After the rat chat, we settled around a couple of tables to eat. I rarely talk when in a group and didn't here as usual. Instead I ate my eggs and toast and studied the 11 people with whom I was to take this course. All of them had been stationed at Langley, and not one of their faces was familiar to me. They all looked older than me—that was often the case then. If we hadn't been sitting at the mess hall at The Farm, you might have thought this was the softball team for a bank: tellers, bank managers, the slightly overweight man who does investing for the people with big accounts. One guy may have been gay, but nobody ever asked, nobody ever cared. Because of the importance of what we were doing, because of the intensity of the work, the CIA felt like a true meritocracy. If you could do a brilliant job, then you were necessary. Nothing outside of that—not race, religion, or sexual orientation—mattered.

After breakfast we assembled in a classroom with Buck, the director of Crash and Bang. Buck was short and stocky, with a shaved head. He had to have been around fifty years old, but I imagined he could tackle and kill a team of armed men charging him. Along the length of his forearm was a ropey pink scar the width of my wrist. It looked like he'd been skinned with a dull razor blade.

"See this?" Buck held up his arm and waved it slowly from side to side. "That's what you get when you let your arm dangle out the window of a car." Buck laughed, and we did, too.

"Seriously?" Annie, the only other woman, asked. I liked Annie. She had short hair, spoke in short sentences, and seemed as direct as a pointed arrow.

"Yes, seriously. So, don't ever dangle your arm out a window." Buck nodded and went on.

We watched some movies that day. It felt a bit like junior high or high school when your teacher turned off the lights and you watched a movie in class. No matter what grade you were in, there were the kids who sat in the back who felt they were undetectable in the dark as they whispered, or passed notes, or doodled in their notebooks. I wasn't one of them. Always the good girl, I did what the teacher expected. And no one in this group was one of *those* kids, either—or at least not now. We were all grown up, working to save the world.

After lunch that day, we were each handed the keys to the cars we'd drive during our week at The Farm. All were white Ford Focuses. Buck instructed us to meet at the track—an actual full-sized car racing track—where we'd do a few speed laps and sudden stops. Most people got in their cars and drove off. Buck got in the passenger side of a car belonging to a guy named Nick. I ran to the window. Buck's arm was hanging out. I pointed at his forearm, and he laughed and pulled it in.

"Hey," I said. "I had back surgery a while ago, so I'm going to drive back to the dorm and put on a brace. That okay?"

"Yup. But hurry," Buck said. "And there're no speed limits and no other cars but ours, so you can hustle down that dirt road as fast as you want." Buck smiled, then he and Nick took off after everyone else who had already left.

I got in my car, stuck the key in the ignition, and then glared down at the stick shift. I'd never driven a stick. Never even tried.

My heart thumped a single knock, like a fist on a door. I whispered and muttered to myself as I examined the three pedals. Brake. Gas. And . . . oh yeah, the clutch. This had to be the clutch. I ran though movies, TV shows, afternoons with friends in Los Angeles, trying to re-create the image of someone driving a stick shift. I put my foot on the brake and started the car. Then I tried to move the stick shift into first. It wouldn't go.

"Clutch?" I said aloud, then pushed it in with my left foot and wiggled that stick and ball until I'd moved it into first. I pushed the gas, with my foot still on the clutch, and nothing happened. I pulled my foot off the clutch, and the car jerked once and then died. After about five tries, I figured out that you ease off the clutch while you ease onto the gas. I stalled out three more times before I figured out how to get to second gear. Third came easily, and by the time I had reached the dorm, I was okay with moving forward, but I wasn't sure how to stop. I cruised in a couple circles and then swerved to miss the single car parked near the dorm. Next, I pulled onto the small patch of grass in front of the dorm, where I pushed the clutch in, threw the stick into neutral, and slammed on the brakes so that I suddenly stopped. I felt triumphant!

I left the keys in the car, ran into the dorm, and pulled out the black Velcro-bound brace that I'd removed from my glovebox and shoved into my suitcase for use at The Farm. I'd rarely worn it the past year, but now seemed like a wise time to put it on.

The brace was barely noticeable under my black Gap t-shirt. It felt and looked sort of like a corset. I rushed out of the dorm, my torso firm, and got back in the car. I was parked on the lawn facing the dorm. With my foot on the clutch, I started the car. Then I stared at the stick shift. R had to be reverse, of course. But, no matter how hard I pushed, no matter how hard my foot was on that clutch, I couldn't get the stick to slide into R. Buck didn't seem like the kind of guy who would tolerate more than a couple minutes of delay. I had no choice. I pushed the gear into first, hit the gas, and tore across the lawn, releasing a spray of shredded grass in my wake. I shifted all the way up to fifth gear on that bumpy, gravelly road and came to a screeching stop on the track, where the other Fords were lined up. I was only a few minutes late.

That afternoon we raced around the track, two cars at a time so we wouldn't hit each other. The goal for the day was to go from zero to . . . well, as fast as you could, before coming to a complete stop. I was thrilled there was no reverse involved, and so I happily stomped on the gas, zooming fast enough to shift into fifth, before I'd boot the clutch, throw the shift into neutral, and brake so hard that the car would spin in circles. It was like a roller coaster and the Mad Tea Party ride at Disneyland at once.

Each time I stopped, when the car finally stilled, I'd burst out laughing. After so much serious work, after focus so intense that I sometimes forgot to eat or even drink water, it felt great to spin circles in a Ford Focus. It was a relief to feel like I was just playing.

When Annie and I were sitting with a few others, including Buck, on the side of the track watching two guys zoom and stop, Annie said, "It doesn't look as scary as it feels."

"I wasn't scared," I said. I had figured the CIA wasn't going to invest all this time and money into me and then let me die on a racetrack in the middle of the woods.

"Buck," Annie said. "Anyone ever die doing this?"

"Not on my watch," Buck said.

If I was fearless before, I was even more so now. Buck made me feel immortal, even in a car I had yet to master.

The next day there were more movies and classroom work. We met the other Crash and Bang instructors, Judy, Larry, and Mo. They were each just as tough looking as Buck. Defensive driving must be a skill that attracts a certain kind of person: the kind who seems to be made of hard rubber and doesn't mind a few gaping, visible scars.

Back at the track again, we found two rows of beat-to-hell Crown Victorias and Buicks. It was like the parking lot for a meeting of eighties drug lords.

"Pick your car, keys are inside," Buck said. "And there are no airbags to get in your way."

I had fallen into a fun foursome with Annie and two guys: Nick and Danny. They all had a great sense of humor, and none of them was full of themselves, in spite of their impressive credentials. Annie was about to be deployed to Africa; Nick would soon return to the Middle East; and Danny was off to Latin

America. We stood together, staring at four cars parked facing each other, two by two.

"I'll be Starsky," Nick said, and he pointed to the oldest of the four cars.

"I'm calling Hutch," Annie said, and she walked to the car facing Nick's.

"Bat Girl," I said, and I went to the black car.

Danny looked at the last remaining car; it had a dent in the side the size of a turkey platter. "So who am I?" Danny asked. "Boy Wonder?" He pulled on the door but it wouldn't open.

"Window!" Buck shouted. Danny looked at the open window, then climbed in.

For hours that afternoon we were to practice what is called pursuit intervention technique, or PIT. We'd already watched movies about it; discussed it with Buck and Judy, who also taught that day; studied charts of it on a whiteboard; and asked every *what if* question imaginable. And then Judy and Buck performed a version of it in the classroom with their bodies as stand-ins for cars. Now it was time to take everything that was in our heads and transform it into actions and reflexes.

I volunteered to be the first person pursued. It looked thrilling in the movies and only remotely dangerous. Nick was chosen to knock me off the road.

We stood outside our beat-up cars and Buck went over PIT one more time. I'd drive as fast as I could around the track. Nick would pursue me and then close in on my left. When he was close enough, he'd nip the back left corner of my car with his front right corner and send me spinning. It's sort of like a game of human pool. Nick's car was the rolling ball and mine was the one he was trying to hit into the pocket.

"Don't hurt me," I said, but I was smiling.

"You know I will." Nick flashed a huge grin.

I took off first. This car was an automatic so I didn't have to worry about shifting. Once I was going around 70, Nick drove onto the track to pursue me. My seatbelt was on, the back brace was corseting me upright, and my window was down, blowing my hair straight back from my face. It felt great, liberating. Thrilling.

Each time Nick got close in his Starsky car, I pushed a little harder on the gas just to give him a good chase. We went around the track at least three times before he was finally able to catch up. He swerved toward me once but didn't knock me, and when he pulled away, he almost started spinning out. It took another couple of laps before Nick could catch up. When he did, I could sense that he had placed himself properly. I knew exactly what was coming. The bang was nearly soundless, but the impact felt noisy. I screamed, mostly in joy, as I spun around twice and then landed like a dead bug at the side of the track. Nick had executed a PIT perfectly.

It was even more fun being the person pursuing the runaway car. I chased down and hit a guy named Bill in the first lap around the track. When I backed up to check on him, he leaned out the window and said, "Let's do it again. I'm going to try to outrun you."

He tried. But he couldn't.

By the time it was getting dark, we were practicing two-car tag teams. The first car would knock on the left side and get the pursuant spinning to a stop. The pursuant would then gun the engine again and keep going, only to be knocked on the right side from the second pursuer. When it worked perfectly, the pursued car ended up sandwiched between the two cars, stopped dead on the road.

The coordinated work felt a little like my old dance team. There was a certain choreography and rhythm; you had to sense the bodies—the cars—around you and match yourself to them, synchronize with them. By the end of the day, after hitting and being hit by just about everyone in our group, we'd bonded into a cohesive unit.

I drove my Bat Girl car many times over the week. I finally had to say goodbye to her the afternoon when we practiced driving our eighties drug lord cars into a cement wall that stood at the long end of the track. If the car could still be driven, you did it again. If you totaled it the first time, your job was done.

Near the close of that day, I stood beside my car at the end of the track waiting for my turn to go again. Frankie, a Twizzler-skinny guy with red hair, had just driven into the wall at such a high speed that his Buick had accordioned to the point where he couldn't get out. Buck appeared to be pulling the door off with his hands, ripping the car open like a superhero. When Frankie finally emerged, we all clapped and cheered, and Frankie took a dramatic bow.

I opened my back brace and retightened it. Like the day when we were practicing T-boning parked cars, this exercise worried me a little more than the others. At least when we drove straight into cars, there was give, movement on the other side. But a cement wall? I ran through Newton's three laws of motion, the first being that an object continues to be in motion unless acted upon by a force. The second being that the amount of force is equal to the mass multiplied by the acceleration—so, me and the Bat Girl car, times whatever speed I hit, would decide how much force would be exerted. And the third being that when one body (me and the car) exerts force on a second body (the cement wall), the second body (the wall) exerts a force equal in magnitude and the opposite direction of the force (me and the car). In other words, my guts, my heart, my organs, and my two-year-repaired spine would push back in my body with the same force as I pushed forward into the wall.

I unwrapped and retightened the back brace once more. No matter what Newton had proven, I wasn't going to slow down and give anything less than my best.

Buck pointed at the bare area of the wall next to Frankie's wasted heap of metal. I got in my car, started it up, and focused on the open spot. Buck trotted to the side of the track, and then I took off. I wanted to smash into that wall at a speed somewhat less than what Frankie had done, but more than my last run, which left my front bumper barely scraped.

When I hit the cement, there was a wonderful metallic, crunching sound. I flew forward. I flew back. I settled into my seat. Everything felt fine. I had nailed it.

□ □ □

One evening, Buck, Judy, Larry, and Mo showed up at the dorm. A few of us were in the sitting area watching *The Bachelor* on TV and heckling the contestants. We weren't drinking, but we were pretending to, taking pantomimed shots each time someone said the word "journey." We all looked up when the instructors walked in. Annie picked up the remote and muted the TV.

"Meeting down at the mess hall," Buck said. Then he turned to me and said, "Tracy, I'll ride with you."

The keys to the Ford were in my pocket. I pushed myself off the couch and walked out of the dorm with Buck.

The darkness was astounding. If it weren't for the sheet of white stars, I would have thought I was in a sealed velvet bag. There were no streetlights at The Farm. No city lights. No empty buildings lit up. No sirens throwing sound and light out into the landscape. It was just thick blackness with the eerie sense of the trees closing in around you. And above that was only sky—that beautiful, vast, and starry sky.

"It's not like this in D.C.," I said. Part of my chatter was to make up for my nervousness. The day we'd been handed the keys to the Fords we'd been instructed to always park "ass-in." This allows for a quick getaway, of course, but it also requires that you use reverse, which remained beyond my abilities. I'd figured out about eight different ways to get ass-in to most spots at The Farm, all of which required circling other parked cars, driving over rocks, dirt, and grass, and banging over parking bumpers so that I'd end up face out. My *circle and drive-over* technique proved hardest at the dorm, however, where the building position, along with the small parking lot, led me to usually park at some strange angle that made it look like I'd been drinking.

Buck looked up at the sky, moved his chin as if he were outlining the Milky Way, and then nodded at me. "Yeah, we're all alone out here. Not a soul other than the people in that building right now." Buck pointed at the dorm. No one else was coming out, so I figured they all had to fetch their keys from their rooms.

We got in the Ford. I was relieved that Buck had said nothing about the crooked-tooth angle in which I was parked. Buck rolled down his window and hung his arm out. I laughed.

"I was hit by a car speeding in the opposite direction," he said, shaking his arm and then letting it dangle. "But that's impossible right now. Even the cleaning crew isn't here. Even Bernetta, that woman who checked you into your room, isn't here. It's just us and the stars."

I put the car in first and did the usual high-propulsion take-off over the lawn and out of the parking area.

Buck gave a closemouthed smile. "I guess no one will get you like that," he said.

"Mess hall, right?" I was avoiding conversation about my parking position, lest I had to admit my handicap.

"Yeah," Buck said. "Take a left up at the fork, we'll follow the scenic route."

"Nothing really to see," I said as I veered onto the left fork. "Just another mass of darkness with all those looming trees." I went fairly fast even though I could only make out the road as far as my headlights.

"Yup," Buck said. "Not even a moon tonight."

"Do you ever look into the woods," I asked, "and wonder how many pairs of eyes are looking back out at you?"

"Of course," Buck said. "I'm in intelligence. Like you."

Something scurried in front of the car, and I slammed on the brakes.

"Tracy!" Buck said. "You've learned how to drive straight into a cement wall, and you're braking for a—" Buck paused; he looked like he was trying to find a word.

"Yeah, what was that?" We were moving again, and I quickly picked up speed.

"I don't know, maybe a badger?" Buck said.

"What even is a badger?" I shifted into fourth gear. "I mean, I know the word, but, like, I can't quite picture a *badger*."

"I think *that* was a badger," Buck said. "But listen, rule number one, if it's the size of a goat or smaller, hit the damn animal! You put yourself in greater danger braking or swerving around it than you do when you just—"

I slammed on the brakes again. In the light of my beams was a roadblock. Two cement posts with a rail crossed between them. I no sooner had registered this odd sight when a man dressed in black, with a ski mask pulled over his face, slammed a pistol into the window, pointing it right at my head.

Before he could speak, I threw the car into first, stomped on the gas, and drove straight through the barricade, smashing it with a satisfying pop as I shifted higher and higher until I was racing down the black, bumpy road in fifth gear.

Buck smiled and nodded. "Pull over, pull over," he said.

I shifted down and then threw the car in neutral to stop. I turned and looked at Buck.

"That was perfect," Buck said.

"You planned that?" I hadn't even had time to be afraid. It was a moment of pure reaction. And I think, really, with Buck in the car, I simply wasn't going to be afraid. I mean, the man was missing a chunk of his arm, and he regularly joked about it.

"Yeah. And you passed perfectly. That is *exactly* what you were supposed to do."

"Cool." I smiled.

"Yeah, cool," Buck said. "Now get us to the mess hall."

Over the next hour or so, the rest of the group filtered into the mess hall. Most people grabbed a beer from the fridge as they clearly needed a little help to decompress. People were laughing as each one of us shared the story of what he or she did when held up at gunpoint at the roadblock.

"I swear I almost shit my pants," Frankie said.

"I peed a little," Nick admitted. "I know that's something women usually do, but it just leaked out of me."

"Maybe everyone does it, but women are the only ones who admit it," Annie said.

More than one person had rolled down the window and tried to negotiate with the gunman. A few people had thrown the car in reverse and backed up. As a group, we had covered almost every option to save ourselves. After the initial couple seconds of shock, no one really thought they were being held up. We each had been in the car with an instructor, and none of those instructors had screamed or reacted as if it were a holdup.

Once we'd all told our stories, Buck gave the entire holdup lesson in just a few sentences.

"You all should have done what Tracy did," he said. "Drive forward. Crash the gate. Run over anyone who's in your way. And get the hell outta there. The second you stop, the second you try to negotiate, the second you take off in reverse, the second you try to drive around the barricade and through the trees . . . you are dead. Bang. Bang. Dead. If that had been real, only one of you would be alive right now."

Of course, I couldn't help but wonder: if I had known how to shift into reverse, would I have simply backed up?

□ □ □

Surveillance was an ongoing part of the course that week. We were required to continually use a surveillance detection route—SDR—every time we drove from one place to the next on The Farm. This meant we could never take the same route twice. And each time we went anywhere, we were to make false turns, start off in the wrong direction, circle around, enter from different angles . . . you get the picture. It's driving in a way that makes following nearly impossible.

There were multiple roads, multiple turns, and a few dead-ends to help facilitate SDR. I'd pretty much memorized the map I'd been handed the first day and usually had an innate sense of where I was and where I was going. Of course, I was the only one who had trained for a year in map reading, so maybe I had an advantage over the others. Also, with my usual diligence, I looked at the map before bed each night and planned all my routes for the next day. Others may have done this, too. When anyone was caught taking the same route twice (most people claimed it was by accident), they were ambushed by people—instructors and their assistants—who shot at them with what are called Simunition rounds. Simunition guns are fake semiautomatic weapons that look real and require the same shooting skills as a working gun. Instead of bullets, they release paintballs. By the end of each day, some of the white Fords were as speckle-colored as an Easter egg. Mine, and Annie's, remained "pure as the driven snow" throughout the week.

□ □ □

Before I'd arrived at The Farm, I'd thought the *Bang* part of Crash and Bang was what we'd feel each time we smashed the cars into something. It turned out, the *Bang* was about BANG! Explosives.

The first day of Bang I drove a new circuitous route that led me across a low gurgling stream to the explosives building. It was the most peaceful entrance to a place that would be anything but.

At the start of each class we were issued goggles, a vest, and gloves. There were fewer movies and discussions than there had been in our Crash lessons. Instead we focused on lab work. Like poison school, there was a lot of chemistry involved and a whole lot of focus. One slipup, one serving of too much picric acid or nitrogen trichloride, and the building could be brought down.

Our failures or successes in the lab were tested at the end of each day just a short walk outside the building. The 12 of us, along with some of the instructors, stood in a half-buried, fortified bunker with an impenetrable plexiglass window. From this viewing post, we'd look out to the field, where old, inoperable cars had been lined up. Sometimes there was a dummy sitting in the driver's seat. Someone had a sense of humor and usually put an unlit cigarette in the dummy's mouth, or a beer bottle in his or her hand. And there was always an arm hanging out the window, waiting to be skinned.

It seemed to take forever between the time the explosives were set up and the time we watched them blow. No matter how many times we did it, the sound of the bang always surprised me. And there was an eerie satisfaction in seeing something almost disappear. Was this human nature? The urge to want the power of destruction equal to that of the power of creation? I couldn't watch those explosions without thinking of terrorists, al-Qaeda, the perverse joy of those who were on the sidelines as they witnessed the creation of ash and rubble through the decimation of people and the buildings that held them.

Of all my visits to The Farm, Crash and Bang was, admittedly, the most fun. But there wasn't a moment that went by when I didn't connect what we were doing to what I was, and would be, doing out in the field. Drive a serpentine, backward route so that no one can follow me. Park ass-in so I can get the heck outta there. Crash the barricade and kill the badger so that no one can kill me first.

And understand that if I end up in the explosion zone, I better hope my affairs are in order.

NINE

TRUTH AND CONSEQUENCES

**Langley, Virginia, and the Middle East
March–May 2003**

Johnny Rivers, from the office of the president, made regular visits to my cubicle, looking for a connection between Saddam Hussein and Zarqawi's chemical terror group. I'd eye him from across the room, his tie knotted too high on his neck, gamboling toward me.

"Anything?" he'd ask.

"Nope," I'd say, and I'd point to my cubicle wall where I had taped up the latest copy of the al-Qaeda poison chart, which clearly laid out who was leading what poison cell and where. Not one person on this chart was connected to Saddam Hussein.

President Bush was angling to invade Iraq and wanted evidence to justify it. He was like a spouse in a bitter divorce, trying to gather up whatever scraps he could to make his case. But in this instance, the collateral damage wouldn't be the kids, the house, the RV, or the boat. It would turn out to be the whole world.

As directed, Ben, David, and I, along with our contacts on the ground, searched and searched for ties between Zarqawi and his chemical cells and Saddam Hussein. We came up with nothing. It didn't matter how many times someone from the White House asked for a connection; we weren't going to give one when it simply didn't exist.

One day Bud Smyth from the vice president's office said to me, "We saw in your report that Zarqawi was in Baghdad for medical treatment."

I said, "Yes, he visited a doctor there."

"Seems to me," he said, "that his time in Baghdad would show a direct link between him and Hussein."

"Uh, well, I'm sorry," I said. "It doesn't."

Later, when Ben, David, Graham, Sally, Victor, and I met in Graham's office, I relayed Bud's supposition that a few days in Baghdad had created a connection to Hussein.

"I was in Baghdad a few days last month," Victor said. "Does that mean I'm working with Hussein?"

"Yes," David said, smiling.

I said, "It's sort of like when someone asks me if I know their friend in California simply because we're from the same state."

"California and Iraq are pretty much the same size," Graham said. "So it's exactly like that."

"Twenty-five million Iraqis . . ." Ben said. "Aren't there more Californians?"

"Thirty-five million," Sally said, "but he's talking square miles."

"Keep your heads down," Graham said. "And don't let what they want to be true persuade you into seeing something that isn't really there."

Bud returned a couple days later with the same questions. I answered him politely and stuck to what was real and true.

Far more troubling than these visits was the fact that we had located crude poison labs in Iraq that were remotely related to Zarqawi. These labs were started around September 2001 by a terrorist group of Iraqi Kurds who called themselves Ansar al-Islam. Some intel suggested they consulted with Zarqawi to create the labs. And sources on the ground had placed Zarqawi as hiding there in the months before the invasion. Still, that didn't connect Zarqawi to Hussein. In fact, it did the opposite.

The Kurdish people had been routinely murdered in Saddam Hussein's genocide. In theory, the members of Ansar al-Islam were on our side, as they wanted to get rid of Hussein as much as we did, if not more so. In practice, however, they were terrorists, and the very people many of us in the CIA feared would rise out of the morass if the United States were to take out Hussein. Everyone I spoke with in counterterrorism wanted to quickly pick up Zarqawi while we had him pinpointed and eliminate the Ansar al-Islam labs. We needed to dismantle this armed group before the country was thrown into chaos.

██
██

████████████ If that wasn't enough to keep me up at night, there was the fact that African terrorists were rapidly becoming the greatest threat to peace. An invasion of Iraq would suck up America's resources and take all the focus off Africa, giving the terrorists there plenty of room to thrive.

The whole thing felt like a nutty funhouse game. Only dangerous. No matter what we reported to the administration, they turned it around, turned it inside out, and spat it back out into some non-truth version of what had been said. Zarqawi with Ansar al-Islam became Zarqawi working for Hussein. Ansar Al-Islam's crude, barely functioning poison labs in northern Iraq became nuclear testing grounds. Terrorists who weren't even fractionally smart enough or wealthy enough to develop tools of mass destruction were turned into feared enemies. And terrorists who were organized, funded, and just then plotting to destroy people all over Europe, the Middle East, and Africa were virtually ignored.

The morning huddle with the Poison Trio, Sally, Graham and Victor, became an ongoing analysis and critique of the White House. There was a certain relief in venting each day. It was our way of not feeling gaslighted, not feeling that we were insane for believing the truths we were finding.

I continued to update and print copies of the poison chart, which I taped to the walls of my cubicle. People from the office of the president, the office of the vice president, or the office of Donald Rumsfeld or Condoleezza Rice or Colin Powell continued to approach me, question me, and then walk away with a copy of that chart.

The information on the chart was factual. The chart was only altered by us when we found new cells, or when terrorists within the cells rose in rank or died.

On Monday, February 4, I handed a finished chart to the office of the White House. On Wednesday, February 5, Colin Powell made a speech to the United Nations in an effort to garner support for the invasion of Iraq. My colleagues and I watched the speech on television. As Powell presented his case, he held up the chemical terrorists chart. But it *was not the chart I had turned in.* The words *Iraqi-Linked* had been added to my words *Terrorist Chart.*

Now I understood why the CIA had been denied approval to pick up Zarqawi and take out the Ansar al-Islam labs in northern Iraq. All our information was being reframed and then submitted as proof that Hussein had weapons of mass destruction. Zarqawi, *who had no known connections to Hussein,* was mentioned 21 times in that one speech. Yes, 21. Suddenly, our guy hanging out with the terrorists who wanted to kill Hussein, and more importantly, the guy running the poison networks for Europe and Africa, was allegedly building chemical labs for the state of Iraq. In one speech, this demented thug—who had been little known outside of intelligence agencies—became the justification for the invasion of Iraq by the United States and the allies we'd gathered—which at that point were England and Spain. With his newfound prominence, before the war even started, the man we could have nabbed went into deep cover.

Someone in charge of things somewhere—though my gut says it wasn't Bush, Cheney, or Rumsfeld—knew it wasn't good to jump in and overthrow a government without any plans for how to run the joint once we were in charge. In a last-ditch, late-start effort, no fewer than 17 different groups, which included people from the CIA and Iraqis who were currently living in the United States, did a fast study of past wars, past invasions, and past regime changes in an effort to prepare the United States for all possible outcomes.

The reports detailed likely scenarios and laid out how to respond. There were entire binders on things such as how to avoid the looting and destruction of places of worship and buildings of historic significance. The thousands of pages of work, however, appear to have been virtually ignored. A civilian on the ground after Baghdad had fallen is quoted in James Fallows's *Atlantic* article "Blind into Baghdad" as saying, "People are used to *someone* being in charge, and when they realize no one is, the fabric rips."

We invaded. The fabric ripped. And there was a gaping, muddy hole that sucked in many of the unmoored men of Iraq: some from the disbanded military (unemployed and armed); some members of the Ba'ath Party (the minority in Iraq and the former ruling party), who were soon banned from public office; some of those who (as predicted in many of the reports) viewed the liberation as an occupation; all the former members of Ansar al-Islam (whom, as I said before, the CIA had wanted to disband for exactly this reason before the war started); along with the usual Islamic extremists who already believed America was occupying the Middle East because of our presence in Saudi Arabia and our support for Israel. From this mud rose new legions of terrorists. (Soon enough, they'd congeal with the Bush-anointed Zarqawi as their leader and rebrand themselves as ISIS or ISIL.)

When it became clear that this war was a lot messier than most people had expected, and that there were no WMDs in Iraq, the CIA was blamed for the whole shebang, falsely accused of having provided faulty intelligence.

I must say this in response to that accusation: I was there. I'm one of the people who supplied the intelligence. *Not a single bit of anything my team turned in was faulty.* How it was changed and twisted by the White House was faulty.

The CIA did not betray the White House. The White House betrayed the CIA.

Everyone I worked with in the CIA was outraged. But there was no time to wallow in despair over what had already gone down. If my altered chart had started this war, then I was going to devote my life to undoing as much damage as I could. I had to simply double my efforts and focus on what was real and sure: 1. Chemical weapons in the hands of al-Qaeda in Europe and Africa. 2. Al-Qaeda's plans to use those chemical weapons against Westerners and Jews.

□ □ □

Just a couple months after the start of the war, Ben and I flew to the Middle East to visit a prison where several of al-Qaeda's chemical team members were being held. This prison was where many key al-Qaeda leaders had entered years earlier as common hoodlums and, after coming in contact with influential imprisoned jihadists, exited as radicalized Islamists. Some of the men held in the prison might know where Zarqawi, X, or anyone else on their team was. And they also might know what chemical plots were currently being cooked up by the WMD crew. At the very least, they might have the phone numbers or email addresses of people who were of great interest to the CIA.

On the flight overseas, I wore a new suit I'd bought in California on my last trip home. My mother loves to shop as much as I do, and we'd picked it out together. It was tuxedo-looking and had a high waist that looked like a satin cummerbund. I felt confident in this suit. It was like putting on a costume and playing a part: the grown-up woman taking down terrorists wherever she could find them.

I slept fine in that suit. A few minutes before we landed, I went to the airplane lavatory, brushed my hair, put on pink lipstick, and then sprinkled some water on my camisole so that the wrinkles would fall out by the time we went through customs.

The airport in this country was clean and modern-seeming. As we walked out of customs and into the terminal, I saw two distinct lines for security. One for men, the other for women. I pulled my pashmina from my bag and slipped it over my head, though really, there were so many people of different nationalities in the airport, it didn't feel like a requirement.

A driver was waiting for us. We were supposed to go straight to the CIA offices, but Ben wanted to see the area where a Western man had recently been assassinated. His killers hadn't been caught yet, but everything pointed to al-Qaeda. Bush had been preparing for war at the time of this assassination, which appeared to cause a reactionary amp-up of al-Qaeda's jihad.

The area where the man had been killed was clean. It looked like a place where one would feel entirely safe going for a walk. Yet, in the past two years, in addition to this assassination, three other Westerners had also been killed.

"There," the driver said as he stopped the car on a modern-looking street with comfortable houses that I could imagine living in.

The two of us looked out the window. It was a peaceful, bright, quiet day. A couple strolled by with a well-groomed dog on a leash. In my imagination, I watched a middle-aged man walk to his brightly colored car, reach for the door handle, and then turn to face two men who gunned him down for no reason other than the fact that he held an American passport.

"Did he have kids?" I asked.

"Yes," Ben said.

"Don't tell me how many." I needed to shut off the horror film that was running in my head.

□ □ □

The CIA offices here were among the most populous outside of Langley. I'd cabled with many people there and found all of them helpful, friendly, and cooperative. Well, almost all. There was Fred. The cables I got from Fred had an attitude, a gruffness and bossiness, that I'd never seen in any other cables.

"Can't wait to meet Fred," I whispered to Ben as we made our way to the counterterrorism offices.

"Ah, Fred," Ben said. "The barking underling."

People stood and introduced themselves to us. And then, from across the room, I saw a toadish-looking man with pink skin and yellow-blond hair lean out from his cubicle and stare us down. He made brief eye contact and then walked toward us with a wide-legged waddle, which reminded me of a cowboy.

"Fred?" I stuck out my hand. He was shorter than me and had a belly that projected like an awning over a porch.

Fred didn't shake my hand. Instead he looked me up and down and said, "What kind of ridiculous outfit is this?"

"My suit?" I thought it was sharp. Stylish. The wrinkles had even fallen out since the flight.

"You're in the Middle East, for fucksake," he said, "not on a shopping trip at Saks Fifth Avenue."

"So, what have you got on Zarqawi's team?" Ben looked down at Fred with his eyes tensely slitted.

"My desk is back there," Fred snapped. "Come see me and I'll give you what you need for the prison visit." Fred waddled away quickly.

Once he was out of earshot, I leaned into Ben and said, "Definitely sexually frustrated."

"Roger that," Ben said.

"Can you imagine actually having sex with someone who continually barks like that?" I asked.

Ben looked at me and laughed.

As repellent as Fred was, he did at least provide good intel. He appeared to be pouring all that pent-up hormonal energy into finding Zarqawi. I had a feeling he wouldn't rest, and probably wouldn't stop berating his colleagues, until Zarqawi was eliminated. Ben and I stood near Fred's desk for over two hours exchanging information. When we were done, I was grateful. Still, I didn't want to try to shake his hand, so I just turned and walked away.

In my fabulous suit.

Ben and I were put up at the Four Seasons because there were no rooms at the Hyatt, where people from the agency usually stayed. ████████████████████████████████████ ██ ███████████████████████████████ The country, and the Hyatt in particular, was full of diplomats, aid workers, some military, and probably a lot of intelligence workers from all nations. The Four Seasons had many of those same people. And so many British guests that when I sat in the lobby and didn't look out the window, I felt like I was in London.

The prison was a few hours away, so we'd be going there first thing in the morning. In the meantime, Ben wanted to nap for a couple hours in his nice room. I was happy to have two hours alone in my room.

When the call to prayer started, I slid open my balcony doors and stood at the rail looking down at the bright city. The call was beautiful and slightly melancholy sounding. Much better in person than what we had listened to from a computer when I was in The Vault.

Most people down on the street continued to go about their business. One car stopped in the right lane and put on the hazard lights. Five men got out, unrolled mats on the sidewalk, and prayed. People walked around them without paying much attention to them. Cars honked quickly—not a New York City lean on the horn, more of a tap-tap—and then drove around their vehicle.

When the call to prayer was over, I turned on the BBC and then sat on the balcony and listened to the news. It was Thursday, May 15, 2003, and not much good was happening, particularly in the Middle East. Only three days earlier, three compounds in Riyadh, Saudi Arabia, had been attacked by truck-driving suicide bombers. This was a well-orchestrated al-Qaeda attack that had to have had some insider involvement, as the terrorists knew the systems to get past the gates of each compound once the guards had been killed. ███████████ ██—there had been enough chatter to know that something was in the works, but we hadn't had the specifics of where.

It all seemed part of the messy, bloody web of warring nations, factions, people, beliefs. More and more, the United States was seen as occupying Iraq, rather than trying to save it. This bolstered al-Qaeda's entrenched ideas that we'd been occupying Saudi Arabia since 1991, when American troops were stationed there during the first Gulf War, waged by Bush Senior.

I was glad I was only listening to the news. I didn't want to see the images I'd already taken in of the smoking rubble, the 39 dead, the 160 injured, and the dozens of children who were injured or killed. One of the compounds was owned by an American company that was training the Saudi National Guard, one was owned by a London-based company, and the third was a housing compound where mostly Westerners resided.

The news moved on to a speech by Paul Bremer, who five days prior had been named by President Bush as the head of the coalition provisional authority of Iraq. This meant Bremer was essentially in charge of the place. When asked about a replacement for Saddam Hussein, who had gone into hiding, Bremer talked only of getting rid of the Ba'ath Party members who were still active in government. When asked about restoring order to chaos, Bremer quoted the exact number of men who had been arrested within the last 48 hours. He spoke as if everything was now under control.

But nothing was under control.

I went back into the room, turned off the TV, then returned to the peacefulness of the balcony. I had to focus on the things I could control, the things and people I could reach, the terrorist plots I could take down before they took down innocent civilians.

With my feet resting up on the rail and the sun beating down on my face, I went over all the information Fred the barking cowboy toad had given me. I sorted it in my head, prioritized, and prepared for my meeting with the local intelligence at the prison.

Once I felt saturated with what I knew, I fetched the magazines I'd bought at the airport in D.C.—*Vanity Fair, US Weekly*, and *Glamour*. Back on the balcony with the magazines stacked in my lap, I entered a realm that didn't even remotely acknowledge the bloody, violent, and chaotic terrors of the world. It was a beautiful, shallow, star-studded escape.

□ □ □

Late that afternoon, Ben and I had plans to go to a souk, a large open market in the center of the city. One of the guys from the CIA, a Texan named Randy, was coming with us. We'd cabled often with Randy, had talked to him a bit in the office earlier in the day, and felt like we knew him well, even though we'd only seen his face for the first time that morning.

Randy picked us up in a cab, and we rode over together. He spoke Arabic and was loving everything about being in the Middle East.

Before we got out of the cab, I pulled my pashmina from my purse, tossed it over my head, and wrapped the loose ends around my neck. I'd seen some women on the street uncovered. But none were blond. And none looked very Western.

"Sorry it's so hot for that thing," Randy said, as if he were responsible for the weather.

It was above 80 degrees and I was in a long-sleeved black t-shirt and loose black pants. But I had no choice. I was about to step foot in the real city and not the Western-flooded places I'd already been: the airport, the hotel, and the CIA offices.

When I got out of the cab, a man on the street stopped mid-stride, whipped his head toward me, and stared. He was just the first. No matter that I covered my hair, bits of it fell out and flashed like Christmas lights on my shoulders. As we walked along the stalls, a kid scrambled up a tree and pointed at me while shouting something.

Randy translated. "He said, look at her green eyes!"

As much as I was taking in the souk, people seemed to be taking in me. As an introvert, it's not a comfortable feeling. I thought about new immigrants to America, people of color in all-white neighborhoods, and people wearing hijabs after September 11 when an anti-Muslim mania swept through parts of the country. To be stared at like that is to double down on the outsider feeling. You feel it inside already, and then, when you are looked at the way I was as I walked through the crowded market, it's like you are being told, *you're not one of us.* I made a note to store this feeling somewhere in my brain. To pull it out and think about it the next time I noticed someone who looked different from everyone else around them. We are all the same, I thought. Green eyes, brown eyes, hijab, no hijab, we want the same things. Peace. A purpose. To love and be loved.

And I really wanted a necklace I found at one of the stands.

There were crowds at every stall, but this one was worse, with people crammed in shoulder to shoulder. Some were looking at me and some were looking at the handmade jewelry. I held in my hand a fine gold chain with an intricately woven gold hamsa amulet hanging from it. The hamsa, in the shape of an open right palm, had a blue evil eye in the center. Like the simple evil eye alone, a hamsa is believed to protect the wearer from the malevolent glare of others. I don't think the people who were pointing and staring at me were malevolent at all. Just curious. Still, I wanted the magic of the hamsa near me. Randy negotiated the price, and I walked away with the hamsa hanging from my neck.

Had I lived there I would have bought so much more. The spice vendor's display was beautiful for the colors alone. There were handbags, clothing, food, shoes . . . whatever you can think of was there. Some of the aisles were covered with draped awnings to keep out the glaring heat, and some were open to the sky. Families shopped together. Women and girls walked in groups, leaning into each other, talking continuously. Men walked down the aisles holding hands, as most Middle Eastern men do. It was interesting to me that in a country where men and women are separated in so many ways and places, a physical affection between same-sex friends and family comes out in public.

"You two should hold hands," I said to Ben and Randy.

Ben looked at me and shook his head. But he was smiling.

Randy said, in his charming Texas accent, "That's for deep cover. Right now, I'm just Randy being Randy."

□ □ □

A car picked Ben and me up at six in the morning for the long drive to the prison.

Ben and I both sat in the backseat, each looking out our own window. The buildings we passed seemed to reflect the people of this city: modern and traditional, every shape and size, all packed in together.

It wasn't long before the chaos and sounds of cars and horns gave way to silence and emptiness. Desert as far as I could see. There were a few men with camels along the road and tourists riding the camels' backs for a small fee. And then, when we were even farther from the city, there was nothing but golden ocher sand, with patches of green popping up at random like whiskers on the chin of a teenage boy. From time to time we passed big rock formations, beautifully round and wind-carved.

The prison appeared suddenly like an apparition. It was encircled with towers, barbed wire, fences, guards. It looked impossible to escape. And then, even if one did escape, where would you go? It would be like escaping on the moon—how long could you last without a spacesuit and the mother ship?

Ben and I were led to a small, blandly beige, conference room. Mounted on the four walls were clocks set to the time zones of major cities around the world. Ben slowly turned in a circle, looking at the clocks and trying to translate the city name beneath each one. I looked at the door, anxious to meet the local operatives who would be arriving shortly. The people of this intelligence force are known to be intense, stringent, relentless, and somewhat terrifying. They are the people you want working on your side and never working against you.

When eight men finally filed into the room, I had to stop myself from audibly reacting. It wasn't as if they looked like buffoons. They just looked like plain nice guys. In suits. Men who, in America, might loosen a tie, crack open a Bud, and stoke up the barbeque. Or maybe pretend to nap on a lawn chair as they watched their fifteen-year-old kid mow the grass.

The ten of us sat around a table and were served thick, dark, sweet coffee in small glass cups. As soon as the conversation started rolling, everyone was animated, intense. Except Ben, who always had a calm, reserved poise to him. If there was any group who could match the CIA's zealotry in tracking Zarqawi and the chemical guys, these guys were it. Just the mention of Zarqawi caused commotion at the table—fist banging, shouting, fiery eyes.

Ben and I discussed the information we needed to get from a terrorist they were holding. He was someone we knew had intimate knowledge of the chemical terror world. If he gave us the right contacts and information, we could find out what major plans were in the works and who exactly was involved in them.

"Tell me specifically what you want to know," one guy said. Of all the men in the room, he looked the most put together, with thick, shiny hair parted and combed to the side and a suit that must have been pressed with starch.

Ben and I went through our list of questions. Using a short, tooth-bitten pencil, the operative translated our words into his language and wrote them in a little spiral notebook. He nodded his head at each inquiry, as if to agree that it would be useful information.

When we were done, he flipped the book shut and stood.

"One moment," he said, and left the room.

Less than an hour later, the man returned. His hair was sticking up in all directions like an electrocuted cartoon cat. And that stiff suit appeared to have been dragged behind a car on a dirt road. His tie was gone and his shirt collar was open, revealing glistening sweat on the top of his furry chest.

Ben scooted back his chair and watched him, almost smiling. I leaned forward on the table as he sat down.

"I have all your answers." He picked up the cup of coffee in front of him and chugged it.

"You have all our answers?" Now I was smiling. I'd expected we'd get some answers in a few weeks. Maybe even months. As I've said before, breaking down a terrorist and getting information is done over a period of time.

But not here. These men had just secured their reputation. With us, at least.

□ □ □

After many hours in a car that day, Ben and I both wanted to exercise before going out for the night. I went into the women's gym, which I had to myself. I had just settled onto a bike and was flipping through the channels on the TV when Ben stuck his head in the door.

"There are only two British special forces guys in the men's gym if you want to come work out there," Ben said.

I did indeed. Not because I had a particular interest in British soldiers but because information, intelligence, comes from all sorts of places, and I certainly wasn't going to get any alone on a bike in the empty women's gym.

I got on a StairMaster near the door but close enough to everyone else that we could talk. I wanted to be able to quickly slip out if a non-Westerner came in.

Ben told the English soldiers ███████████████████

██

███████████. They weren't too interested and didn't ask many questions. This is human nature's gift to intelligence workers: most people would rather talk about themselves. We asked what was happening on the ground in Iraq. They had just been in Baghdad and were on a break before they were to return.

"It's a total cock-up," one guy said. He was on his back lifting a rack of weights.

"Your president's a fucking wanker," the guy spotting him said.

I guessed at the translation of their words. Actually, I had to guess at much of what they said. I never asked for translations, though, because I didn't want to slow them down and stop them as they volleyed in a diatribe against the war. Ben never stopped them either. He just kept nodding and prodding for more.

The British soldiers made it clear that the overriding feeling was that they had all been drawn into a personal battle between George W. Bush and Saddam Hussein. And though Hussein had tortured, murdered, locked up, and repressed his people for decades, the belief among Iraqis appeared to be that the soldiers who had come in with the desire to save them were simply replacing Hussein, with the United States as the new dictator. In other words, *no good deed goes unpunished*, and this one, the good deed of getting rid of Hussein, was being severely punished.

No matter who my source was, the story was similar. Westerners in Iraq were stirring up a frenzy of anti-Western sentiment. The only place to get a different story was through White House briefings and press releases and the news outlets that relied on the White House press.

As I said before, if President Bush had run for reelection in the months following September 11, I would have voted for him without a second thought. The man who had chatted with me in The Vault was attentive, aware of what was happening in the world, and very much had America and Americans' best interests at heart. But just then, after the invasion of Iraq on false pretenses, I had a queasy feeling that this whole war—all these lives, all these resources, all this destruction—was going down just so W. could do that which his father had failed to do in 1991: take out Hussein. I hated Hussein as much as anyone else who values freedom. But I also wanted Bush impeached for treason.

□ □ □

Before the sun came up the next morning, before Ben and I were to meet with a European case officer, I hired a driver to take me all the way ███████████████████████. Just like when I sit with a hairdresser, I established immediately when I got in the car that I didn't want to talk. The driver respected this, and so the silent ride up the mountain, through desert monotony, felt like a prolonged meditation. When we got to the top, the driver put the car in park, pushed his seat back, and closed his eyes. We were the only ones there. I got out of the car and walked through the quiet to the edge of a low, serpentine stone wall. There were divots and gaps in the wall, which looked like it had been laid by hand a thousand years ago. Loose boulders and squares of stone were scattered on the ground. There was the sound of birds, and the rustling-paper sound of small things crawling in the brush and dirt at my feet. All the land in front of me was cast in the glowing, sumptuous light of the low sun. Golden dirt rolled out below my feet all the way down to the Red Sea. From where I stood, I could see Israel.

███
███
███
███
███
███
███

████████████████ I remained still yet relaxed, my arms hanging loosely at my sides. My breathing slowed and deepened, and I was flooded with a perfect peace, a moment of feeling complete. I knew that below me some of the most long-lasting and violent clashes were being played out by people of all religions. But here, where Christianity, Judaism, and Islam met, there was nothing but serenity.

Back in the car, before we left, I asked the driver, "How do we get everyone up here so they can feel this peacefulness and stop trying to kill each other?"

He shrugged and threw his hands up, then reached down and turned the ignition.

Ben was waiting for me when I returned just before noon. I quickly changed into business clothes, and then we took a cab to the Hyatt, which was so filled with Westerners that I didn't need to wear the pashmina on my head. We met in the sitting room of a suite with a European case officer, Cheryl, whom we had only known through cables. Cheryl had beautiful strawberry blond hair pulled back into a thick bun at her neck. I wondered if when she walked the streets of this city, she, too, got the pointing, the gaping, the tree climbing. I didn't ask, though. Cheryl was all business.

And beer.

Cheryl had six beers sent to the room for the three of us. When they arrived, she reached into her slouchy carryall and pulled out a giant bag of salt-and-vinegar potato chips.

"I always bring my own food," Cheryl said casually. It wasn't a bad plan to avoid dysentery. Though I'm not sure a diet of chips and alcohol would give one the energy needed to chase down terrorists.

I skipped the beer but dug into the chips. The three of us talked for three hours, exchanging intel. Ben and I had a great deal more information than Cheryl. In fact, she didn't have much that we didn't already know. But the operatives of her country were always good to us, always helpful, and I was happy to give her what we had.

████████ Toward the end of our meeting, Cheryl suggested we meet up later with other operatives from the CIA. It was our last night there; the next day Ben and I were going on to another country, where we were to spend a month following up on the new intel. I wanted to see the nightlife, and Ben was game, so the three of us reconvened that evening at a hookah lounge with a few people from the local office, including Randy, the Texan.

The club was dark, hip, youthful. Only about half the women were veiled. Arabic music played on enormous speakers hanging from the corners of the ceiling. Like everything I'd experienced here so far, the music was a mixture of old and new. Some of the songs were modern, thumping, rap-sounding. The others were wailing ballads and dinner-club-sounding tunes that felt like they were from the 1950s.

Seven of us crowded into a low, half-circular booth with a round table in the center on which sat several three-foot-high hookahs. The pipes were made of purple or magenta glass on the bottom with silver necks and a burning, smoking dome at the top. We were given our own tubes, which attached to the top of the glass bulb and had a silver tip to suck out the smoke. The pipes were beautifully ornate, like they belonged in a mosque or a church.

I'd never smoked anything in my life. Not even a cigarette. But I was overseas. With a rowdy group of people who needed to burn off the pressure of finding terrorists who were multiplying and reproducing like a metastasized cancer. Between the war, the recent attacks in Saudi Arabia, the intel we'd gotten from the prisoners, and the growing African terrorist cells, I desperately needed that smoke.

It was apple flavored. And it made my head a little spinny.

For a few hours I let go of everything and just let myself sit. Eat falafel. Smoke hookah. And laugh about things simply because it felt good to laugh. It was as if I were floating in a different universe for a while—one without the guys who wanted to kill people like Ben, Randy, Cheryl, and me.

On that very same evening, in an African country, a coordinated suicide bomb attack took place.

It was the deadliest attack in that country's history.

TEN

MALIBU BARBIE

Africa
2003

The images came at the strangest times. Like when I was looking out at the sea—a robin's-egg blue canvas, the perfect background for something beautiful and light. But, no. As soon as
there was a visual blank space, or a moment of silence, my brain
pulled up the heads I had been shown. They floated before my
mind's eye like the bouncing balls in a karaoke video. The eyes
were wide, mouths gaped open, necklines like a ragged t-shirt.
There were bits of brain spattered on them like the splashings
from a dropped platter of spaghetti, and their cheeks were
smutted with black debris. It was a like watching a film on a
continuous loop. I couldn't stop myself from seeing them any
more than I could stop myself from breathing or sneezing. The
suicide bombers probably hadn't known at the time that when
you wear a body bomb, the energy from the blow rolls up and
out, popping a head off like a cork. Just as I didn't know that
looking at those unmoored heads lined up on a cart would etch
the vision deep into the neural pathways in my brain, forever
binding me with these five misguided murderers.

The young men whose heads I had seen had caused much
more damage to others than what I was suffering. I had every-
day, common-in-war-zones PTSD. But more than a hundred
people had been killed or maimed by this group. They hit an

African capital with the stated intention to kill Westerners and Jews. Not one Jewish person was among the victims, and most of the people they murdered or hurt were Muslims. No, it never made much sense. Just like the fact that the detached arms I'd seen didn't haunt me the way the heads did. Each arm was adorned with a Casio watch. The Japanese watch, which sells for less than $20, was—and still is—as commonly found on terrorists as an iPhone on an American teen.

Sometimes, to try to erase the image of those heads, I'd replace it with the faces of the men who had shown them to me. They were operatives from the African country where Ben and I were working for the month. There were no women in this bureau, and I wondered at the time if showing me the heads was revenge for simply having presented myself in their office. One of the first men I met there, a slouchy-looking guy with dark, short teeth, refused to use my proper name. Instead, to the delight of his colleagues, he called me *Malibu Barbie*. It amazed me at the time that the idea and image of Malibu Barbie would travel all the way across the globe to a passel of operatives in a country where most people didn't have a working television, let alone a Barbie doll. But these men, boldly macho in their voices and how they took up the space in any room— legs spread wide, arms flailing—knew who Malibu Barbie was. Maybe the only way they could contain me mentally was to equate me to a hard plastic doll with a waist so small that, if she were real, a man could encircle her with his hands. And to show me those heads.

At over six feet tall and with that helmet of perfect, shiny hair, Ben reminded me of a movie star. But they didn't call him Ken, or Brad Pitt, or, with Ben's attractive-but-big nose, Adrien Brody. Ben and I both knew this wasn't about being American, and it wasn't about being in the CIA. It was about being a woman and their need to assert dominance. They weren't threatened by Ben. They even appeared to admire him, everyone hushing up each time Ben spoke. But they were terrified of me: a woman doing the same work they did.

Day after day, Ben and I sat in their grungy offices, drinking their thick black coffee and abiding their insults to me, so we could eventually get what we needed from them: information, details, and answers to the many questions we had after having followed a lead to their country's capital.

Essentially, they weren't willing to help us until we helped them bring in the people who had planned the attack that gave us the heads. At first they even blamed us for it. Yes, the CIA should have known. But these men should have known, too. This was their country after all.

Blame and unrecognized achievements were part of the job. Anytime a bomb went off, it was a public failure on our part. But every time a bomb didn't go off, every time a suicide bomber didn't walk into a restaurant, or community center, or Jewish cemetery, or subway station because we had stopped him—no one heard about it. Most of our successes were kept secret. This was fine by me. But it wasn't fine by the men in this country who wanted to point fingers at us because their citizens had been harmed.

Also stuck in my mind were the faces of the terrorists I was tracking. A money trail had led us to this city, and we needed names to go with some of the satellite images we had, so we could find every single person involved in the plot. It was enough money to finance something huge—bin Laden style. I felt like a giant clock was ticking in the sky above me, and every second I wasn't getting closer to finding the terrorists, they were getting closer to executing their chemical plot.

So, yeah. There was a ticking clock. And there were those damn heads.

□　□　□

The differences between the Middle Eastern country where Ben and I had visited the prison and this African country became apparent to me before I'd even viewed the heads. Before I'd even met the man who dubbed me Malibu Barbie.

I had started tallying comparisons on the flight over when I noticed that most of the women on the plane weren't covered. In fact, there had been a woman wearing a belly shirt—her flesh flashing out between her breasts and the top of her pants. A few women were in skimpy, low-cut tops. Immediately, I folded my pashmina into a tight square and stuffed it into my backpack. I was happy I'd packed a bathing suit. This new city, I thought, might be a place where I could lie in the sun, in my bikini, on the single half-day I'd planned to take off each week over the next month there.

In the cab on the way to the hotel, Ben pointed out the window at two women jogging in shorts and tank tops. He was as surprised as I to see this here. We could have been in a Florida resort town. I felt like I was on vacation.

That vacation feeling only intensified when we got to our pink stucco hotel with the blue shutters on every window. It looked like an expensive tropical resort. The hotel was intimate and only two stories high. Ben was given a room on the second floor. I was put on the first floor.

And that was when the vacation feeling ended.

You know that slight chill that comes over you when you're somewhere alone—a cafe, a library, a bus, a grocery store—and you sense someone staring at you? When it happens, you turn in the direction from which you feel that gaze and you catch the person, just for a second, before their eyes dart away. Has it ever happened that you sensed this and turned to find no one? No, probably not. The chances are, 100 percent of the time you felt someone watching you, when you turned to look, voila, *someone was indeed watching you*. I don't know how humans feel this. It's probably a mammalian trait and goes back to our ancestors needing to detect predators to survive.

When I entered my hotel room, for the first time in all my

travels for the CIA, I felt in my gut, in my mind, and on the surface of my skin that I was being watched. As I have never been wrong when sensing a gaze, I assumed I wasn't wrong this time either.

I did a thorough search of the room and the bathroom but didn't come up with anything. Still, I couldn't shake the feeling of being observed. I called the front desk and asked for a different room. They claimed they were fully booked. I called Ben and asked him to call the front desk and ask for a different room. They told him the same thing: not a vacancy in the place. Ben said he'd switch rooms with me, but we both knew if there were eyes on me, there were eyes on him, too. I called housekeeping and ordered eight towels. The woman on the phone didn't ask why, which was good since I hadn't taken the time to think up an excuse. When the stack of towels was delivered I threw one over the TV set, one over the clock radio, one over a decorative bronze camel, one over the painting hanging over the bed, and two on the tiles along the gaping crack between the floor and the wall. The rest I carried with me into the bathroom.

My plan was to shower before Ben and I started our working day, but as I stood in the bathroom that feeling of being watched intensified. I went back to the room with a towel, opened my suitcase, and took out my bathing suit. With great care—as if I were feeling shy in a public dressing room—I slipped on my suit under cover of the towel. Then I returned to the shower and washed with my bikini on.

Once clean, I dressed under the cover of two towels.

After I'd dried my hair, I rushed out of the room. As soon as I was in the tiled corridor, walking toward the courtyard where I was to meet Ben, the "watched" feeling was gone.

Ben and I took a cab to meet Scott, an agent in the local CIA office we had been trying to work with. In my correspondence with Scott I had found him to be inscrutable, a little laconic, and stingy with intel. I assumed the best, though, and figured he just wasn't good at communicating through writing. After all, we were from the same country and presumably had the same goals.

Presumably.

As Ben and I stood in Scott's cubicle, his supervisor only a few yards away in his office, Scott let his feelings be known.

"Sucks here," he said. "He's a dick." Scott nodded toward his boss's open door. I looked over my shoulder to see if he had heard. It didn't seem wise to call one's boss a dick while at work, no matter how far away that boss might be. Which, in this small office, wasn't far at all.

"Oh, yeah? Bummer, man." Ben was playing the bro part. I knew where he was going. He would try to find equal ground with Scott so we could get the information we needed out of him and do our job.

"It's a miserable post. This country? Not my thing, man. I'd rather be back in Langley. I need a Royal Farms store, I need Taco Bell! I mean, when's the last time you had Taco Bell?"

"I prefer Jack-in-the-Box—" I didn't finish my sentence. I wanted to yell, *Human lives depend on the work we're doing, so you better be doing your job, not dreaming about a chalupa!*

"Dunderhead over there couldn't make it more miserable. The guy is constantly up my ass."

I leaned out of the cubicle to get a better view of the alleged *dunderhead*. He was on the phone, his feet crossed on top of his desk. When I leaned back in, I felt Ben's arm twitch against my hip. I looked down to see him rubbing his fingers together. A gesture for me. A tiny violin, meaning, *cry me a river, dude, and just do your job!*

"Hey, we'll run with anything you got, man," Ben said. "We need to close in on these guys fast."

"I got nothin'," Scott said.

"What about the local intelligence offices?" I asked. "Who's our best source there?"

"Those guys are a bunch of dicks." Scott shrugged, and I

wondered, *if everyone you're surrounded by is a dick, does that make you one, too?*

"Did you follow up on any of our cables?" I asked.

"Everything I know is from what you guys sent me," Scott said. "Seems like you two are pulling up a lot of shit."

Ben and I were silent for a moment. I was flabbergasted. And furious. This was the first person I'd met in the CIA who didn't appear to want to do his job, who seemed to take the task of saving human lives lightly. Yeah, it's hard to bat 100 percent. But the CIA came pretty damn close as far as I'd seen. This guy, however, was the outlier one would hope to never encounter when working counterterrorism.

Finally I said, "Why don't we go talk to local intelligence guys together and see what we can get from them."

"Yeah, right." Scott threw his chin up, laughing. "You two go. I'm not on the best terms with those guys."

"Oh, yeah." I said. "Dicks."

"Total," Scott said.

"Not one guy who will help us out?" Ben's eyes were starting to slit.

"Nah." Scott was sneering now.

"Wait," I said, "are you saying you won't show up in their offices?"

"At the assembly of dicks?" Scott shrugged. "No way. You go ahead and I'm gonna get me some shawarma from the guy on the corner. It's not Taco Bell, but it's okay. Oh, and my wife invited you both to dinner tonight." Scott handed me a folded piece of paper with his address. At least he was following protocol here. It was rare not to spend your first night dining with your counterparts in the host city. The person in charge often was the first to extend the invitation, but he—the alleged dick among many in this country—hadn't even come out of his office to introduce himself to us. Like it or not, we'd be stuck with Scott that night.

In the cab on the way to the local intelligence headquarters,

Ben and I unloaded. We had to speak in code so that our cab driver wouldn't understand. Ben started with, "My Taco Bell– loving uncle is an asshole." And it went from there. Talk of a lazy uncle who was bringing the hardworking family down.

I figured no one could be as bad as Scott and maintained high hopes for the work we might be able to do with this country's counterterrorism officers. Also, the great number of uncovered women on the street implied there was more choice, freedom, here. So, I assumed the intelligence agents would also support women's individual choice and freedom.

The building was fairly new and looked clean and efficient. My hopes soared even higher: modern building, modern-thinking people. After checking in with the receptionist, I dashed into the restroom. I'd been so eager to get away from Scott that I hadn't wanted to take time to use the restroom at the CIA office. This bathroom was spotless. It looked like it had just been built and had never been used. After I washed my hands, I used a paper towel to wipe up the water spots along the counter. I didn't want to leave it any less pristine than it had been when I had walked in.

Ben and I were led into the main office where the agents had their desks in modern cubicles, just like at the CIA. Immediately I knew why the bathroom had looked brand-new. Other than the receptionist who led us down the hall, there were no women. It was disheartening, but I simply had to carry on and do my work. Still, I remained optimistic.

A man with hair slicked back like an eighties TV star approached us and shook Ben's hand. He reeked of cigarette smoke and had a small gray heap of ash on the lapel of his shiny suit.

"Welcome," he said.

He barely glanced at me and ignored my extended hand. And then his colleague approached. The one with the blackened corn-nib teeth. He shook Ben's hand, then looked at me and said, "It's Malibu Barbie!"

There was laughter from the cubicles nearby, and soon we were surrounded by a group of men, none of whom looked me in the eye, all of whom appeared to think Malibu Barbie was the most clever nickname they'd ever heard.

Only a few minutes later, I saw the heads. Those damn, floating heads.

□ □ □

Scott's house looked like it could have been in California. It was a 1970s tract home with warm wood floors. Outside the office, Scott wasn't such a bad guy. I was frustrated that, to my mind, he wasn't doing his job properly but had to forgive him, at least for the night, so I could relax and enjoy myself.

There was a nanny who took care of Scott and his wife's child during our visit. But there was no guard or other domestic help. I stood in the kitchen and talked to Gina while she finished getting dinner ready. Spaghetti was cooking in a large, deep pot of boiling water, and she was working on a homemade tomato sauce into which she was dropping fragrant crushed cloves of garlic.

"Good for your blood," Gina said as she added another wet-looking clove to the sauce.

Gina was born and raised in the States. Her parents were both from an island nation. She was a professional who had worked for a few years in D.C. while Scott was in grad school and then at Langley.

"I hate it here," Gina said as we set the table.

"You do?" I waved a plate in the air toward Ben. It made me angry to see him sitting on the couch having a beer with Scott while I set the table. Ben jumped up and rushed over to us.

"I'll set the table," he said.

"No!" Gina said. "You sit. You worked all day."

"She worked all day, too." Ben nodded toward me. "You both did."

"We'll clean up!" Scott offered from the couch. Ben looked

at me with imploring eyes. I knew he was trying to schmooze Scott into doing some work for us. I had to give him a break.

"Okay, you guys clean up," I said.

Gina's spaghetti, even with all that garlic, was pretty great. And after traveling for so long, it was nice to eat something that felt like home; something that I knew wouldn't send me digging through my toiletry kit for Imodium.

Ben and Scott did clean up while Gina and I sat on the couch and looked through her photo albums. I could see that her married life was divided into two parts. Part One was Gina as a working mother in America, who felt productive and purposeful in her life. She had friends. Her child had friends whose parents were a part of her life. She had a community. Part Two was Gina as Scott's wife overseas. She had no friends. She didn't speak the language and was having trouble picking up even the most basic words. Her child had few friends. Gina felt like an outsider with no community to wrap around herself and her family.

"Everyone in the agency here is divorced or single," Gina said. "They don't want to do dinners in with spaghetti and the noise of kids. I mean, as far as I'm concerned, the only good thing I have going here is the noise of my kid and my husband in the rare times he's home."

"He doesn't seem very happy either," I said.

"He's miserable," Gina said. "I mean, it would be one thing if I were sacrificing everything I worked toward and want in life so that he could have some ultimate experience or do great work—"

"But this *is* great work." I chose not to point out that Scott didn't seem to be doing the work that needed to be done. That he had, in fact, made my job more difficult in so many ways— the least of which was that the local intelligence officers appeared to assume that all Americans were like Scott and so far didn't seem to trust, or like, me or Ben.

"Do you love the work?" Gina asked. No one had ever put this question to me. Probably because no one, outside of those already in the agency, knew what I did.

"I do," I said. "I love the people. I love the agency. I believe in what we're doing. We're saving lives. Or trying to."

"Yeah, but you're all alone." She quickly covered her mouth as if she'd said something wrong. I just smiled, but her words clanged around inside me.

In the cab on the way back to the hotel, Ben told me he was warming up to Scott. He felt bad for the guy, an American homebody, stuck overseas.

"He's misplaced," Ben said.

"Yeah, I guess." I was off in my head, thinking about Gina and her before-and-after lives. Thinking about her child, who had demanded snuggle time and a kiss goodnight from both parents at bedtime. Thinking about how she saw her family as a tight little tribe where everyone counted on everyone else. Together, they had created their own lifeboat.

I realized then that I wanted to feel enclosed by something more intimate than the agency. I was alone. And a family one day sounded wonderful. But if I had that family, I'd want us all to live in a solid home where we didn't need a safe room or a driver. None of that would be easy to achieve while working for the CIA.

With Gina's words, the seeds of a different future life had been planted in my mind. I could feel it in me. What had previously been unnamed and unrecognized was now letting itself be known. And imagined. Still, I couldn't fathom giving up the fight against terrorists. I'd have to find a way to do it from the States. I could become an analyst for the CIA, but that was not my style. I had to move, take action. *The FBI*, I thought. They fight terrorism in the homeland. I'd encountered a few FBI agents in Langley, and they didn't seem so bad.

As if there were a file in my brain, I took my thoughts of

the FBI and slotted them away. For now, there was work to do. I only had the names of three of the people on the money trail we'd been following, and no one's whereabouts yet. If Gina wanted to be sure she could kiss her child goodnight every single evening, I needed to find the rest of that deadly crew soon. Because, it seemed to me, Scott had other things on his mind.

□ □ □

It's funny how quickly the unusual becomes routine. Putting on my bathing suit to shower was second nature now, as if that was how I'd done it my whole life. The Barbie commentary came and went as Ben and I spent our first of four planned weeks simply getting to know the local intelligence operatives, building relationships with them, showing them we could be trusted, and sussing out who among the agents we could trust. It was a hard week to start work with them as they were trying to identify the recent bombers and bring down the al-Qaeda cell behind that attack. But we knew it was bigger than that. That attack was only one item on al-Qaeda's lengthy agenda, and though we wanted to close up and seal that case as much as local intelligence did, we also wanted to look further out into the future, out into the radiating arms of al-Qaeda, and stop all potential oncoming attacks.

Over the next few days, with David back in Langley triangulating our intel, we located one of the people we'd been searching for: a terrorist named H. Currently he was living outside Africa and applying for the equivalent of a green card in a European capital. Like what had happened in London with the police and the ricin plot, we'd seen all the evidence of his plan, but none of what we'd seen—before it was combined to make poison—was illegal. Still, there was no imaginable circumstance in which H would have this stuff and *not* be making WMDs. Think of it this way: if you came home and found the KitchenAid mixer, a bag of flour, a stick of butter, two eggs, brown and white sugars, a bottle of vanilla, a shaker of salt, a box of baking soda, and a bag of Nestlé's Semi-Sweet Morsels on the counter, you'd be pretty darned sure someone was about to make chocolate chip cookies. If the baker then walked in the kitchen and denied they were making cookies, or anything even remotely like cookies, if they accused you of jumping to conclusions, you . . . well, you'd assume they were lying. As certain as you'd be that cookies were about to be baked, we were certain that WMDs were being built. On top of all that, we'd identified H earlier at an al-Qaeda training camp, so we were sure of what his ideological beliefs were and how he intended to spread those beliefs (from al-Qaeda's written materials I'd read, "the dialogue of bullets, the ideals of assassination, bombing and destruction, and the diplomacy of the cannon and machine gun").

What we didn't know was who was helping H with this plot, who would deploy the poison; we also weren't sure exactly when and where he planned to have it deployed. If H were arrested and we could talk to him, we'd break down this plot before it moved any further than production in his grubby apartment. But it was up to the people in the country where he was currently residing to arrest him.

Unfortunately, no one there was willing to do that. The only thing official records showed was that H was so committed to the values of the West that he was completing all the paperwork to legally work and go to school there. His application was fully in process, and none of the evidence we handed over could convince anyone to stop it.

He was still, however, a citizen of the African nation where we were staying. He could be extradited back to Africa where we could speak to him, or he could speak to the local intelligence and then we would speak to them.

Our difficulties in getting H were multisided; I felt like I was in a room with the walls slowly closing in on me. There were Scott and his boss, who appeared to have no interest in al-Qaeda even after the recent bombing in the country where they now lived. They were not officially banned, but no other word better describes how unwelcome they were at the local intelligence offices. And the local men we'd met were not about to do any favors for *those two*, or implore their countrymen to extradite a guy we—the Americans—wanted to speak with. Ben and I had managed to get a few of them to warm up to us, but even though they liked us, they didn't like the idea of identifying a terrorist from their country. In spite of what had recently gone down, they maintained the line that there were *no African terrorists*. Only Middle Easterners. It was like an intense college football rivalry to the death: the USC Trojans vs. the UCLA Bruins. You'd be hard-pressed to find a Trojan who didn't want to call the Bruins for a penalty on every play. And vice versa. These men saw themselves as the modern good guys. They liked to depict other countries as barbaric breeding grounds for terrorists. Neither one of those generalizations was true, of course.

In under two weeks, Ben and I had helped identify every single detached head, and everyone associated with that attack. With the rest of that crew taken in or under surveillance, we could get more people to focus on our current crises at hand: H, the money he had backing him, and the plan he was brewing. We called a meeting at the local intelligence office. Ben even brought in some pastries.

"We've now conclusively identified every terrorist in the recent coordinated bombings," I said. "And every single one was from your country. Are you still maintaining that you have no terrorists?" I looked directly at the man who had first dubbed me Malibu Barbie. I was daring him to say those words now that he'd seen how serious I was about this work, and how much I could accomplish in relatively little time.

"They are . . ." he paused. "Rare." He pulled a crumpled unfiltered cigarette from his breast pocket, smoothed it out with his thick fingers, then stuck it in his mouth and lit it. I scooted my chair back so I wouldn't have to breathe in the smoke I knew he'd blow toward me.

"Well, yes," Ben said. "Islamic extremism when measured against the millions of Muslims in the world is very rare. But that's our job. We're here to find the rare extremists. It only takes one of them to blow up a building, or spray ricin powder in a movie theater."

There were mumblings and gesticulations from the men in the room. They spoke in a dialect I couldn't understand, with some English words thrown in.

"You need to look at the Middle East!" the smoking agent said. I imagined he was translating all they were saying into one pithy sentence.

"H is a citizen of your country." I was stating the obvious. They already knew this. But it was as if they believed that if they didn't pick up H and bring him in, he wouldn't exist, and they could carry on thinking that the men we'd identified who were responsible for the recent attack were the very last of their country's rare terrorists.

"We will think about this." Little clouds of smoke puffed from the agent's mouth with each word.

There was silence for a moment. And those damn floating heads appeared, taunting me; compelling me to work faster, harder. Until my mind was so full, there was no room for them.

□ □ □

When they weren't calling me Malibu Barbie, the local operatives were calling me *ma'am*, which was fine by me. To be *ma'am* in this country made me feel grown-up, in control of my life, like someone who would never have been called *Zidiot* while in school. *Ma'am* would definitely never endure more than 30 hours of travel to stand in the wedding of someone who wasn't really her friend.

But Tracy Schandler, aka *Zidiot*, did.

The bride and I had started out as friends at the age of three. By the time we were in third grade she was one of the ringleaders of a gang of girls who bullied me at school. This went on to such an extent that I retreated into my head; I became quiet, an observer, and utterly friendless until high school. The first month of ninth grade, the bullying future bride called me at her mother's insistence. She apologized for the years of schoolyard terror and asked if I would be her pal. We both were interested in dance, so we knew we'd be placed together often in high school. Though I'd acclimated to my internal life by then, I was still a kid and desperate to hang out with other people. I said yes, and we were friends through high school. To a degree. I had never felt safe enough to open up and reveal to my former torturer the person I'd developed into during my years of solitude. She got a very flimsy version of me, an outer layer that didn't resemble the person I felt I was inside.

I landed at Dulles Airport after two days of travel, and then took a cab directly to the CIA headquarters. I wouldn't be using that passport or those ID cards in California and didn't want to have them on me or in my bags.

Afterward, I grabbed a Starbucks coffee (the usual) and got in a cab to return to Dulles for the last leg of this marathon voyage. With the half-full cup in my hand, I fell asleep in the back of the cab and was awoken when my head bonked against the window. The coffee didn't spill but my consciousness did, and I began to wonder why I was making this effort for someone whom I didn't genuinely know. And who absolutely didn't know me. Or appreciate me.

Thirty minutes later, I skirted through the airport again, shadowing my face behind hanging hair. I didn't want to be recognized by anyone in airport security as the woman who had just disembarked from a flight that had originated in a country to which Americans don't normally travel. I was an American on American soil, though, so a bureaucratic SNAFU—being questioned—would be the worst that could happen.

It wasn't until I was standing on the flattened carpet of a Los Angeles hotel ballroom, wearing a poufy blue dress that I'd donate to the Salvation Army the next day, that I had total clarity. I understood then that I'd made this ridiculously exhausting effort to be in the wedding only so I could have a do-over from childhood. I'd wanted people to see that Tracy Schandler, the girl they'd called *Zidiot*, had been included. Was a bridesmaid even! Was no longer their victim.

But for whom, exactly, did I make all that effort? The people who weren't my friends now any more than they'd been back then? The people who didn't matter in my life? The people who had nothing to do with me currently and nothing to do with all the ways in which my life was rewarding and thrilling?

It was as if I'd added water to an old, shriveled plant hoping it would spring to life all over again as a bushy, flowering shrub.

The only person who was bullying me now was me. I was the one who had compelled myself to dart halfway across the globe for people with whom my single point of connection was the fact that they had been my tormentors.

The bride was fabulously happy.

I was not.

My parents, too, were invited to this wedding but were seated at a different table during dinner. Instead of catching up with them, I was stuck between a man who spoke while chewing his food and a woman who turned her face away from me. *Never again*, I thought as I picked at a piece of chicken. I realized I didn't need these people to like me. I didn't need to be included. Yes, as Gina had pointed out, I was alone. But just then, I was complete in my aloneness. My needs had nothing to do with anyone at that wedding and couldn't be satisfied by anyone there. My needs could only be met by me.

Driving away from the wedding, I sat in the backseat of my parents' car as if I were a little kid again. It was warm, and the sun was beating in through the sunroof. My mother started talking about the goings-on in her circle of friends, people I'd known most of my life. Her voice was comforting, calming, so much so that I looked out the window at the ocean along the freeway and for once didn't see the untethered heads. Without those tattered faces, I was free to think about other things. Like how wide that expanse of water was. I floated above the sea in my head and zoomed out until I could see the Pacific glimmering all the way to Japan. From there, I followed the water through the Philippine Sea, into the Indian Ocean, and then into the Arabian Sea. I drifted up the Red Sea, with Africa on one side of me and the Middle East on the other.

That was where my mind was. That was where my purpose was. The shy girl with braces and acne hiding by her locker was still inside me. But she was no longer afraid. Not of any bullies anywhere in the world.

ELEVEN

BANG, BANG, BOOM!

War Zone, Middle East
2003

Before I flew off to the office in the Middle East for a five-month stay, I downloaded an application for the FBI. I wasn't sure if I'd fill it out and send it in or not. But I'd printed it. I loved the CIA so much that I couldn't imagine leaving. In my mind, I tried to reframe going into the FBI as a transfer rather than a change. I'd continue tracking terrorists, but from a single home base. I left the blank application in my apartment in the States and decided I'd deal with it, or not, when I returned.

Once I was in the war zone, I forgot about the FBI. I forgot about everything outside my work. I didn't even have a photo or memento from home on my desk in my shared office. We worked in what was once a hotel; it was the same space where we took our meals. My office was a former hotel room, exactly that size, but where a bathroom used to be was open, rusted plumbing and a half-chipped-away mosaic marble floor.

Time in the war zone moved differently than time anywhere else. Because we were all living where we were working, there was no sense of a break or even a rest. It was like a continuous, cluttered, noisy symphony where the notes go on and on and on. You might change from the horns to the strings, but the music never stops playing. Even when I lay in the relative calm and peacefulness of my trailer, I knew there was a war happening not far from me. I couldn't forget that while I slept, bombs were going off, missiles were being fired, IEDs were being planted beside rocks in the dirt roads, and terrorists were plotting their next move.

While I slept, people were dying.

Each morning, the moment I woke up, I already felt like I had fallen behind.

The office psychologist, a woman who lived in the trailer beside mine, appeared to be slowly losing her spirit, her optimism. I sat with her at breakfast one morning and watched as she stared down at her plate. I was having my usual, a PowerBar brought from home and black coffee. She was eating scrambled eggs that kept falling off the fork she held in her limp hand. At around forty, she seemed like a person whom I had expected could and would handle anything. Yet there she was, clearly depressed. Between the Navy SEALs, the CIA, and the terrorists, she was dealing with three sides of a brutally acute, blade-edged triangle.

"I'm just . . . I'm just not sure how much more I can take," she said, re-forking the same jiggly wad of egg she'd already dropped once. I felt bad for her, but I also worried a little for myself. If she's feeling undone by all this, I thought, then there's a chance I could become unraveled by it, too. I decided then that I better do everything I could to maintain optimum mental health.

That night, around midnight, I hadn't changed out of my work clothes and sat up on my bed, wide awake with a book open in front of me. I hoped that reading would shut down my brain, close up shop in a sense, so I could release the pressure of trying to track chemical cells and actually go to sleep. I was reading the same page over and over again when there was a knock on the door. I called for whoever it was to come in. Larry, a Navy SEAL from San Diego, popped in his head. He was tall, with a big toothy smile, and always appeared to be bouncing on the tips of his toes as if he were in the middle of a tennis match.

"Wanna go have some fun?"

"Hmm . . . will I get killed, maimed, or in trouble?" I closed the book.

"Nope. Just pure fun."

"Okay, I'm in." Fun is always the best therapy for me.

"Vest and head covering," he said. "Meet me in five."

It took less than five minutes for me to strap on my bullet-proof vest and throw a scarf over my head. The bomb-sniffing dogs were at the SUV, where five other guys were waiting when I arrived.

"I knew you'd come!" A Navy SEAL named Daniel threw up his palm, and we slapped hands.

I hid in the way-back, as usual, and the six of us drove to a nearby airport that had been repurposed and was now an American military base. A shipment of night-vision goggles, called NVGs, had just come in, and the SEALs wanted to test them out and get used to them.

We drove through the usual security checks, parked, and then Larry helped me out of the back. The six of us jogged across the pitch-black tarmac to a canvas tent where the ship-ment had been placed. There were other military there, and the SEALs seemed to know them all. Or maybe they didn't know each other, and it was just the intimacy of being in this strange desert airport, in the middle of a war, in the middle of the night, that made it seem like they were old friends.

Larry opened a crate with the claw end of a hammer and handed us each what looked like a helmet with binoculars at-tached to the front. One of the soldiers fitted me in one and adjusted the strap. The goggles lifted and lowered on a hinge above my face. He raised and lowered them, adjusted the hel-met, and then said, "Good to go."

The five SEALs from the office and I left the tent and crossed the tarmac again to where a couple of ATVs were sitting.

"Ladies first," a guy named Alex said.

I sat on the seat of one of the ATVs. It was about the size of a dune buggy with an open top and four thick wheels that looked like they could roll over anything. Alex showed me the ignition, brakes, and gas. Then he got in the ATV beside me.

"Drivers ready?" Daniel asked.

Alex and I lowered our night goggles. When I looked out, everything was party-balloon green. The places that were illuminated, like the tent where we'd just been, screamed with white light. I looked at the runway and watched a rabbit skitter across.

"You see that?" Alex asked.

"Yeah, that was cool."

"On your mark . . . get set . . ." Daniel started. And before he shouted *go*, I had pulled away and was racing down the tarmac as fast as that vehicle could go. In the neon green light, there was nothing ahead of me but paved blacktop with some arrows on it. I kept the ATV moving forward and looked back to see Alex catching up. And then I stood on the gas, actually stood, so that my butt was out of the seat, as I raced toward nowhere.

It must have been after three in the morning by the time we returned to the trailers. I took off my clothes, pulled on my sweats and t-shirt, slipped under the covers, and finally fell into a deep, pure, thoughtless sleep.

□ □ □

The next day I felt on fire, alert. It was like I'd gone on a mini-vacation. I was at my desk in my office all morning, sending and receiving cables from other agencies in regard to H, the terrorist I had started tracking while I was working in Africa. He had recently gained citizenship in a European country, so I had lost the chance to have him extradited back to his homeland. Over the past several days, I'd been speaking to FM, a man being held at another site. FM's cousin lived in the same European city as H, and regularly prayed at the mosque where H was spreading his "charms" and trying to recruit new followers. According to FM's cousin, H was being heavily financed by X to plot a "big" poison attack that would change the way Westerners thought of al-Qaeda. It was as if these guys were trying to make a name for themselves; they wanted to stand on the world stage, with everyone watching, and be awarded gold medals for killing. After several days of talking and negotiations, FM had given me his cousin's address and phone number, which I immediately passed on to the Poison Trio and undercover operatives in Europe. To thank him for this information, I had given FM fresh figs, pomegranates, and a photo of his mother. The photo was the hardest item to procure, but through a string of contacts I did it.

Around noon, I shut down my computer and locked up my desk. I had a 12:30 meeting with an asset who had a tangential relationship with another individual I was looking for in relation to H. I ripped open a PowerBar and ate it while putting on my bulletproof vest. I was off to find Johnny, to take me to, and stay with me during, my meeting. With my vest dangling open and the PowerBar in my hand, I rushed out of my office and started jogging down the wavy marble steps to the first floor.

I can't tell you exactly what happened. But something did. I tripped and plummeted straight down the stone steps to the stone landing, where I ended up unconscious on my back.

When I came to, I was surrounded by Navy SEALs and the office bureau chief, Redmond, a no-nonsense, square-jawed man.

"Don't move," Redmond said. He, like all my supervisors, knew I'd had surgery on my spine.

"I think I'm okay." I wasn't in pain. Just woozy. And tired. I wanted to sleep more than anything.

I started to sit up and was gently pushed down to my back and then lifted onto a stretcher.

There was a lot of chatter and directions, as if this was a life-or-death situation. I felt fine. More than anything, I was embarrassed to be the center of all this fuss.

"Really, I'm not in pain—"

Commands were snapped over my head, and I was carried out of the hotel office to a waiting military helicopter. Redmond wouldn't take any chances. He wanted me flown to a nearby Air Force base where there was a hospital and doctors who could X-ray me to make sure everything in my spine and my head was undamaged.

There was something relaxing about that bumpy ride with the rhythmic chugging whir of the chopper's blades. I closed my eyes and drifted off to sleep, only to be awoken by a Navy SEAL who shouted at me, "No you don't! Eyes open!"

It happened three more times. Finally I said, "Come on, just five minutes. I swear I don't have a concussion."

"Are you kidding me?!" he yelled. "There's a war going on, you're on an open-air helicopter, and you want to SLEEP? If you're not concussed then you're the most relaxed person I've ever seen."

"Well, I am from California," I said. "We're mellow people."

He smiled and nodded as if that just might be true.

We landed at the Air Force base, me on my back, the sun beating straight down onto my face. From where I lay, it looked like an enormous city of canvas tents lined up on a field of gray gravel. I was hustled, on a stretcher, to the trauma tent, which had enough equipment in there that I imagined anything could be accomplished there: surgery, X-rays, delivering a baby if necessary.

I was the only patient and was seen to by a doctor, a tall, sturdy-looking man, and a nurse, a soft-faced woman. They each wore beige-and-brown camouflage scrubs; her top had a v-neck and was almost stylish. There was something of a different era to them—as if they were from a 1950s TV show about a brilliant doctor and his kind nurse. Both were efficient and swift. He asked questions while she took my vitals. Her hands were warm, and when she touched me I had the urge to close my eyes and go to sleep again.

"Nuh-uh," she said, gently squeezing my arm. "You've got to stay awake."

The doctor left, and the nurse attached an IV to my arm. I didn't ask why, or what it was, but I did feel more awake once that fluid was flowing into me. She left with a promise to return soon so they could do X-rays and a CT scan.

I lay in that tent, the canvas walls almost glowing from the intense sunlight, and listened to everything beyond the open flaps. There was the sound of trucks, people talking, mechanical beeping from equipment operating or things being moved, and then, suddenly, a wailing of sirens that drowned out all other noises. My mind tried to fill in the blanks: whatever just happened, it was far enough away that I didn't hear it. An IED could have gone off; a chemical bomb could have been launched over the barbed-wire fence, past the barricade of armed security, and into the base; a suicide bomber could have blown up at the other end of the base.

The nurse rushed into the room and rolled me so that I was at the edge of the flaps, but with room for people to roll past me.

"You're about to get lots of company," she said. "A bomb went off just outside the base and hit a group of women walking to the market down the road." Her voice was calm, but she was speaking quickly, and her hands were moving like darting flames as she arranged IV poles and attached bags to them.

"You can just let me go—"

"Absolutely not!" she said. "You need to be cared for, but first—"

A team of men and women, everyone speaking in a flurry of shouts, rolled in six people and lined them up beside me. Everyone looked charred, many were faceless. Their skin glistened like freshly burnt paper, and there were exposed chunks of red flesh from their cheeks to their feet. There were areas where I expected an arm or leg but just saw a raw, tattered opening. Bright bits of color, like large confetti, were pasted here and there over each of them. Maybe they'd been wearing colorful hijabs? The scent of burnt hair and blood was overwhelming. I could taste that smell, like a copper penny in my mouth.

The woman right next to me moaned and groaned. The rest were silent. The nurse who had helped me went to the moaning woman and hooked her up to the IV. Then she took her hand and held it. I hoped the injured woman could feel how warm the nurse's hands were through the gloves she was now wearing. It was doubtful the patient understood English, but the nurse spoke to her as if she did. Her voice was soothing, gentle, reassuring. She looked into the woman's face and told her she was in good care now and everything would be fine. The moaning slowed. Other people in the room silently tended to the others, but they all seemed to fall away out of focus as I watched the nurse and the woman.

"I'm sorry," I whispered. I was so angry at whomever had placed that bomb outside the base. It was meant for American soldiers, or any American, but no one stepped foot outside the base unless they were in an armored car. So, naturally, it would hit villagers; maybe even the mother, aunt, wife, or sister of the terrorist who placed it there.

People quietly filtered out of the room, and the nurse went down the row of gurneys and silently checked on each person. None of them were attached to an IV.

The woman beside me turned her face toward me. Her skin was blackened, shiny, and there were bits of bright blue fabric embedded in her flesh. She stared at me, and the whites of her eyes glowed. I stared back and stuck out my arm toward her. She didn't, or couldn't, move, and I pulled my arm back in.

"I'm so sorry," I whispered again. I stayed with her like that;

eyes locked to let her know she wasn't alone, that she wasn't just a body. I could see her and would hold her in my mind. Her chest rose and fell as she breathed, and soon my breathing synchronized with hers.

The nurse returned and took her hand once more. Again she talked to her gently and calmly—the way people talk to those they love. Then she tucked the woman's hand by her side and checked my IV bag.

"She going to be okay? Are they all going to be okay?" It was too quiet in there. Eerie.

"Everyone else has passed. She's getting morphine so she can go out peacefully." She blinked both eyes shut for a second as if the thought pained her.

"That's it?" I asked.

"There's nothing that can be done," she said. "Except to make it easier than it might otherwise be."

She patted my shoulder and then turned to the woman and squeezed her hand once more before leaving the tent. It was now just the newly dead, the single survivor, and me. I looked back at the woman. We locked eyes again and breathed together. I didn't know how long it might take, but if what she wanted was this—to die in the gaze of another human—then I would provide that.

It wasn't long before the woman's eyes flickered, and I knew we were no longer seeing each other.

"I'm sorry," I whispered once more, before I looked the other way, out the flaps of the tent, where the living seemed even busier than when I'd first been wheeled in.

Soon the sirens were wailing again, though the pattern and length of each howl seemed different than the last time. The nurse, along with a few other people, ran into the tent. They weren't talking much, but they all seemed to know what they were doing as they transferred me to a backboard and ran with me to another tent. We passed other people who were running—some pushing patients, some just with their heads down. Through the limited conversation, I knew that there was a bomb threat. Something, allegedly, was headed right toward us.

In the new tent, there was a wide, square hole in the ground—like a grave for more than one person. I was lowered into it. A doctor yelled, "Vest!" And then I watched as a bullet-proof vest flew from one hand, to the next, to the doctor. The doctor laid the vest across my chest and then lay on top of me, facedown. The sirens continued to wail, the other people in the room scattered. To different graves? To other tents? I had no idea; all I knew was I was on my back with a vest between my torso and the doctor who lay over me. He was heavy on me, but not so much that I couldn't breathe. I wasn't scared, but I did think about dying and how if I were to go just then, I wouldn't be looking anyone in the eye, but I also wouldn't be alone. It struck me how at a time of need, the presence of a stranger can stand in for family, the people you love.

When the sirens stopped—maybe 30 or 40 minutes later—it was business as usual. I was carted by two new people to the imaging tent, where they did the X-rays and a CT scan. It wasn't long before the first doctor I saw came into the tent to give me the results. My head was fine, but I had two new bulging discs on my spine.

"You kinda took a one-two punch," he said. "First the fall, and then moving you into that hole without your back secured." He shook his head.

I could stay on the base and look into treatment for the discs, or I could refuse treatment and go back to the office. Either way, I was to lie on my back and do nothing for three days.

I refused treatment.

The medics wanted me supine for the helicopter ride back. But the sun was starting to set and I didn't want to miss it. I sat up and looked out into the open sky that was red and orange and liquid-looking. Then I looked down to the beige blond, beautifully monotone landscape. I was glad I was alive to see it all.

I didn't take three days off.

I didn't even take that night off.

The bombed woman's face was imprinted in my mind; I could feel her image as a permanent part of me. I decided that I had to amp up my efforts once again. I had to catch the terrorists who would do that to any woman. Any man. Any human. Anywhere in the world.

TWELVE

TROJANS RULE!

Europe
February–April 2004

A new guy, Jerry, had joined the Poison Trio; now we were a Poison Quartet. There was nothing wrong with Jerry; he seemed smart and determined. He was older than me, but under thirty, with a youthfully tousled mess of blond hair. I didn't particularly like him or dislike him. But I was having a difficult time acclimating to him—it's hard to get used to a fourth leg when you've been balancing pretty darn well on three. I had no objection, however, to a fourth set of eyes on the growing African terrorism cells.

At Jerry's first meeting in the cubicles, with Graham, Sally, Victor, David, Ben, and me, he spoke up right away. Jerry talked loudly, forcefully, as if he had to convince the rest of us of what he was capable of. Sally pursed her lips. I had a feeling she was stopping herself from interrupting him. Graham calmly nodded. Victor did the same and then looked at me and said, "What do you think, Tracy?"

After all the work I'd done in Africa and the Middle East, we now knew definitively what H, the African-born terrorist now living in Europe, was up to. All my sources, collected together, showed that a multiplatform chemical attack led by H—most likely in Europe—was imminent. I knew, however, that the chemical intel wasn't enough for operatives in his new country of residence to arrest him. My group looked beyond those chemicals, charted H's movements across the globe as well as the movements of his known connections, and found that he had been involved in planning the coordinated bombing in Africa that had created those haunting and unbearable floating heads. I didn't care why H was arrested. I just wanted him off the streets, out of the mosque, and unreachable to his followers so that his plan would be disrupted. Unfortunately, the intelligence agency in his new country of citizenship claimed that even the bombing connection proved too circumstantial to warrant an arrest.

There was still hope, though, as H had recently bought a plane ticket to another Western country. I immediately started cabling all the contacts I had in that country. If they looked at the evidence carefully enough, they might find it too hard to let this man roam free. Still, even if they detained H, his European country of residence would have to okay it as he was officially one of their own.

"Someone has to get over there," I said to Victor. "We have to lay out all the evidence and present our case until people understand the consequences of *not* taking in H."

"Which are?" Sally was baiting me. She wanted me to state the obvious.

"There *will* be an attack. Al-Qaeda is fully funding him. Also, he's proselytizing new followers from the local coffee shops and the mosque every week. He seems to have incredible charisma."

Jerry started speaking again. Everyone listened. It wasn't that he was saying the wrong things. It was that he was using too many words. We all spoke in quick, concise terms. There wasn't time for endless palaver.

███████████████████████████████████

███████████████████████████████████████

██████████████████████████████████

Graham cut Jerry short. "Okay, Jerry, Tracy. Go get the job done."

And that was the end of the meeting.

□ □ □

Many European intelligence agencies have plenty of women. But few have as many women as the agency of H's new homeland did. The intelligence operatives from that country were always helpful, smart, and their written English was flawless. The problem wasn't going to be one of communication or respect, as it had been in the country where they called me Malibu Barbie. I just needed to prove to them that my sources were legitimate and my leads were solid. To assist on this end, a counterterrorism analyst, Gigi, was to come abroad with Jerry and me.

I'd first noticed Gigi simply because she was gorgeous. It wasn't a self-conscious gorgeous, not a put-on that she created. Rather, it was the luck of nature: thick curly hair; dark flawless skin; and bright, light eyes. The beauty of contrasts. I admired Gigi's style, too. She wore sweaters with fur collars, lipstick the color of blood, and shoes you could never run in. It all came together as this: Gigi was confident, unselfconscious, and easygoing in a way that I envied. On top of all that beauty and style, it turned out she was incredibly smart, kind, and funny. We quickly became friends.

The flight to Europe was easy, but we landed at an hour that made it too late to talk with the operatives there. Gigi, Jerry, and I agreed that we'd check into our hotel rooms and then meet in the lobby and go out to explore the city for the evening. We were all curious and energized. Also, none of us had ever been to this particular capital.

The hotel was nothing remarkable, like any corporate American hotel. I threw my suitcase onto the luggage stand, brushed my hair and teeth, put on lipstick, and left the room. Gigi's room was near the elevator. I pushed the call button and then stood there, listening at her door. Madonna's "Like a Virgin" was blasting beyond the walls. I imagined Gigi having a party in there. For a second, I considered knocking on her door and joining the party, but I felt too shy. Instead, I got on the elevator and headed toward the lobby.

I don't know how people travel without a book to read. I always carry one, and I'd even brought one with me to the lobby to pass what I thought would only be a few minutes as I waited for Gigi and Jerry. It was longer than a few minutes when Gigi finally showed up. Even half-obscured in her hooded coat, she looked spectacular. I watched people watching her as she traversed the lobby, took off her coat, and then sat across from me.

"Madonna?"

"You heard?" She smiled. "I was dancing. You know, waking myself up after the flight."

We talked about both H and Madonna. At that age, our brains were flexible enough to volley between the two in a single conversation. After an hour, Jerry still had not come down. This seemed odd to me, as my amateur analysis of CIA placement came down to only one question everyone had been asked at the first interview: *Do you prefer a bath or a shower?* I had picked shower. Who has time for a bath? In my mind, operatives—those who are running around the world at breakneck speed, tracking the bad guys—were the shower people. And the bath-takers— those who liked to sit still in one place—were the analysts. Analysts were the brilliant, home-base people we counted on to shed light on the data we were collecting. Jerry and I were operatives. Gigi was an analyst. According to my calculations, Gigi should have been the last one to arrive and Jerry should have been downstairs when I was.

"He's probably watching porn," Gigi said, of Jerry.

"You really think he'd charge porn to his room?" I wouldn't even order *Look Who's Talking* and expect the agency to pay for it.

"It's free on regular TV here. I saw it when I was looking for a music channel."

"Wow. Okay. But, still, can you imagine, sitting in your room and looking at porn when you know your colleagues are waiting for you?" I couldn't.

"Men seem to have less shame with this stuff." Gigi looked toward the elevators where Jerry was walking toward us wearing a puffy green down coat.

Jerry dropped into the seat beside me.

"Were you enjoying that free porn?" Gigi was smiling as she asked.

Jerry didn't smile back. He simply stood, looked at his watch, and said, "Let's go see the town."

That's the thing about intelligence workers. They're trained to read liars. Jerry wasn't even going to try.

I zipped up my coat and put on my hat and mittens. We walked out of the hotel and into the dark and cold. Like other European cities I had visited, the locals didn't seem to notice the temperature. Only about half the people I saw wore hats, some were pushing baby carriages, others were strolling hand in hand. It was the beginning of March, however, so warmer than it had been in a while for them. For me, it was as cold as D.C. ever got, hovering in the thirties.

Almost immediately we were along the water, looking out at the glittery lights of an island across from us. ██████████

█████████████ Jerry was leading. He turned so we were headed away from the water. We were on a cobblestone street now, lined with pretty yellow, orange, and green brick row houses that had roofs that staircased up like a wedding cake. Gigi and I continued to discuss Madonna and ████. Jerry was saying relatively little. In fact, he'd barely spoken since Gigi had mentioned his porn session in the hotel room.

Jerry vanished around a corner, then paused and waited for us to catch up. We were by the water again. Jerry looked at me and asked, "What kind of shit school is USC anyway?"

"Pardon?" I was twenty-five. Only four years out of college. I still identified myself by my school. I had pride in it.

Jerry started walking again with Gigi and me on either side of him. He turned his head toward me. "I've just never met anyone of substance from California. And especially from USC."

"Uh, Ronald Reagan was from California," Gigi said. "You know, that guy who ended up as president?"

"Not a brilliant man, and he was an *actor*."

"I think he might have been from Illinois." I knew it as fact, but was trying to mellow my tone. "Nixon was from California."

"Okay, you both just named two very average presidents. You're not helping your case."

"Joan Didion's from California," I said.

"And John Steinbeck." Gigi clearly was on my side.

"No idea who Didion is, and I guarantee you that Steinbeck is the only Californian writer people outside of California have heard of."

"What's your problem?" I stopped walking and turned to Jerry.

"I'm just pointing out a fact that California, and USC in particular, have not produced any great people. It's a shit state with shit schools, and I'm shocked the agency let you in."

"You have no idea what you're talking about!" Now I was angry. "You've probably never been there! If you spent one day on the USC campus you'd be bawling your eyes out, running away with your tail between your legs because you couldn't understand anything!"

"ARE YOU KIDDING ME?" Jerry yelled. "IT'S A STATE FULL OF IDIOT SURFERS AND SUNBATHERS, AND I GUARANTEE YOU'RE THE ONLY PERSON IN THE AGENCY WHO'S FROM THERE—"

I looked around to see if anyone was watching. We were supposed to blend into the landscape. Be invisible! But here was the head-turning Gigi and now the yelling Jerry. But the locals seemed unbothered; no one was watching us.

"Go fuck yourself!" Saying those words was rare for me. In fact, this was a first. I'd never told anyone, not even the gang of bullies in school, to fuck themselves. It's ridiculous that I even cared what Jerry, the necessary-but-intrusive fourth leg, said about California or USC. But, as I stated before, I was only twenty-five.

And so I went nuts.

Jerry yelled. I yelled louder. Jerry leaned into my face. I leaned in too, so close that my lips were only inches from his. Jerry insulted me, my school, my state; I insulted his taste, his lack of knowledge, his provincial and limited thinking.

We were both ridiculous. Me because I was still defining myself by my family, my school, my hometown. Also, after having flown home for the least-important-to-me wedding ever, I was determined to never again let anyone bully me. Anywhere. Anyhow.

As for Jerry, I had a feeling this whole thing had to do with insecurities: feeling intimidated by the powerful Gigi, and feeling more humiliation than either she or I could have then guessed over having been outed about the porn-a-thon in his room. Insecure bullies know how to pick their victims, though. Gigi probably had never been victimized, and Jerry could see that from the start. So he picked me. He sensed a vulnerability;

a gap where he could wedge in a hard, metal-toed boot and deliver a swift kick.

The only problem was, Jerry was sensing my past, and not who I was on that day.

The fight escalated to the point where people did stop to watch. I wanted to shut it down immediately. My job was more important than anything I had to prove to Jerry. But he was new in the agency and didn't seem to understand the priorities. I had stopped talking, but Jerry carried on. Still, my heart was banging, and my chest heaved up and down as if I'd just run a race.

And then Gigi stepped between the two of us and put a hand on each of our shoulders.

"Enough!" she said. And Jerry finally went silent.

I had an urge to push him into the icy water.

"Fine." Jerry brushed Gigi's hand away.

"Tracy, you walk in front, I'm in the middle. Jerry, you're in the back. You two aren't allowed to talk."

"Fine." I took off with the two of them trailing. I meandered around the city, trying to take in as much as possible in the few free hours we would have there. But I was still so angry that I couldn't see much; I had no focus. We hadn't had dinner yet, so I walked us straight into a crowded restaurant where it looked like people were having fun. People who didn't insult each other's education and probably wouldn't give a damn if someone did anyway.

"I'll eat elsewhere," Jerry said, and he turned and walked back in the direction from which we came.

Once he was out of sight, he was mostly out of mind. Gigi and I had a great time eating seafood and still talking about Madonna and H.

□ □ □

Jerry avoided both of us the next morning, and we didn't see him again until our meeting at the intelligence agency. Jerry and

I both acted as if nothing had gone down the night before. I was certainly embarrassed and regretted that we'd drawn any attention to ourselves. He may have been new in the agency, but he surely had to have known how dumb that was.

Jerry's disregard for USC and the entire state of California was utterly meaningless when held up beside the fact that ███ ███ ███ ███ ███████████████████████████████. The local intelligence let it be known that they had been closely tracking H and knew his whereabouts at all times. But they still wouldn't arrest him with all the evidence we—themselves included—had amassed.

And so we spent days with our foreign counterparts connecting the pieces each agency had and stringing them all out together so we could have one clear, complete image of what and who we were dealing with. More information poured in from sources around the globe—every hour we worked together, the situation became more and more clear.

Before we went home, just before his scheduled flight out of his country of residence, H was arrested for his connection to the bombings that created those free-floating heads. Gigi, Jerry, and I felt utterly victorious. The Madonna-dancing stunner, the anti-California porn watcher, and the sorority girl from USC had helped stop what could have been one of the largest chemical attacks in al-Qaeda's history.

□ □ □

On the flight home, Jerry changed seats and sat a few rows behind me and Gigi. She and I mulled over what the next greatest threat was now that H was out of commission. We agreed it remained the newer African terrorist cells, but we were unsure of who within those cells was going to direct the next big chemical attack. Certainly Zarqawi already had someone lined up to step in for H. As I said before, hunting terrorists was a lot like cutting an arm off a starfish. Another one—or maybe even two—will grow in its place soon enough. Hopefully we could identify the new starfish arm before he put any plans into action.

Victor and Graham had been taking our intel on the ███

███
███
███
███
███
███
███
███
███
███
███
███
███
███
███
███
███
███. Unfor-

tunately, I missed something big. Huge. An oversight for which I still cannot forgive myself.

□ □ □

Gigi, Jerry, and I landed back in D.C. on March 10. On March 11, I got to my office at 6:30 a.m., then went to the food court and picked up my venti black Starbucks. With my coffee in one hand and my purse flung over my shoulder, I crossed the room, saying hello to the other early comers. At my desk, I sipped the coffee and waited for my computer to start up. The first thing I saw was a cable from Europe. At 1:30 a.m. D.C. time, 7:30 a.m.

in Madrid, multiple bombs had gone off on several commuter trains. The press was already blaming Basque separatists, but I knew it was far more likely that the perpetrators had been the individuals we had been tracking.

I felt ill. Shaken. How could I have not seen something that would have taken dozens of people to execute? There had to have been some chatter, some scrap of intel floating around about it. I sat at my desk for a long time, reading and rereading the cable. Then I got up and went to the morning meeting, which was taking place at David's cubicle. Even Jerry was speechless.

As the media went on about Basque separatists, the CIA followed every lead. In the end, 190 people died from ten bombs that went off on four different trains at three different stations. Over 1,800 people were wounded. By March 14, the Basque theory was dead, and five al-Qaeda operatives were arrested. Three were ███████████████████████████████████ ██████████████. A few days later, four more al-Qaeda terrorists were arrested. By March 30, after multiple arrests and releases, charges were brought against 12 men. ███████████████ ███████████████████████████████████████ ███████████████████████████████████████

██████ The next day, warrants were issued for five more men associated with that particular terror cell. And then, in April, seven more associates of those already arrested were located by Spanish police at a home in Madrid. As the police were breaking down the door, the terrorists set off explosives and killed themselves and one police officer.

The March 11 bombing was the deadliest terrorist attack on European soil since the bombing of Pan Am flight 103 over Lockerbie, Scotland, in 1988.

This felt more personal than either 9/11 or the altered al-Qaeda poison chart. I took it as a great failure in my career.

□ □ □

Sometime after the Madrid bombings, I dug up that FBI application I'd had lying around my apartment. On a Sunday when I wasn't working, I filled it out and mailed it in. Again, I put it entirely out of my mind and left to work for a few weeks overseas. When I was home again I was interviewed by the FBI.

It was only a few days later when I got the call: I'd been accepted to the FBI and needed to show up at Quantico, Virginia, on May 1.

I loved the CIA. I had, and still have, incredible respect for the agency and the women and men who work there. I believe in what they do and know, for a fact, that they are saving lives every day. But I needed to save myself, too. I needed to have a home where I felt settled, safe, nested. Where I could see my family more regularly and date someone who wasn't undercover. And more than that, I needed to let go of feeling responsible for every act of terror in Europe, the Middle East, and Africa.

It was a heartbreaking choice. But I made it.

THIRTEEN

TRIGGER ALERT

Quantico, Virginia
May–August 2004

It was like going to boot camp and law school while also studying human behavior and psychology. An all-or-nothing deal,
too. In or out. Win or lose. If you could make it through the four
and a half months of training at Quantico, there was a position
with the FBI waiting.

We were always referred to by our last names. I had ceased
to be Tracy and was now Schandler. A name that sounds more
masculine than feminine, but that was just as well, as getting
through the training took a lot of . . . well, it took guts and other
things normally associated with men but easily summoned up
by women, too. As a group we were called NAC 04-13. This
meant we were the thirteenth New Agent Class to start the FBI
academy in the year 2004.

I had given up the lease on my apartment near Langley. My
mother had flown out and helped me sort, pack, and put the
few things I was keeping in storage. My furniture was passed
on to my cousin, who had recently moved to D.C. for his new
job. When I drove to Quantico—an hour and a half straight into
Virginia—I felt unburdened. I was hopeful and forward looking. Light, both emotionally and physically. With the radio
turned up and the windows rolled down, I sang the whole way
there. It was the first week of May, and the trees were lush and

leafy; a continuous green blur going by. The wind whipped my hair into my face, into my eyes; I wished I'd pulled it into a ponytail. But not much could bother me right then. I was thrilled to be joining the FBI.

Before parking the car, I circled the facilities so I could get a quick mental map of where I was. There were open fields, sniper ranges, and military barracks. The U.S. Marines train at Quantico, too. Surrounding it all were acres and acres of woods, trees, streams, and ponds. You could get easily lost there if you weren't good with directions.

I showed up at the exact time assigned to me for check-in. A woman gave me a map of the facilities and a key to my room. I would be housed on the second floor of the dorms with everyone else in my class. It was a multistory building, but trainees were forbidden to use elevators. I didn't mind taking the stairs, but I knew there'd be some intense physical training and figured I wouldn't want to march up eight or nine floors at the end of each day. At that moment, a room on the second floor felt like a great start to this new iteration of a career in counterterrorism. My first stroke of good luck.

My roommate, Amelia, had already arrived. She had taken the bed by the window, which was fine with me. The place was set up like a typical dorm room: two single beds, two desks, one closet, and a little walking space in between.

Amelia jumped off the bed and grabbed my bag as I entered. She had a big smile, big white teeth, and straight blond hair. She looked like she belonged on the campus of USC, like a Delta Gamma girl to the core. She had a Southern accent, Southern charm, and talked to me like we'd known each other forever. Or more like we would know each other forever. Good luck stroke number two: the best possible roommate.

In the free time before the whole class was to meet up, Amelia and I sat on our beds, high-speed chatting as we caught each other up on our lives so far. I told her about the CIA; she thought that was the coolest thing ever. She mentioned that she had been working in the Park Service. And then she told me about a woman, Lisa, whom she referred to as her wife (gay marriage wasn't legal then). They'd been together seven years, and Amelia was missing Lisa like mad already. She would keep her wife a secret, Amelia let me know, until she had sussed out the rest of our class. Based on the people I'd worked with in the CIA, I didn't think this was going to be a problem. Though, what did I know?

"I realize we haven't even started training yet," Amelia said. "But I'm already thinking about graduation, when you'll meet Lisa. Y'all will love each other."

"Can't wait!" I said, and the conversation was stopped as our suitemates, whose bedrooms were on the other side of the bathroom, popped in and introduced themselves.

Donna and Molly were both CPAs. Donna was from Connecticut and Molly was from Seattle. Both sported deep tans, as if they'd just returned from a vacation in the Caribbean. I wondered just then if roommates were assigned according to how they looked: Amelia and I were blonds; Donna and Molly were well-tanned, well-toned women in their thirties.

Donna and Molly seemed friendly. There were only six women in my class of 40, so the other two must have been down the hall somewhere. I'd meet them soon enough, but if these three turned out to be as good as they seemed, the female corps should prove to be pretty darn fabulous. This I considered the third stroke of great luck.

Amelia was friendly and chatty with Donna and Molly, but I could tell she didn't trust them yet as she never mentioned Lisa. Even when Donna and Molly each revealed that they were engaged to be married, Amelia didn't say she was in a relationship. The suitemates didn't ask me any questions about the CIA—they didn't appear to be interested the way Amelia had been. This was fine with me. After living a secret life for so many years, I felt uncomfortable talking about myself and rarely did unless I was asked a direct or specific question.

Just before we had to meet in the lecture hall, the last two women joined the party in our room. Betsy was blond and wore powder blue eye shadow, like someone from a seventies disco film. She bore a vague resemblance to Tonya Harding, the skater. She talked loudly about her life back home, the boyfriend she left behind, how cheap the sheets on the dorm bed seemed. All the while, Betsy never looked at me or even turned her body toward me. Josie, Betsy's roommate, was quiet and watchful. Maybe she was dreading the fact that Betsy, the talker, was her roommate. Josie was Asian, which didn't strike me as unusual until the six of us walked to the lecture hall to meet the other recruits.

As a group, these trainees resembled a predominately white USC fraternity more than they did the people of any American city where they might soon be placed.

Amelia and I sat and then realized there were name tags on the seats. We got up and each moved to where we'd been placed alphabetically in the amphitheater. Overhead were fluorescent lights and ceiling panels. I couldn't help but wonder if there were cameras up there. I sat next to a guy named Ralph who was friendly and kind. He had the face of a former boxer: beaten-in looking. On the other side of me was Jay, from Kansas. He was laser focused on the instructor at the front of the room, as if he were already being judged on his performance.

Cliches are rarely interesting, but that's what the instructors at Quantico seemed like. They were what you'd expect: middle-aged, stocky white men with short hair who barked orders. Even the one female instructor mostly fit that stereotype. (She certainly never looked out for the six women trainees.)

The first order barked was from Troy. We were instructed to stand up, one by one, and state our names and what we'd been doing—career wise—before we joined the FBI. Some people answered in a sentence. Many answered in a paragraph. A few answered in several paragraphs, as if they were Atticus Finch in the courtroom, showing the world their brilliance and commitment to doing good. When all that palaver was boiled down to single words, it sounded something like this: Lawyer, accountant, lawyer, accountant. Police officer. Lawyer, lawyer, lawyer. Accountant, accountant, accountant. Police officer. Park Service (Amelia). Lawyer, accountant. Former professional football player(!). Lawyer, accountant. Police officer. Lawyer, lawyer, lawyer.

With very few exceptions, these were the law-and-order people of the world; the ones who want to make sure all the rules have been followed and everything adds up. I'm saying this in praise of them, in gratitude. We need these people to keep the country safe and running smoothly. But as I listened to the voices in the room, I couldn't help but wonder if the system, the way things work in the United States, might be enhanced— problems more easily addressed—by bringing in people with more varied backgrounds who might better understand the multifabric, patchwork quilt that is the United States.

The letter *S* is in the last third of the alphabet, so it wasn't until this exercise was almost over that my turn came.

"My name's Tracy Schandler, and I was a counterterrorism operative in the CIA," I said.

"Where were you posted?" Troy asked.

"War zone, overseas." I paused for a second and then added, "I can't be more specific."

I looked down at my desk to avoid the eyes staring at me. There was a moment of silence before I heard a grumbling male voice in the corner of the room say, "Yeah, and I worked as Superman on the planet Krypton." A smattering of laughter followed, and then the lawyer next to me started speaking and I was able to disappear again.

Once the introductions were over, Bart took the stage. He

was our supervisory special agent, meaning we'd work directly with him throughout training.

Bart had a throaty New York accent. The gold chain around his neck was thick enough that if someone grabbed it and twisted, Bart might be choked to death before the chain broke. With fat, jeweled fingers punctuating the air, Bart detailed how things were going to work over the next four months. It was clear he was in the final stretch of his career in the FBI, and he wanted no glitches, no burps, no hangnails, not even a hiccup.

"Most of you understand order. You're cops, lawyers. You know that if we don't all play by the same rules, chaos ensues." Then Bart looked at me. "This isn't the CIA, Schandler. No going rogue."

I smiled; my usual reaction to adversity.

"Everything we do here," Bart continued, "we do right. There are no undercover SNAFUs. In the FBI, unlike the CIA, we get the job done."

I started making a mental list: all the poison plots and bombing plots the CIA had stopped. Operations that the public never had and never would hear about. It was enough for me to know about them. I didn't feel the need to prove anything to Bart.

Next Bart splattered the room with blathering misogyny. He said it was going to be hard for *the ladies in the room* to keep up with the men, but that's what they'd have to do if they were to make it through the academy. The more Bart spoke, the more I imagined that he believed that women should not be a part of the FBI.

I felt sorry for Bart's wife and kids, whom he'd mentioned earlier, who'd had to tolerate—and probably obey—this man for years. Following orders isn't necessarily a bad thing. But following orders from someone with less than stellar intelligence is painful. I kept smiling, and Bart kept talking. He wrapped it all up with a simple declaration that the CIA was responsible for September 11.

After Bart's baffling speech, we were issued computers, backpacks, and our uniforms. For daily work, cargo pants and a blue polo shirt. For physical training, blue elastic-waist shorts and a gray t-shirt. The only items of clothing we'd been instructed to bring were suits, the kind of thing we'd wear on the job once we'd graduated. And footwear: boots and running shoes. I brought the boots I'd been wearing at the last war zone where I'd been stationed. When I packed them, I couldn't help but look at the tread on the bottom, still caked with golden sand and rust-colored dirt from a faraway and dangerous place.

Once we'd collected our uniforms, we were each given an FBI baseball hat, a bulletproof vest, a holster, handcuffs, and an orange dummy gun that was the same size and weight as the gun we'd carry as agents.

"Your gun is part of your body now," Bart said. "You walk, eat, piss, and shit with that gun. Get used to it. Learn how to sit and move so that no one notices it's there. And ladies—" Bart looked directly at me. "I don't care if doesn't match your outfit. I don't care if it doesn't match your hairdo. Wear the gun!"

I glanced two rows down toward Amelia. She widened her eyes at me, I rolled mine. Did Bart really think that someone who voluntarily joined the FBI would even think about their orange fake gun matching or not matching the FBI-issued training uniform? And hairdo? How do you match a gun to a hairdo anyway? Also, who says "hairdo"?

□ □ □

Amelia and I were instantly inseparable. She could do a perfect imitation of Bart that never failed to make me laugh. Donna and Molly, on the other hand, seemed entirely unbothered by the daily insults hurled at the women in our group by Bart and the two other instructors, Ted and Marge. Josie never spoke, so I couldn't figure out how she felt about any of this. And Betsy, with the daily smear of shimmering blue across her eyes, also appeared unbothered by the blatant misogyny. In fact, she'd adopted Bart's apparent dislike of me and often brought up the CIA with a condescending eye roll as if I had simply invented my past.

"We've just got to get through this," Amelia said on day five, as we were getting ready for our first physical fitness test (PFT).

"Yup," I said. "As long as we have each other as venting partners, this will be fine." I double-knotted my running shoes.

"It's like prison," Amelia said. "Just have to do the time and then we'll be free."

I laughed. "Uh, yeah, it's really nothing like prison." I'd seen plenty of prisons and prisoners in the Middle East and Africa. If you took the time I had to pee in a bucket in a closet, added unexpected beatings and intermittent rape, and then a continuous fear for one's life (like an unending, high-stress fever), then you might be approaching what I'd seen in prisons.

Amelia smiled. "Well, it's close!"

"Nope." I smiled back and stood at the door, waiting for her to tie her shoes. "Not even close."

"Okay." Amelia yanked her laces tight. "But I'm really effing miserable and feel like they are really effing nasty to us."

"I'll agree to that," I said.

As we walked to the field where we were to take the PFT, I told Amelia about the ideas that had been percolating in my mind since our first encounter with Bart. I started with the story of having been bullied in school by girls. That experience, in part, had instilled a desire to be a teacher as a way to change the way women treat each other, change how they're treated by others, and, in that way, change the world. Within the agency, I was able to thrive and achieve with little resistance to the fact that I am a woman (yes, foreign agencies were rattled by my presence, but the people in the CIA were not). This gave me a sense of myself, of my power; it was something I'd never felt before. Now, in the FBI, the cycle of meanness and oppression was up and running again. This time, I wouldn't stand for it. I would resist. And I was determined to find a way to change it.

"What if you taught in a school, like you'd always planned?" Amelia asked. We had reached the field and needed to shut down the conversation soon.

"I was thinking about that," I said. "I'd want to teach girls. Empower *them* to change the world so that places like this are packed with women who—"

Like a movie scene, Marge pointed toward me at that very moment and shouted, "Schandler! This isn't a coffee klatch, shut your trap and get over here!"

Amelia burst out laughing. I held it in, and we jogged to get in our places.

The first part of the PFT was sit-ups. With someone kneeling at our feet—hands on the tongues of our shoes—we had to do as many sit-ups as possible in a minute. This was no problem for me. It wouldn't be a problem for me still, today. After sit-ups we did the 300-meter sprint. I was running every day at the time, but I just couldn't sprint very well. Fortunately, I was able to pass the sprinting test, though by a hair. Push-ups were next. If I stopped typing right now and dropped to the floor, I wouldn't be able to do a single one. But at that time, by dint of determination and maybe rage at Bart, Ted, and Marge, I did 19. This was the minimum number required to pass the push-up test. The 1.5-mile run was next. I wasn't worried about it and just ran as I usually did, though with a little more fire under my feet. Amelia passed everything but the run. She would be on lockdown at Quantico, unable to leave the premises—even on the weekend—until she passed the test. And if she failed again, she was out.

"I won't let you fail," I told her as we walked to the showers. "Just come running with me every morning before classes start." This was more of a sacrifice than she knew, as I needed that running time, those long stints when there were no voices around and just the gentle *ch-ch-ch* sound of my feet on the ground, for peace of mind. In the CIA, there was no stress, worry, or anxiety that couldn't be temporarily quelled by a long run. The rhythm, like an external heartbeat, puts everything in my mind and body at rest.

Amelia easily agreed to the early morning runs.

"But hey"—I had to say it or I'd resent the offer—"I don't like to talk when I run. I just run."

"Totally on board with that," Amelia said. And she was.

At five thirty the next morning, in the damp, cool air, Amelia and I took off into the woods of Quantico. There was a double heartbeat now, her shoes slapping against the ground, just a few steps behind mine. I trusted her, was comfortable with her, and was easily able to float off into that empty head-space that brings me peace.

We did this run every day for the next two weeks. Amelia increased her running time, and we both felt confident that she would easily pass the PFT.

But before we were required to take the physical test again, Amelia quit.

"I can't take another minute." Amelia folded a shirt that was turned inside-out and shoved it into her bag.

"I get it," I said. "But if we stay, we're the people who could change this."

In the past few days, Bart, Ted, and Marge kept a sharp eye on Amelia and me. Everyone in the academy had to perform everything well; there was no slacking off. Amelia and I had to do better than that. Way better, lest we be called out, pointed out, mocked, and humiliated. In law class, each time Marge asked a question, she called on me to answer it, whether my hand was up or not. I loved reading about law and continually had the highest test grades of this class. This seemed to drive Marge mad as she threw trick questions at me, or questions from the chapter that hadn't yet been assigned (and yes, I always read ahead). When I answered correctly, Marge appeared distraught. The one time I got an answer wrong, Marge thumped her hand on the desk and said, "See, Schandler! You're not as smart as you think you are!"

It went beyond small insults like that. There was an emotional aggression directed toward us by the supervisory special agents that made their feelings clear. We were disliked and unwanted. And maybe mob mentality took over, or it might have been a life-saving effort by the others to stay in the good graces of those in charge, but soon enough almost everyone—including three of the four other women (Josie still expressed nothing)—seemed to loathe me and Amelia. The two people who did not join in this gang hostility were Darren and Jake. They happened to be the only African American people in our class. Were people being hostile to them, too? I didn't catch it, though it's highly likely that I was so caught up in my own nightmare, I was unable to see theirs. Either way, we had two sympathizers who never jumped on the dog pile and who always extended a hand of friendship.

In addition to having to endure the mass wave of people who appeared to dislike us, Amelia was also uncomfortable with the gun training. Just that morning, she'd been mocked by Bart for not having enough enthusiasm about hitting the cutout man straight in the head.

When her suitcase was packed and zipped, Amelia unlocked the dummy gun from the holster on her hip and laid it on the desk.

"I can't be a part of this gun culture," she said.

I didn't want Amelia to leave, but I had to agree it was best for her. Guns—the assembling, disassembling, cleaning, handling, and shooting—were an enormous part of our training. I'm all for greater gun control, but I do think guns should be in the hands of law enforcement. If there's anyone I trust with a gun, it is an FBI agent who has undergone months of daily practice with the weapon.

Once Amelia left, it felt like all that fury was trained on me with the pinpoint of a laser. I didn't attempt to fight it. And I refused to try to make them like me. I simply retreated to my head, worked at my highest level—including being a total and complete team player when necessary—and looked toward the endgame: graduating, being placed in an office, continuing the work of tracking terrorists. And, maybe just as important, creating a stronger, smarter representation of women in the FBI. As I'd said to Amelia, it wasn't anything like prison. It was like junior high school. But this time, the bullying started with the teachers rather than stopped there. And I refused to collapse into victimhood.

□ □ □

The FBI at Quantico maintains that people are in or out, pass or fail. But, really, there is a sort of forgiveness offered to some people some of the time. That is, if you don't quite pass the academy, you can have a certain amount of do-over and can join the class behind you. This is how I got a new roommate when Amelia moved out. Brandy moved in with the grace of a bulldozer. Her husband was in the FBI so she was already inculcated into the agency point of view. Brandy was small and flailed her forearms as she spoke in a way that made me think of T. rex dinosaurs and their disproportionately tiny, grasping arms. She talked rapidly and continuously about everything, ranging from how to properly make a bed to how to properly load a firearm (even though she had previously failed firearm tests) to how to properly relate to Bart, whom she adored and had witnessed belittling me ("Schandler, just because you've already been trained in firearms doesn't mean you're any better than anyone here! You're not even good when I only compare you to the girls! In fact, you're worse—you have confidence where you shouldn't!"). Brandy had no interest in what I had to say, or what I might know, or how I might help her. She viewed herself as the authority. The right side of everything. The final word. And she conveyed this authority in a twittery little chipmunk voice with her arms flapping and a tense, false smile. If you've ever read the book or seen the movie *Election*, think of Tracy Flick. That's who I was dealing with. Only Brandy was armed. And dangerous.

□ □ □

With the exception of law, most classes at the academy were taught both in the classroom and through acting out scenarios. After many classes on psychology, manipulation, and reading body language, we were each sent into a room to interview one of the instructors who was playing the part of a suspect. For this exercise, and others like it, we were to dress in the clothes we'd wear to work. I put on the one suit I'd brought to Quantico, something I'd often worn into the office at Langley. The pants and jacket were black with a tiny, almost-invisible red stripe. Beneath the jacket I wore a red ribbed shirt, my holster, the orange dummy gun, and my cuffs. On my feet were the same black peep-toe pumps I'd been sporting to work the past four-plus years. I had stayed up late the night before, closely studying the case material. I wanted to be exact, demanding. I wanted my questions to encircle the suspect without his knowing it, like a lasso that cinched tight before he even felt the rope at his side.

I strode into the room with my notepad in hand and took a seat across from Bart, who was playing the part of a white-collar criminal. I spoke calmly and with a certain friendliness intended to put him at ease so he'd open up. I pretended to know more than I did so I could instill both fear and a way out of that fear by presenting myself as the person who could save him from his predicament. I did everything exactly as it had been taught, and when I walked out of there, I felt secure that I had nailed the interview. No matter how much he disliked me,

Bart—and whoever was observing the interview through one-way glass—couldn't find fault with my methodology.

I was so happy with how the interview went, I could barely be bothered by the intrusions of the day, such as Betsy approaching me in the shower (blue eye shadow intact; it must have been waterproof) and saying, "So, like, why do you even keep up the charade that you were in the CIA? Everyone knows you weren't." It was so odd, so immature, as to be more baffling than insulting. I turned my back and continued to wash my hair.

At dinner that night, I sat alone, as I had every night since Amelia left. This always gave me time to think and to go over what we'd learned during the day. Marge, one of the instructors, approached me at the table. She stood still and stout as a fireplug.

"Schandler," she said.

I looked up, as if to ask what she needed.

"I need to see you in my office. ASAP." The way she said ASAP made it sound like Aesop, the man who wrote the fables.

"Should I just come now?" I looked down at my plate of food, barely touched.

"What exactly does *ASAP* mean to you, Schandler?"

"Okay." I picked up my plate, dropped it off at the busing station, and then walked to Marge's office, where I waited for her for at least 15 minutes.

When Marge finally showed up, she said nothing about having made me wait. She simply opened the door, walked in, and sat behind her desk. I sat at the chair across from her.

"We had a problem with your interview."

"You did?" I had felt so confident in my performance, this was almost as baffling as Betsy asking me to stop pretending I'd been in the CIA.

"Bart found your suit distracting."

"Distracting?" It wasn't ripped, dirty, or wrinkled. Yeah, it was a few years old, but it was still fine as far as fashion and fit went.

"It was too tight. It distracted him."

"My suit was too tight?" I still wasn't getting it. Was Marge saying my suit was too small and that clothes worn in the FBI should fit exactly right? My weight had barely changed a pound since my senior year of college. "But the suit is exactly my size."

"Schandler!" Marge's face pulled into a focused pucker; I could see what she'd look like as a very old woman. "Your suit was distracting. It showed too much of your body. You need to wear larger clothes. And you need to write an apology to Bart."

It felt like a snowstorm was blowing through my bones. I was chilled. "You'd like me to apologize to Bart for the fit of my suit?" My voice was calm. I needed to be certain that what she was saying was what I was hearing.

"Special Agent Smith to you."

"Sorry. To be clear: you'd like me to apologize to Special Agent Smith for the fit of my suit. Correct?"

Marge rolled her eyes and shook her head. "How many ways can I say this, Schandler? Don't be the dumb blond everyone thinks you are! Your suit was distracting! Apologize to Bart or leave the program! If you want to be a team player, if you want to succeed as an agent, you need to learn *Aesop* how not to make your coworkers uncomfortable. Got it?"

"Yes, ma'am." I smiled. But from behind that smile, my eyes were raining bullets.

That night, I opened my laptop and composed an email to Bart.

The first draft read:

> Dear Asshole,
> I'm sorry you got off on my four-year-old CIA suit, the sight of which never appeared to ruffle the composure of both men and women from nations all over the world.

The second draft read:

Dear Pervert,
I apologize for triggering your pervy impulses in the face of my old, black suit.

The third draft read:

Dear Tiny, Afraid, Scared, Little Boy in a Man's Body,
I'm sorry that the power I wielded in that suit made you feel impotent and worthless. I'm sorry you are so afraid of women that you need to dominate and belittle them whenever possible.

The email I sent read:

Dear Special Agent Smith,
I'm sorry my suit made you uncomfortable. I drove to the Walmart after dinner and bought a new suit in a larger size.

Sincerely,
Tracy Schandler

□ □ □

Hand-to-hand combat was always fun. How often do you get thrown together with people you don't particularly love with the instructions to beat the breath and blood out of them? Usually we wore punching gloves and padded headgear. The exercise that seemed to mirror how I felt in the academy was Bull in the Ring. Each person was weighed, and then we were sorted into four groups of ten divided by weight. The women all weighed less than the men, so my group was always the six women and the four lightest men. One by one, each member of the group would stand in the center of a circle and fight for

60 seconds straight with each of the other people in the group. In other words, it was nine minutes of fight-for-your-life battle with nine different people coming at you in sequence. What I didn't have in skill, I made up for with determination. We were filmed in many exercises, and when I watched the footage of myself in hand-to-hand combat I thought of wild kangaroos, or the Road Runner, just keeping at it no matter how many anvil weights and bundles of dynamite get thrown in his way. I was a punching machine, and that kept my ribs, teeth, and nose in place while others had theirs knocked loose.

I'm too self-critical to ever be proud, but when I watch the footage of myself at the daily shooting practice, I'm always surprised by my skill with the 9-millimeter Glock. I was so continuously criticized during target practice that I never realized that I wasn't bad at it. We were assigned particular shooting patterns: three shots with your right hand, three shots with your left, one with your right, one with your left, and so on. With the ear protectors and goggles on, I was sealed off from the world outside my head. As I single-mindedly focused on the targets, I was able to flow with the shooting rhythm in the same way I performed dance routines all throughout school.

We practiced with shotguns, too. They were just as fun, and my scores were even higher, as it's much easier to hit a target with buckshot than with a 9-millimeter Glock. The only person who didn't use the Glock was the former professional football player. He was issued something more proportionate to his frying-pan palms and baguette fingers.

□ □ □

Hogan's Alley is a dummy town built at Quantico over 30 years ago with the help of Hollywood set designers. It's named after a comic strip of the same name from the 1890s. The comic was about mischievous kids from the wrong side of the tracks in New York City. The FBI-created town looks more like suburban

Maryland than New York City. Hogan's Alley features apartment buildings and tract houses with garages and sidewalks. There's a quaint downtown with a bank, doughnut shop, drugstore, diner, bowling alley, and more. There's a trailer park at Hogan's Alley. And naturally, there's a motel, as who could imagine crime without thinking of some motel by the side of the freeway with bloodstained carpets and a bedspread you'd never touch without wearing gloves? If aliens ever landed in Hogan's Alley in the middle of the night, they'd be utterly confounded by this complete little town, mostly furnished, but with no money in the Bank of Hogan, no hot doughnuts in the doughnut shop, no running water, and no living human inhabitants.

With outside actors hired to play criminals, we conducted raids and takedowns, and negotiated for hostages in Hogan's Alley. Each scenario enacted was taken from an actual FBI case. We wore plastic face masks and bulletproof vests and were armed with guns that looked and felt real but shot only paintballs (which hurt when they hit and can easily take an eye out). Lined up outside the bank—or bowling alley, motel, wherever—an instructor talked us through exactly what we should do, step by step, person by person, shot by shot. The goals were always the same: don't get hit; disarm and capture the suspect.

Brandy claimed her heart was banging with fear, that it felt like a real raid every time we got out the guns and went to Hogan's Alley. I found it to be a foggy imitation of the actual experience. It was more like being fifteen and driving in a car with one of your parents in the passenger seat continuously snapping at you, "Stay away from the curb! Put your blinker on! Not that blinker, the other blinker! Slow down! Speed up! Right lane, right lane! You can't make a goddamned right turn from the left lane!" When you first drove without a parent, you could still hear them saying those things. It took a few months for the correct moves to become instinct. The same was true for FBI raids.

Forensics class occupied the two hours before lunch. I often wondered whose idea of a joke that was, as the images we saw in forensics were enough to make most people ill. After the severed heads in a trough that I'd seen in Africa, though, there was little that could spoil my appetite. Brandy's chattering voice carried above the crowd murmur, and every day as we walked from the forensics room to the cafeteria, she yammered on about how her stomach was tumbling. Even if I was ten people behind her in the food line, I could hear her claim she could *never eat a thing* after forensics. I'd pop my head out to look, and sure enough, her tray was always piled as high as mine.

The forensics teacher, Special Agent Kotter, had wild curly hair and a mustache. He came across as more of an intellectual than a law enforcement official, and this offered some relief from the ways and manners of the rest of the trainers. Kotter had done some of the forensics on United Airlines flight 93—the one that heroic passengers had crashed into a Pennsylvania field on September 11. What he found, and how he pieced together information from the wreckage, fascinated me. The appearance alone of the wreckage conveyed useful information: the giant dismembered tail the shape of a fish fin that lay in the field behind the blackened, ash-crumbled body. It was as if some enormous animal had chewed up the plane and then spat out that chunk of tail. I found the image of the plane gruesome but forced myself to take it in, and particularly to acknowledge those brave passengers who chose to crash into a field rather than into the U.S. Capitol, as the terrorists had planned.

Kotter was fond of throwing slides up on the projector as he spoke. There were often autopsy photos, bodies dissected with the exactitude of frogs in a science lab. And there were bodies prior to the autopsy: people who had been shot, knifed, bludgeoned, poisoned, burned, drowned, or run over. And then there were the many who had been strangled to death, their hyoid bone broken. The hyoid bone is unique in that it's the only one in the body that isn't attached to another bone; it sort of floats in your neck, glued to muscle. It's easy for a man with large hands to surround and then crush it. The bruising and red marks left behind, the way a neck looks after a strangulation, make the human body seem frail and light. When I looked at those images, I felt grateful for my beating heart, my legs that could run, my lungs that took in air.

The men were squirming in their seats, uncomfortably jocular, the day we discussed the Lorena and John Wayne Bobbitt case. Lorena cut off her husband's penis as he slept. She got in her car, drove away with the untethered phallus, and then Frisbee-tossed it out the window into a field. The police and FBI searched the field until they found the dismembered . . . um, member. It was later reattached, and even later than that enlarged, as John Wayne Bobbitt launched a career as a porn star. Though Kotter had never censored photos before (we'd seen raped and mutilated women, and children against whom crimes had been committed that are too gruesome for me to name), on the Bobbitt day, there was what would now be called a "trigger warning."

"If you want to see the photo of John Wayne Bobbitt's detached penis," Kotter said, "stay after class, and I'll show you."

When class ended, it appeared that everyone was filing out.

"Really?" I said to the former professional football player. "You can handle everything else we've seen but not John Wayne Bobbitt's penis?"

"Hell no!" He laughed and went out with the rest of them.

The photo was interesting in that the stump was jagged and ragged. It hadn't been a clean cut; Lorena had to have sawed away at it for a while.

"How could he have slept through that?" I asked Kotter. It was just the two of us; everyone else was off to the lunchroom.

"Drugs. Alcohol." His head was tilted as we looked down at the photo together. And then he looked up at me and said, "Doesn't it bother you to look?"

"No," I said. "It's a body part of a particular person who suffered at the hands of another particular person: his wife. It's not a threat to the nation. Nothing really to be horrified about."

"You've got a strong gut, Schandler," Kotter said, smiling. It was a rare and small compliment, but I was very happy to hear it.

The second time I was called in an office to be disciplined was even more baffling than the first. I knew it couldn't be my suit, as I'd been wearing my baggy clown sack (I looked like David Byrne from the Talking Heads) ever since I'd made Bart uncomfortable. This time Ted called me in. I'd come to think of him as Junior Bart, as he seemed to mirror Bart in everything but the New York accent and the gold chain.

"Schandler, sit," Ted ordered.

I sat and looked at him, waiting.

"Are you wondering why you're here?"

"Of course."

"Can you tell that the other members of your class have a problem with you?"

"Yes." As far as I could see, the group was simply mirroring our three supervisors. Taken as a microcosm for world history, it seemed amazing to me that humanity has ever been able to rise above the lowest common denominator.

"Do you know what that problem is exactly?"

"Can't say that I do." Surely it would do no good to point out that I was singled out on the first day as a traitor to our country because I was in the CIA on September 11. Also, I often wondered if my security clearance, which was higher than that of everyone at Quantico, had anything to do with my instructors' dislike for me.

"It's your constant yakking about the CIA," Ted said.

I never spoke of the CIA. There was nothing to say. Everything I did was undercover. Bart, though, brought it up often and worked it into each lesson. ("We don't shoot from the hip, Schandler, not like you did in the CIA!")

"Okay," I said.

"The biggest problem is that no one believes you. They don't understand why you'd make up this crazy story about being some overseas spy. Everyone thinks you're full of it."

Once again, I was speechless. Confused. The FBI had done background checks on me. They interviewed my supervisors at the CIA. They visited me in my office at Langley!

I said nothing.

"Could you just walk me through exactly what you did in the CIA?" Ted's face was still. Sincere. I could only presume he was serious.

"Sir." I paused. "Isn't it all in my file?"

"I suppose so." Ted nodded. "Let me look into it and see if I can get some clarity for the group."

"Okay," I said. "And maybe you should ask Bart—"

"Special Agent Smith."

"So sorry," I said. "Maybe you should ask Special Agent Smith to stop referring to my career in the CIA during lessons. I certainly have no interest in talking about it."

"Schandler, how 'bout we start with making sure you really are who you say you are?" Ted nodded. "Let's put your little make-believe identity to rest."

"Okay." I smiled. It was a painful smile, aching in the corners. "Thank you, sir."

"We good? You going to keep quiet about this?" Ted stuck his hand out to shake mine.

"Quiet about this meeting?" Again I was confused.

"About your alleged spy career," Ted said. His hand was still out, he was grinning. And then he winked. "What's the truth now? You can tell me. Were you a secretary there or something?"

I reached out, shook Ted's hand, and said, "Yeah, something like that, sir. I'm sure it's in my file."

"Good, good," Ted said. "You're excused now."

I rushed out of there, slightly breathless from the exchange. It seemed so ludicrous, I couldn't imagine even telling this story to someone. So I didn't. I held it in my head and thought about it over and over and over again, imagining what I would have said had I felt free enough to speak the truth. Also, I couldn't stop thinking about what I could do in the future to help girls and women, people like me, to find the power to say what's real and true, to speak up in the face of injustices.

About three days later, I was eating lunch alone when Ted approached my table. My stomach dropped. What was it now? Did I need to testify as to the natural color of my hair?

"Schandler," Ted barked.

"Yes, sir?" I put down my fork and waited.

"We looked through your files, and then we sent an agent over to Langley to get to the bottom of this."

"Yes, sir." I was waiting.

"Amazingly, you really were a goddamned spy." He nodded enthusiastically, as if I should have been thrilled to find out that I hadn't been a secretary after all. In truth, I would have been proud to have been a secretary or administrative assistant at the CIA. They work just as hard as everyone else and deserve as much respect as the operatives and analysts. "I still won't mention it," I said.

"Good then." Ted gave me a thumbs up. "We're on the same page."

Oh no we weren't. And we never would be. In fact, we couldn't have been farther apart, especially when my grandfather, Jack Davis, died while I was at Quantico.

A couple weeks earlier, Jay had lost a grandparent. He flew home to his family in Montana, returned five days later, and quickly crammed and caught up—as far as I knew—on his classes. So I wasn't worried about being able to take time off after my mother called and told me that my grandfather had fallen in the tub and hit his head; he was in a coma and failing.

From the moment I heard about the accident, I didn't put away my cell phone and even slept with it under my pillow. It was three in the morning when my mother next called to tell me my grandfather had passed away. I whispered into the phone; still Brandy woke up. I could sense her watching me even when I threw the covers over my head so I could speak with my mother privately. When we hung up, I stayed like that, under the covers, and cried as quietly as I could. There wasn't a big moment in my life that my grandpa hadn't witnessed in some form. The idea that he would no longer be around was so jarring that I almost couldn't process it. We'd had an entirely uncomplicated relationship. There was none of the fear and anxiety that my parents could project, and none of the difficulties of friends and boyfriends. It was all love, laughter, and joy. No one had been more proud of my career in the CIA than my grandpa. (He had been thrilled when I had told him about visiting his family's neighborhood overseas on my first CIA trip.) Oddly, the only thing my grandfather had been less than enthusiastic about was the FBI. I'd been meaning to sit down with him and find out why it didn't excite him the way the CIA had. Unfortunately, I never had the chance.

I didn't sleep for the rest of the night. Once the sun was up and breakfast had been served, I went to find Marge, Ted, or Bart. If I took a flight to Los Angeles that night, Thursday, I could make the Friday funeral. I'd only miss a single day of training as I'd be back on Sunday.

Bart was in his office, feet up on his desk, laughing on the phone. I waited in the doorway for a good five minutes. By the time Bart hung up, Marge and Ted had come down the hallway and entered Bart's office, too. Together, they felt like a firing squad.

"What can I do you for, Schandler?" Bart asked.

I'd been crying all night and morning. But in the face of these three my emotions went cold, and I was as dry and firm as hard-packed dirt.

"My grandfather passed last night. The funeral is tomorrow. I'd like to take a late-night flight home tonight so I can go to the funeral. I'll return Sunday and will only miss a day of training."

"Can't be done." Bart looked from Marge to Ted.

"Go home Saturday," Marge said.

"The funeral is tomorrow," I said.

"I doubt the funeral is tomorrow, if he just died last night." Ted cracked his knuckles; it reminded me of the *ba-ba-bum* drum taps after a talk-show host tells a joke.

"We're Jewish."

"Well, I'm Catholic," Ted said, "and I've never seen anyone buried less than five days after they pass."

"Jewish law says you have to bury your dead right away," I said.

"Does it now?" Bart dramatically nodded his head toward me. "And you're up on Jewish law?"

"No, not at all," I admitted. "I just know that people get buried right away."

"You can go Saturday," Bart said.

"Jay was gone five days for his grandfather." I had to point it out.

"You're not Jay," Marge said. "Are you?"

"No, ma'am." I held her gaze for a second. "But can you explain why Jay could leave for a funeral and I can't?"

"You're different," Bart said. "'Nuf said."

I looked at each of their faces. No one was going to crack open their heart, even slightly, and give me a break here. Without saying another word, I turned and left the room.

I missed the funeral, but I did get two days with my family to mourn one of the most important people in my life.

□ □ □

No one gets out of Quantico without having suffered in multiple ways. The final pain to be endured was being pepper sprayed directly in the eyes during the last week of academy training. Brandy, my chattering roommate, actively fretted over the coming pepper spray drill. Her husband had said it was the greatest pain he'd ever endured, and he—according to Brandy—was a guy who wouldn't even flinch if he were knifed in the eye.

"Bet you didn't get pepper sprayed as a CIA secretary!" Brandy laughed. I stayed silent. We were each in our beds, the lights were out.

A few seconds passed, and then Brandy said, "And no mascara tomorrow! Even if it's waterproof it can't hold up to the continuous tearing. And you'll be rubbing your eyes, too! You don't want to rub mascara flakes into your eyes and scratch your cornea. That hurts. Not as much as pepper spray, however. Remember: you will cry. I promise you. Not just tears, I mean cry. Like, wa-wa-wa-wa. That kind of cry."

"Do you think Betsy's blue eye shadow will hold up?" I was kidding. Who cared if Betsy's eye shadow held up?

Brandy gasped. "Oh no! Maybe she shouldn't wear the eye shadow tomorrow. And she definitely can't wear mascara. She's going to scratch her cornea! I'm going to tell her!"

Brandy got out of bed and then stuck her tiny feet into her giant fuzzy slippers that made a swooshy sound when she walked. Brandy skated out the door and down the hall to Betsy's room to warn her about mascara and eye shadow. Fortunately, she was gone long enough for the sudden quiet to lull me into a perfectly peaceful sleep.

The next morning we lined up on the blacktop. Bart held an orange punching bag, Ted and Marge held containers of pepper spray. The drill was this: Ted and Marge would spray you directly in the eyes. Once hit, you'd go to the punching bag and battle it as best you could. After 30 seconds or so, the person behind you in line would try to remove your orange dummy gun from the holster, and you would fight him or her. If you lost that fight, you had to do the whole drill all over again. If you won, you were excused to the showers, where you shed and bagged all your clothes to be washed immediately. In the shower, you'd rinse your face, eyes open, in cold water as long as you could stand it. The showers were closed to all other classes as the pepper spray was so potent that just brushing against the clothing of someone who'd been hit could cause distress.

A guy named Gus went first. He was a blue-eyed, stocky guy who walked with widely bowed legs, like he was wearing a diaper. Gus hit on me the first night of the academy, uttering some line about training pals with benefits. I turned him down immediately, as did most of the other women in our group. Brandy seemed impressed by Gus, however, and frequently spoke about him and his feats of strength. I didn't want to know how deep their friendship went; the idea of the two of them together seemed like a movie so awful I wouldn't even watch it while I was folding laundry. Still, I felt bad when Gus bent over his knees, spitting and blubbering in pain. We all cheered him on as he blindly fisted his way to the punching bag and then flailed his arms like a crying madman as the former football player, laughing, tried to disarm him.

One by one it was the same story. Blinding pain. Endless snot, tears, and spitting, as I presume the pepper spray went in people's mouths, or maybe it went down their sinuses and was coming out everywhere. One guy collapsed to his knees and started dry heaving. The crowd backed away in a big circle. Nothing came out, and he blustered his way to the bag, fighting and crying. I didn't care what any of these people had said or done to me. This looked agonizing, and I was going to support them through it.

And then it was my turn.

I stood and faced the nozzles, my eyes wide open. Ted

sprayed from where he already stood; Marge took a couple steps forward so she could get a straight shot into my eyes. I felt it cold and wet on my face and in my eyes.

But nothing hurt. The group was weakly clapping. Yes, they cheered for me.

Still, there was no pain. I glanced at Marge and then turned and ran to the punching bag. Bart, who was holding the bag, screamed something about everyone in the CIA being "pussies" and this was the test of a real American hero. I barely listened; my brain was spinning as I tried to figure out why I felt nothing. Tasted nothing. I wasn't even sniffing or spitting.

A guy named Tony came up behind me and tried to take my gun. I turned, looked him in the eye, and whacked his hands away multiple times, then I kicked at him as well. When it was over, I glanced at Marge and Ted, who had their heads tilted together. They were talking while their hard, beady eyes stayed trained on me. Before they could say anything, I ran, as if I were being chased, to the locker room.

When I got there, Betsy, without eye shadow, was on her knees, blindly feeling around. I bent down and picked her up.

"Oh my god, oh my god," she was crying, actually crying. "How could they do this to us?! I've never been in so much pain in my life and I CAN'T SEE! What if it doesn't go away? What if I'm blind?!"

I could see fine. I helped Betsy off with her clothes, walked her to the shower, and turned on the cold water.

As each of the other women came in, I helped them undress and get to the shower. They were in so much pain, they didn't seem able to take in that I felt nothing. Not the slightest sting.

I took off my clothes anyway. After a leisurely shower, I dressed in the uniform I'd placed in the locker room before the exercise.

Four of the five other women were talking continuously about the hysterical pain, their tears, and the amount of snot that had come out of their noses.

Josie sat with them on the locker-room bench, nodding, agreeing, and repeatedly blowing her nose. She wouldn't have been able to insert a word if she'd wanted to.

Brandy looked up at me. "Tracy, seriously, wasn't that the most agonizing thing you've ever experienced? I mean, that was worse than a knife in your eye, right?"

"Absolutely," I said, and left before there were further questions.

Late that night I Googled: *immune to pepper spray*. It's rare, but it exists. Some people just don't feel it. But there was no way I was going to let anyone in the FBI in on my tiny little secret superpower.

□ □ □

Sometime in the middle of training, we were handed slips of paper that listed the FBI offices in the nation with openings. Sitting in a classroom, we ranked our choices one through ten to indicate where we'd like to be placed. If you put Los Angeles, San Francisco, or New York, you were pretty much guaranteed to get it as those offices always needed more people. Also, most agents didn't want to go to those three cities because of the high cost of living. I put Los Angeles as my first choice; I wanted to be near my family.

A couple of months after we'd ranked our choices, everyone was assembled alphabetically in that same classroom and then called up to the podium, one by one, to be handed an envelope with the information about the office and squad to which we were each assigned. The envelope was opened right then, on the stage, and the results read aloud to the group. People who got their first choice usually hooted, or cheered, or pumped a fist in the air. It was a highly charged, highly emotional gathering that was, for most people, happy.

I was one of the last ones to come up and receive my envelope. I took it from Bart and opened it. It said *Los Angeles Field Office, Santa Ana Resident Agency.*

"Los Angeles!" I said, and waved my arms, smiling.

This was better than I'd hoped as Santa Ana, a city in Los Angeles County, was only ten minutes from my parents. The fact that I was being sent to a resident agency was odd, though. Usually only experienced agents were sent to resident agencies, as they were small units, less supervised but highly active.

Once the class was dismissed, I approached Bart at the front of the room.

"Can I ask you something?" I asked.

Bart tilted his head, eyes rolled toward the ceiling with impatience.

"I can come back another time," I said.

"Schandler, do you know why I'm irritated with you right now?" Bart straightened his head and looked me in the eye.

"Hmmm, can't say that I do." It was anyone's guess. Maybe my teeth were too white and he had issues with the glare.

"Your cheering over Los Angeles was in poor taste considering not everyone got their first choice." Bart nodded once, as if to add force to his words.

"I'm so sorry," I said. Most people got their first choice. And most cheered much louder than I had.

"Think about other people, will you?" Bart said.

"Yes, sir." I looked down at my envelope. "Can you just tell me why I got a residence agency? Do you know what I'll be doing there?"

Bart picked up his binder, which was on the podium, closed it, and mumbled to me as he walked away, "You're in counterintelligence."

And that was the end of the conversation.

No one was in the room. I opened the envelope again and read the paper.

No matter what had gone down at Quantico, in the end, the FBI got it right by putting me in a resident agency in my hometown. I needed a safe home base where I could start the work of changing things for women within the FBI.

FOURTEEN

THE GIRL

Orange County, California
September 2004–August 2005

Hate speech is protected by the U.S. Constitution. But threatening to hang and kill people is not. I was doing a rotation in cybercrime when someone started making death threats on the internet to members of a black sorority. Immediately, I focused in on bringing down this idiot. In my mind, he was worse than any jihadist in al-Qaeda. Statistically, the person who makes these kinds of threats is most likely to be a white man who was born and raised in America. In other words, he'd have had many opportunities and ways to not become a hating, racist moron.

It didn't take long to find the address from which these messages were being sent. The guy I was then working with, Todd, and I drove to the house in my FBI-issued vehicle: a boat-sized white Buick with black-tinted windows. Like something a drug dealer might drive. Todd fiddled with the radio and talked about a movie he'd seen the night before with his girlfriend. She'd come into the office one day, and I was struck by how much she and Todd looked alike. Both had honey-colored hair, square jaws, and tight, compact bodies. So far, Todd had seemed like a fine partner in that he wasn't too bossy or controlling. Since he was more senior than me, Todd was in charge while I was learning the ways of cybercrime.

Our suspect's suburban bungalow was run-down, with

peeling paint and dead shrubs. The lawn was mowed, however, and the cement walkway appeared to have been swept. Also, there was a plastic floral wreath hanging on the front door. Someone was trying to make this feel like a happy home.

"I'm going to let you take the lead on this." A wooden toothpick bobbed in Todd's mouth as he spoke. I knocked on the door, and Todd tossed the toothpick into the dead shrubbery. I watched it sail.

"Wood. Biodegradable," he said.

A stout woman with neatly shorn brownish-gray hair opened the door. If you put an apron and a bonnet on her she might have looked like Old Mother Hubbard. She smiled, her eyes blinking. Todd and I, in suits, couldn't have looked very threatening. And she, with her cheeks folded into little cherry tomatoes and her crinkle-edged eyes, was probably not the white supremacist we were looking for. More likely she was the walk-sweeper and plastic wreath–hanger.

"Hello." Even her singsong voice was Mother Hubbard–like.

"Ma'am." I smiled and flashed the FBI badge that was clipped to my holster. "We're with the FBI. Can we ask you a few questions?"

"Oh!" Her shoulders rose a little, as if she were excited. "Is it about them?" She pointed her chin and eyes to the two-story stucco house across the street.

"May we come in?" I was still smiling at her. Once we were in the house, I could probe deeper. It's much harder to get someone out of your house than it is to dismiss them in the doorway.

"Of course." She leaned her head out a little, as if to see how many of us there were, and then stepped back and opened the door wide.

The inside of the house reflected the outside. Tidied, neatened, but run-down. Order above aesthetics.

She sat on the floral sofa, and I sat on the chair beside her.

Todd remained standing, his body positioned where the living room and hall met. If anyone wanted to run, they'd have to go out a window.

"Do you live alone?" I asked.

Mother Hubbard told me about her lovely nineteen-year-old son, whom she called A.J. He worked at a Quiznos sandwich shop and always helped around the house when asked.

I explained that threatening emails were being sent to a black sorority and that I had traced the server to a computer in her house.

Mother Hubbard brought a hand to her mouth. She looked genuinely surprised.

"No!" she exclaimed. "It couldn't be A.J. A.J. would never do something like that. He loves all people! He even mows the lawn of, you know, those people across the street."

I sensed that I didn't want to know what she had against the neighbors across the street, so I didn't ask.

"Has he fallen in with some new friends lately? People who might influence him?"

"I swear to you on my Bible," Mother Hubbard said. "My son would never, ever do anything as awful as that!" Her eyes were glassy, as if she were about to cry with sincerity.

"Do you mind if we take a look at his room?" I asked.

Mother Hubbard walked Todd and me down the short hallway. The thin hollow door had a patch mark in the middle where maybe it had been punched through and then repaired. She opened the door. I walked in, and Todd remained in the doorway with Mother Hubbard behind him. Hanging over the tightly made bed (one of Mrs. Hubbard's morning chores, I presumed) was a giant Nazi flag: bright red, with a white circle, the center of which had a ruler-sharp, black swastika.

Todd and I looked at each other. I glanced back toward Mother Hubbard, who flashed a closed-mouth smile at me. She was either one of the dumbest people I'd ever met or one of the most cunning.

"Is A.J. at work now?" I asked.

"Yes, he'll be there until three thirty," she said.

"Is it the Quiznos next to the Shell station?" Todd asked.

"Yes, it is," Mother Hubbard said.

I drove fast, as I was worried A.J.'s mother would tip him off before we got there.

"Well, that was a devoted woman," I said.

Todd did his singsong imitation of her voice and said, "Not my son! My son would NEVER do something like that!"

I pulled up as close to the front door as I could get.

"Why don't you go in and get him to talk to us out here?" Todd said. "No reason to make a scene at work."

I got out of the car and looked back at Todd. Why not make a scene at work? The guy was posting statements online saying he wanted to hang black sorority women. A scene at work seemed like an underwhelming response to the gravity of his actions.

Todd waved his hand as if to shoo me in. He got out of the car, and I stepped into the Quiznos. It wasn't hard to pick out A.J. with his blond, closely shorn hair; neckline acne; and stooped shoulders. He was working with an older woman and a girl who couldn't have been older than sixteen. There was a line at the counter. I walked to the front of the line where the young woman was ringing up a sandwich, flashed my badge, and asked if she could send A.J. out to speak to me.

The woman's mouth dropped open. She finished the transaction. Then she turned around and said to A.J., who was putting a layer of meat on 12 inches of bread, "Uh, you need to go outside and talk to this lady right now."

A.J. looked over at me. I flashed the badge. The other customers, strangely, all focused on choosing their ingredients and didn't seem to notice. A.J.'s face reddened from the neck up, like a rising elevator of blood. He abandoned the sandwich and came outside. Todd nodded toward A.J., and the three of us went around the corner so we were at the side of the building, alone. A.J.'s shoulders were even more stooped now. He was taller than both of us, skinny as a piece of licorice.

Todd lifted his hand, thumb up and pointer finger out, making the shape of a gun. He waved that hand in front of A.J.'s face and gave him a stern, angry lecture. Anyone watching this would have thought he was a furious father laying into his kid. But the situation, as I saw it, called for much more than an older man giving a young man the what-for. This kid should have been arrested. And charged. We knew from his posts, and from my research, that he was a lone wolf in his crimes. So we wouldn't have gotten a chain of white supremacists out of him. But still. A finger wagging? This did not sit well with me.

Back in the car I was silent. Enraged. I felt like I'd fallen into the position of the obedient wife who let her husband mete out the punishment he felt was right for the occasion.

"You don't think we should have arrested him?" I finally said, just as we were pulling into the rooftop parking lot of our small office.

"So he could go to prison and learn how to be a real criminal?" Todd got out of the car and waited for me.

"He already is a real criminal," I said. At this point my anger had turned inward. I wished I could have a do-over so I could arrest A.J. myself; let Todd try to unarrest him!

"You keep watching him," Todd said. "I guarantee he'll shut it down."

It seemed to me Todd couldn't guarantee anything of the sort. Yes, I'd keep watching A.J. And Mother Hubbard, too, that sly, plump woman who loved her son. And, maybe, I'd keep an eye on Todd as well.

Todd had no problem arresting the next suspects we

approached just a couple of weeks later. At five in the morning, Todd and I met at a Starbucks a few blocks from the suspects' house. The single Starbucks employee, a sleepy-eyed boy, opened the door, let us in, and poured me my venti dark roast with no room for milk or sugar. Within a few minutes, the 12 other agents we had called for backup filed in as well. Everyone had on a bulletproof vest with an FBI windbreaker over it. I got a second cup of coffee while the others lined up for their first. Armed with caffeine and Glocks, we huddled around a table so that Todd could debrief the group. No one else was in the shop. The employee was trying to do the work of filling napkin dispensers and wiping down tables, but he was having a hard time keeping his eyes off us. Todd only spoke when the employee was behind the counter, out of hearing distance.

The couple we were going to pick up was illegally downloading and then selling theatrical release movies. They lived in a neighborhood of large, two-story, three-car-garage homes. We didn't expect them to have firearms or to shoot at us, but you never know when one's fortune is at stake and prison looms. Hence the vests, the extra bodies, the methodical planning of the takedown.

At 6:00 a.m. exactly, we were in our positions surrounding the house. Every window and door was within sight or reach of an armed agent. Todd and I were at the front door. He knocked, and then we both turned to our sides, out of the range of gunfire if it were to explode through the frosted glass.

There was no explosion. Instead, a shirtless, middle-aged man who had more hair on his belly than on his head opened the door and looked out.

Todd flashed his badge, did the talking, and detained him while I went to find the wife.

She was in the bedroom, standing at the end of the bed in a white cotton nightgown. Her hair was a tangled nest around her head, the way most long hair is after a full night of sleep. The woman's belly jutted out. I had seen her in social media photos all over the internet, and we'd staked out the house, too, so I'd seen her through the windows. I'd even watched her getting in and out of her car. Fully dressed in fashionable swing dresses and drapey tops over leggings, she had hidden this pregnancy beautifully.

I flashed my badge, announced my reason for being there, and then recited the Miranda warning as I handcuffed her. The woman stood, wobbling slightly.

"You've got the wrong people," she said quietly. "We didn't do it. I didn't do it."

"I'm going to have to pat your belly to make sure it's just your belly," I said.

She was tearing up. "It's a girl."

Her belly was hard, taut, and there was a small shifting, a kick, as I ran my hand over it.

"Did you feel that?" she asked.

"Yeah." I had to smile.

And then she started fluttering her eyelids, as if she might pass out. I sat her on the bed and called to a guy named Jose, who was in the hallway outside the bedroom. He leaned his head in.

"Can you stay with her while I get her some orange juice or something?"

Jose came in, and I went to the kitchen. Large, sunny, and white, it was like something out of an ad in a home magazine. There was an open bag of bagels on the cutting board. I took a knife from the holder, sawed one in half, and then went to the fridge to find cream cheese. It was exactly where I keep it: in the butter shelf, a tub of the easily spreadable, fluffy stuff.

There was no orange juice, so I poured a glass of water and took that and the bagel, wrapped in a paper towel, into the bedroom.

Jose stood by as I re-cuffed the woman so her hands were in

front of her, allowing her to eat the bagel. We both watched as she ate, teared up, sniffed, and took another bite. Occasionally she muttered, "It wasn't me. I swear."

Later that day I visited Todd at his desk.

"Hey," I said, and I waited for him to look up from his paperwork.

"Hey." He finally made eye contact, his pen poised above the papers.

"I'd appreciate it if you didn't put me only with women— or the people you think are harmless—during these arrests. I'm perfectly capable of dealing with the bad guys. I mean, I've dealt with the worst." After what had gone down at Quantico, I wasn't about to bring up the CIA and the fact that I'd debriefed some of the most notorious terrorists the world has ever known.

"Alcoholic dad?" Todd asked.

"No, not at all," I said.

"Okay. Whatever." Todd shrugged and looked back at his papers.

The next time we barged into a cozy domestic scene like that was when we went after a plastic surgeon for insurance fraud. Essentially, he was giving breast jobs to women and charging the insurance companies for lumpectomies or other noncosmetic procedures.

It was early morning again. As we swooped into the house, his wife screamed over and over again, "I'm calling the police! I'm calling the police!" She waved her cell phone in the air and then dialed 9-1-1, punching the numbers with great drama and flair.

"Ma'am." I stood beside her.

She was panting into the phone as it rang. "I'm calling the police!" she shouted.

"Ma'am, we are the police." I scanned the room for Todd but couldn't find him. I wanted him to see that, once again, all the guys assumed that I'd be the person to attend to the woman and none of them had even glanced her way.

"I'm calling the police!" she shouted again, then looked at the phone, as someone at 9-1-1 had clearly answered. "Yes, there are people in our house!"

"The FBI," I said. "Tell the person that the FBI is in your house." Everyone, other than she and her husband, was wearing a windbreaker with FBI printed on the back in 3,000-point font.

"I want the police," she said to me. And then she shook her head, confused, and hung up the phone.

"Tracy," Todd called me over to where he stood with the plastic surgeon. The doctor had been half naked when we arrived and was now in a shirt, sweatpants, and even a pair of shoes.

"You want to take this over?" Todd seemed to finally understand that I wanted in on the big action, the challenges.

I cuffed the doctor and read him his rights. Then I led him to the backseat of my car so I could take him to the federal courthouse.

The entire ride there, the plastic surgeon blathered out everything he'd been doing, how it worked and how much money he'd made doing it. He blamed the insurance companies, the current administration, and the cost of malpractice insurance for his wrongdoing. It was everyone's fault but his, he claimed, as he went through his history of bilking the system. I wondered how anyone this dumb could have ever made it through medical school. Did he think I was just a driver? I had Mirandized him! I was in a bulletproof vest and carrying a gun. Everything he said to me would be written up as soon as I got to my desk.

I didn't interrupt. I simply repeated the facts he gave me in my head so I could commit them to memory.

And I drove as slowly as possible.

□ □ □

There were three tracks of ongoing work for the duration of my time at the FBI. The first was going through the cases of Jeannie, who was about to retire. Jeannie, who showed up late and left early, seemed to have simply abandoned her work. None of her cases were closed. And none were actively open. Going through her files meant that I'd read through each case—often five inches thick with papers—and follow up on every lead, every suspect, every witness, and every victim. This could take anywhere from several hours to several weeks. Usually it took a couple weeks. All of it was work Jeannie should have done herself, continuously. Sometimes, as I was sorting through her piles of unfinished business, I imagined Jeannie in her home. I'd pegged her as a hoarder, unable to throw anything away, deeming every ATM receipt, every recyclable water bottle, every newspaper, every Amazon box, every sheet of bubble wrap, every take-out pizza flier as having potential value one day. She'd have to buy red Solo party cups and paper plates because the sink was so overflowing with dirty dishes that there was no access to running water.

The paperwork mess Jeannie had created in the office—the mess I confronted alone—would take longer to sort through than the cluttered home I'd imagined for her.

One day, I paused at the open office door of the special agent in charge of our resident office. He was a nice guy who had the permanent squint-eyed scowl of a football coach in the middle of a game.

"Sir," I said, smiling as was my habit when I was nervous, "so, I'm wondering why Jeannie doesn't just do her own paperwork, or why someone else didn't start in on it earlier?" There was no one else in this small office who had been busied with such non-urgent business.

"Last one in." The special agent shrugged.

But I wasn't the last one in. I was only the last *woman* in. Two men had started at the same time as me. One, Darren, was already deep into cybercrime. The other, Bruce, was rarely in the office, as he was busy infiltrating himself into the gang wars of Los Angeles.

I did work off and on with Bruce in gang crime and sometimes sat in an office and listened to tapped phones. Most of the gang members were too smart to give much information on the phone, so the bulk of what I heard was domestic chores: picking up cream on the way home and did Jesse prefer briefs or trunks because Louise was going to Target after work and would pick some up. Oh, and don't forget toilet paper!

When I saw that Bruce had a gang tattoo chart, I made a copy, put it on my desk, and quickly committed it to memory. It's a fascinating art form; like hieroglyphics, the tattoos represent history, affiliation, and goals. The facial ones were of particular interest to me, the most common being an open or closed teardrop falling from an eye. Some teardrops represent prison time, some represent a murder having been committed, and some an attempted murder. Many of these gang boys were so young, I worried about how they'd ever get their tattoos removed if they were to change their minds.

Often my gang assignment was to sit within view of a gang house and record who was coming and going. I'd count the kids and note what everyone's schedule was. These guys did have guns and they would shoot, so doing a raid took a team of agents strategically entering the home in a way that none of the kids would be hurt. The most difficult bust of this sort was when we raided a tiny two-bedroom bungalow where more than 20 people were living—15 of them skilled with firearms. There were three little kids in the house, all under the age of ten. Bruce, who was directing the team, gave me the job of containing the kids once we had entered. I know it sounds barbaric, but I had to flex-cuff them. I'd heard plenty of stories of brave little kids running out with their dad's gun and trying to shoot down the FBI. To them we were the bad guys. On Bruce's raid, I quickly hustled the three kids into the corner of a bedroom. Mattresses and blankets crisscrossed the floor, like a fort they had made for a slumber party. Once they were cuffed, I had them sit on a mattress facing me. No one cried. No one screamed. They just looked up at me, as if they were waiting to see what else the mean blond lady might do.

"Hey," I said to them, 'it's okay. You're going to be okay. No one's going to hurt you."

The largest of the kids nodded at me.

Once the house was secured and everyone had been cuffed and detained, Child Protective Services arrived to take care of the kids. I had a switchblade in the pocket of my cargo pants. When I pulled it out and let the blade spring forth, none of them even blinked. The smallest one said *cuchillo*, knife. They watched, quietly, as I sliced off their cuffs while praising them for being so good and cooperative. In my head, I was hoping that things would get better for them after this moment, that this—being detained by an FBI agent in their home—was the low point.

□ □ □

The longest case I worked on was one of the biggest counterintelligence cases to be cracked by the FBI. The suspect was a man named Chi Mak, who had emigrated from Hong Kong with his wife, Rebecca, in the seventies and was working for Power Paragon, a company that developed defense systems for the U.S. Navy. FBI agents had enough evidence to get a court-approved clearance to enter the Maks' house and put up hidden cameras as well as tap their phones and cars. Also, their garbage was intercepted before being dropped at the dump. Every week, that garbage was sorted and closely examined in an empty garage.

By me.

The simplicity and compact nature of the Maks' lives was interesting to me. Rebecca appeared to live in self-imposed exile. She hadn't learned English during her decades in California and never partook in the things that make most people happy: movies, museums, the beach, TV, shopping . . . Yes, the world is messed up now, but there really is so much joy to be had by simply walking out the door. Well, she did walk out the door, once a day for a quick, silent stroll around the neighborhood. Other than that, she only left the house with her husband, and mostly to do chores—wash the car and grocery shop. They did play tennis every Saturday, but to me it seemed like a physical education requirement rather than an act of pleasure. I could have been wrong, though. Maybe that was her hour of joy each week. In their home, the Maks were frequently companionably silent. When they did speak it was often about Chinese politics, Mao, and Chinese history. Those things are of great interest to me, too; I was a Chinese history minor in college. But, unfortunately, I was not assigned to read through the translated texts of their conversations.

The salary Mak earned was plenty for two people living in a modest home in Downey, California, but he and Rebecca lived as if they were subsisting on pennies and dimes found in the change slots of vending machines. They dressed in old clothes and never appeared to purchase anything other than groceries. Each Saturday, they went to the same hardware store, where they never bought anything. At first the FBI thought they went there to make a drop and pass off information. Eventually we figured out that they were there to drink the free coffee that was put out in the lumber aisle. Also, they ate off newspaper rather than plates. After their meals, they balled up the paper with the food scraps wrapped inside and threw it all away. This made their garbage easily identifiable for me. I always wondered if the newspaper plate was to save water, to save the cost of dish-washing detergent, or to save the time it took to wash dishes. Maybe it was all three.

Once a week, I put on my cargo pants, boots, and a long-sleeved t-shirt and drove to the garage where I sorted the trash. Wearing a mask and puncture-proof gloves, I opened the Maks' bags and dumped them on a tarp spread on the floor. It was like playing Where's Waldo?, except I wasn't sure what or who Waldo was. Other than the days I was trained to sort garbage, I was alone during this task, which allowed me to do it in a Zen way. With my mind cleared, I would tell myself that I wasn't looking for anything in particular, I was just looking carefully. To look for specific things eliminates the possibility of finding what you don't expect. Everything—every toilet paper tube, or travel brochure, or dietary change (what did it mean the one week they cooked a turkey breast in July?) was fair game for my scrutiny and piercing suspicions.

All printed matter and handwritten matter, usually in Chinese, was of particular interest. As Mak tended to rip up his papers, I often pulled out small squares, like postage stamps, and laid them out on a table. A woman named Fran went through the Chinese-language bits pulled from the trash and translated them. She didn't work in our office but was on this case to help decipher everything.

It was Fran who identified a tasking list from the sorted trash. Written in both Chinese and English, this list clearly identified classified materials that Mak was to supply to the Chinese government. It turned out Mak, the guy everyone at work said was friendly and helpful, had come to the United States solely to pass on classified military information. It was a career-long commitment. Though maybe not lifelong. The Maks owned two houses in China. It was presumed that once his undercover life was over, he and Rebecca would retire there. I couldn't help but wonder: if Mak, who was sixty-four at the time he was caught, had been able to retire with Rebecca in China, would they have continued to eat off newspaper?

Mak and Rebecca were both eventually convicted. Rebecca's charge of acting as an unregistered agent of a foreign government got her three years in prison and then deportation to

China. Mak is still serving his twenty-four-and-a-half-year sentence for conspiring to export U.S. military technology to China.

□ □ □

I did feel like I was being a productive member of society while I was in the FBI, and I'm proud of the work I did there. But throughout my time in the bureau, I couldn't help but note that my skills and talents weren't being properly utilized. I was *The Girl* in the eyes of the agency, and everything I was asked to do reflected that. When there was a misbehaving boy (A.J.), I was the girl-bride who stood by and watched while her husband doled out the punishment. (The words *wait till your father gets home* come to mind in that scenario.) When there were children involved, I was the girl who babysat. When there was a wife, daughter, or mother involved, I was the girl who would be their friend. With Jeannie, I was the girl who would act as her secretary, there to fix her messes and clear her name. And in the Chinese spy case, even though I was the most well-informed person in that office in Chinese history and politics, I was the girl who sorted the trash. The domestic worker. The cleaning lady. The maid.

If I were the only new person in the office, I might have bought the special agent's excuse of *last one in*. But there were Darren and Bruce, both of whom had entered when I did. I would have loved to have plunged deep into the cases they'd been assigned.

In high school, I had decided that I wanted to be a history teacher. I wanted to change the lives of young minds, to inspire them to think broader, deeper, and within a global and historical context. When I joined the CIA, I didn't stop wanting to do that—I just tucked it away while I challenged myself to take a harder road, to do the unexpected, to become someone I hadn't yet realized I could be. My experiences and my achievements in the CIA gave me a sense of myself and a confidence that I'd probably had as a young girl, but had lost during the years of being bullied. I didn't just learn about myself in the CIA. It was an immersive course that gave me a postgraduate-level education in politics, foreign policy, world history, and cultural history. I was dealing with the ugliness of terror and terrorists while surrounded by the great beauty of Muslim culture, art, and architecture. In the end, I gained greater tolerance and compassion for people who, on the surface, appear to be nothing like me.

As an FBI agent, I wanted to learn all I could about counterintelligence, I wanted to find new ways to keep our country safe, and I wanted to become more proficient, smarter—an expert in my field. But my time in the FBI didn't feed into that. I have since discovered that my experiences with the bureau aren't unique. Currently, there are a dozen women who have filed a complaint against the FBI with the Equal Employment Opportunity Commission. All these women claim to have been discriminated against at Quantico, and 7 of the 12 claim they suffered additional discrimination because of their race. None of this surprises me, and I expect that the more public their case becomes, the more women will speak up. Not that there are many to come forward; women still represent less than a fifth of working agents.

I did grow in the FBI, but not in the ways I had expected. Instead, I grew deeper into my true self, where I could see what I really wanted to do with my life and how I should proceed to get there. It became clear to me, as I was pulling greasy chicken bones from the Maks' soiled newspapers, that in order for things to truly be different, the balance of power would have to change.

When I was a kid, there was a bumper sticker on our refrigerator that said, *Stop bitching, start a revolution*. I read those words every day, 10 times a day, 20 times a day! They are embedded in my head just like the sound of my mother's voice. The FBI poured gasoline on a tiny flame that was burning in my heart. That flame blew up and encompassed me so that I could no longer ignore it. I had to stop bitching and start my revolution.

After 15 months, I quit the FBI.

THE REVOLUTION IS NOW

Dallas, Texas
Present Day

Projected on the screen at the front of the room, next to my desk, is a Hate Map. The top of the map says in bold sans serif type, "954 hate groups are currently operating in the U.S. Track them below with our Hate Map." The interactive map would be fun if it weren't so horrifying.

There's a passel of seventeen- and eighteen-year-old girls lying on pillows and blankets in the center of the room, staring up at the screen. The lights are out, the room is a perfect temperature, and everyone is comfortable, at ease. The topic for today is domestic terrorism.

Melia raises her hand. "How many neo-Nazi groups are there?"

I click on the pull-down menu that categorizes the variances of hate and then click on Neo-Nazi. "A hundred and twenty-two. That's the biggest increase of any hate group in the last couple years. Up 22 percent."

"More than the KKK?" Amity asks. Back at the pull-down menu, I click on the KKK. We all see that there are 77 chapters now, down 17.

"More than the KKK. But isn't the presence of only a single group enough for us to take action?"

"Yeah," Amity says.

"Can you click on just the hate groups in Dallas?" Harper asks.

I scroll over the map of the United States, down to Texas, and then click on Dallas. Circular symbols are clumped and layered. I click on each symbol so we can see which hate groups are in this city, their city, and my city, too, now. I can't help but note that the girls in the room, wearing their plaid skirts and white blazers, represent the target of every single hate group in the United States: African Americans, Jews, Muslims, immigrants, women, and LGBT.

"Consider the reading you've done this week," I say. "Look through the different groups on this map. Now ask yourself, *Is this terrorism? Are these groups equal? Do we feel stronger about some than others, and if so, why?*"

Immediately there's a cacophony of voices. It appears that everyone has an opinion.

We are in week seven of this class, which I have named Spycraft. The girls have read about the Oklahoma City bomber, events leading up to and following 9/11, the creation of ISIS, the hunt for bin Laden, and EIT (torture). They spent one month each extensively researching a different terrorist group (ISIS, Boko Haram, al-Qaeda, etc.). Unfortunately, no matter how many girls I have in the class, there are enough terrorist groups in the world for each to have her own. Each student wrote a threat assessment report on the group she was assigned, analyzing the likelihood and capabilities of that organization to deploy biological weapons, along with the statistical likelihood of where and when those weapons might be used. Every year, the reports have been so thorough, insightful, and intelligent that I have bound them into a binder, made multiple copies, and mailed them to the Department of Homeland Security and senators, particularly those who are on intelligence committees.

□ □ □

Going forward, my students will learn code cracking, "masked writing" (where the message one intends to send is camouflaged within a meaningless message), and how to get information out of someone who would rather die than speak. They will write a paper analyzing the current administration's policy on domestic terrorism; a paper analyzing the events of September 11 and proposing if, and how, those attacks could have been prevented; and a paper on the effective and ineffective ways to wage war today.

The work, the reading, the content of this class is heavy stuff. But in asking the girls to analyze it and to find solutions, they don't get overwhelmed or terrified of what they find. Rather, they become engaged and empowered.

"Mrs. Walder," Austen says, "will you click on the other cities in Texas so we can see who has the most hate groups?"

"I hope Dallas loses that one," I say, and I start clicking as the girls start talking. The opinions in this room are strong; these girls are fierce and outspoken. As I expect them to be. And they are respectful and kind to each other. As I also expect them to be. There is no tolerating bullies here.

□ □ □

In the fall of 2010, when I had just started teaching at this all-girls school, I felt I was firmly walking the track I'd set for myself after leaving the FBI and earning a graduate degree. I was a history teacher who planned to throw a lot of current events and politics onto her syllabi. It was the nine-year anniversary of September 11 that year when the headmistress came on the loudspeaker and asked that everyone sit in silence for one minute to remember the victims of the terror attacks. The girls of that class were freshmen; they'd been in kindergarten when the towers went down. I imagined it was one of the first vivid memories for each of them. I watched their faces: a couple of girls had closed their eyes, and then I noticed that one girl, Ruby, was crying. I motioned for her to follow me into the hall. No one was around and there was utter silence as the minute ticked down. It was only in the past summer that Ruby and her family had moved to Dallas from New York City.

"I was five years old and going to so many funerals," Ruby said, sobbing. I hugged her and couldn't help but cry, too.

That afternoon when I drove home, I thought about my work in the CIA following the 9/11 attacks. I had been swimming through a murky sea of guilt, driven and singularly focused on finding the perpetrators. But instead of seeing through swim goggles, my sights were streamlined into the vision of night goggles. It's a limited point of view that doesn't allow for peripheral vision, color other than green, nuances, or even the particular features on a face. Thinking of Ruby's experience of 9/11 helped me take off those night goggles. It put a face on a form and directed me toward a broader place of empathy where I could see the echoing effects of that act of terror and not just the terrorists and those they'd murdered. I understood then that my focus in teaching had to come from a broader place than my focus in the CIA. I needed to open up and turn toward the people whose lives were, and are, changed because of terrorism. I needed to examine things from the outside in, rather than from the constricted tunnel of undercover work.

That week, I wrote down my thoughts so I could clarify to myself what I wished to accomplish with my teaching. I decided that I wanted my students to fully grasp American politics and policies from a global perspective. I wanted them to understand the interconnectedness of the world—why a boy in Yemen who had only seen American soldiers once in his town at night might have ideas about Americans that could lead to destruction. I wanted them to understand how and where systems and policies work, and how, why, and where they don't work. I wanted to show the girls that the skills, intelligence, and perspective they have to offer *as women* are desperately needed in places like the

FBI, the CIA, the State Department, the Senate, and the White House. I wanted to inspire as many of them as possible to go out into the world and occupy positions of power so they could help shape and influence policy and action. And I wanted the results of their work, the aim of their work, not to be for the greater good of a few men, but for the greater good of humankind.

It seemed a lot to ask from my position as upper-school history teacher. And then I realized two things:

1. I could show them and tell them about my life before teaching. And,
2. I could teach a class that would specifically inspire them to pursue careers that would help change the tilt of the world, that would shut down hatred and crank up compassion.

Yeah, I had big goals. But I'm not afraid of big goals.

□ □ □

After class, I turn up the lights and remind the girls to get their tweets out this week. Another requirement for Spycraft is that they read the news every day from a major American newspaper and tweet one story a week that is of great interest to them. At the start of each class, we pull up the tweets that have been hashtagged for Spycraft and the tweeters explain the essence of the news they sent out. This Twitter thread is now a serious newsfeed that links former students, future students, and present students. It is a chain of relevant information collected, curated, and critiqued by women of all ages.

As they leave the room, the girls continue a raucous debate between those who think all hate crimes are forms of terror and those who think only hate groups that commit murder can be called terrorists. That alone, that the subject didn't immediately change to what's on TV or what they did over the weekend, gives me a flush across my skin that I can only describe as pride. One girl, Anna, has stayed in the room as she's in my next class, too. Anna goes to a desk, opens her computer, and starts typing. I toss pillows and blankets into one corner of the room.

Within a few minutes, the girls in my next class, Advanced Placement U.S. History, enter in pairs or alone. Some are talking, animated. Some appear to be lost in their thoughts. A couple of girls open their notebooks and start doing homework from their previous class. Anna is so caught up in whatever she's writing that she hasn't appeared to notice that her two best friends are sitting beside her with a third girl, braiding each other's hair. I walk behind Anna, glance over her shoulder, and see that she's working on her paper for Spycraft. From what I've seen in her this semester, she is as obsessed with politics and current events as I was at her age.

A few girls congregate in the corner of the room where snacks are kept. There are Cheez-Its, York Peppermint Patties, gummy things, pretzels, and granola bars. There's a carton of goldfish crackers bigger than a gallon jug of milk. A girl named Ava picks up the goldfish crackers and pours them directly into her mouth. I shoot her a look and she stops. They know I hate when they do that.

I return to my desk, where I keep framed photos of my young daughter and my husband. On a shelf near my desk are photos of me with some well-known politicians and me on the job in the CIA and the FBI. My t-shirts and baseball caps from the CIA and the FBI are hanging on the walls of the room. I put them up the semester I started teaching Spycraft. Also hanging on the wall is an American flag that has written in the stripes the names of every person killed on September 11.

A girl named Ellie runs into the room.

"You're not late," I say.

"I'm not?" She's so happy she runs to the corner and jumps into the giant pink pillow. It is an act that is familiar to me, as I remember throwing myself around like that. In fact, everything in this room is familiar; it's all a version of me. The pink cushions remind me of my pink beanbag chair in the Delta Gamma house. The snacks are like the snacks I hoarded in my drawer at Langley. And the t-shirts and photos are visual representations of everything that came out of that time.

"Mrs. Walder?" Anna says, and I look at her so she'll continue. "Can I ask you something not school related?"

"Of course," I say. The girls often ask about non-school-related things. They want to know if I wore disguises when I was undercover, if I've ever shot anyone, ever feared for my life, or ever seen a bomb go off.

"So, I'm thinking that when I'm done with college, I'll join the CIA. And, like, is there ever fun in the CIA? I mean, are people just dead serious all the time?"

"It's a serious job, and it's hard work, but there are smart people there, and many of them are loads of fun. I mean, you could work as a clown in the circus and not be a fun person, right?"

"Yeah, you're right," Anna says.

Anna's best friend, Bella, speaks up. "She wants to be just like you, Mrs. Walder."

"Don't tell her that!" Anna's embarrassed.

"But it's true," Bella says.

"You'll all be amazing going out and being yourselves," I say. And then I wonder, *What does it mean to be like me? What does someone like Anna think of when she says she wants to be like me?*

Late that afternoon I pick up my daughter from nursery school and turn all my focus on her. She is a small miracle, having started off as the single survivor from a crop of 13 embryos created by my husband and me. I had been on a run, clearing my mind from the stress of trying to make a baby after having had a hysterectomy, when the doctor called to say there was only one embryo that could be implanted in the surrogate. My first thought was, I really hope this is a girl because she is already showing how tough, strong, and determined she can be.

After a few minutes in the car, my daughter tunes me out, decides she will no longer answer my questions, and starts singing. Her voice is warbly and birdlike, sweet as sugar. *I'm a little teapot, short and stout . . .*

She sings the song over and over again until my thoughts drift back to my day at school, what went down, and what I need to prepare for tomorrow. And then I remember Anna, working on her Spycraft paper from the moment it was assigned. Anna, who imagines she wants to be like me. I wonder, if she had seen me dealing with my daughter's temper tantrum last night, or picking up after the dog who ate a shish kebab off the counter and got ill from it this morning, or using five minutes between classes to try and call the credit-card company but getting caught in the abyss of a robot telling me to press numbers, or grading papers today while shoving room-temperature pasta in my mouth in the faculty lunchroom, would she still want to be like me?

My daughter starts up once more, *I'm a little teapot . . .* I think about all the people I've been. There has always been *me* inside, but there have been different ways in which the inside *me* has come out. I was the floppy baby. The bullied girl. The reluctant Homecoming princess. All those selves are true and real, but I have rejected them as my identity.

My daughter sings louder, *When I get all steamed up, hear me shout! Tip me over and pour me out!* I glance at her in the rearview mirror and decide that I will choose to see myself, what I've done, and what I'm doing today through the most powerful lens, that of the young women who might want to follow in my place.

I am a Delta Gamma girl who joined the CIA, hunted down terrorists, and stopped WMD plots before they could kill. I am a California girl who joined the FBI and helped catch foreign spies on American soil. I am a teacher at an all-girls school, a woman who is daring to try to change the world.

I am armed with students.

I am armed with a daughter.

This is my revolution.

ACKNOWLEDGMENTS

Writing a book like this took more than just digging deep into my memory, journals, and datebooks. It took the kindness, understanding, generosity, and support of dozens of people.

My parents, Steve and Judy Schandler, have applauded everything from my first steps to my daughter's first steps. I want to thank them for this and for simply having the faith in my strength. Thank you to Bunny and Howard Walder, David and Rebekah Walder, Matt and Kat Schandler for your enduring love and support. My cousins Karen Glassman and Dina Litt have been my cheerleaders throughout this process; I know we will be cheering each other on for life.

Alexis and Kazzye are brilliant women without whom I could not have made it through some very difficult times. Everyone needs friends with whom she can feel safe, and Lisa Moloshok, Laura Hodge, and Alexis Willis have been that for me for many, many years.

For having the courage to go out and meet Osama bin Laden, I'd like to thank Peter Bergen. He inspired me to take on the fight against terrorism, and I imagine many others have been inspired as well. Thank you to Sarah Carlson for paving the way for me in the publication process and giving me such sound advice.

There are many people in the CIA who believed in my strengths when I was only learning to use them. These people can't be named for obvious reasons, but I hope they know who they are and know the depth of my gratitude.

The people of Macmillan and St. Martin's Press have worked so hard on this book with unending generosity and almost-unimaginable detail. I had no idea how much incredible work goes into actually making a book until I encountered Alan Bradshaw, Rima Weinberg, Meryl Levavi, Karen Lumley, Kevin Gilligan, Mark Lerner, Sara Beth Haring, Laura Clark, Rebecca Lang, Kathryn Hough, and Olga Grlic.

And I owe huge thanks in particular to Elisabeth Dyssegaard, who showed her faith in this book when it was nothing more than a proposal.

Laura Holstein, Ellen Pompeo, and all the creative powerhouses at Calamity Jane Productions, as well as Katie DiMento and Sarah Timberman of Timberman/Beverly Productions and Elizabeth Newman of CAA, must be thanked for their patience, faith, and endurance as they have waited for this book.

None of this would have been possible without my brilliant literary agent, Gail Hochman.

Huge thanks to Cheryl Hogue Smith, Ron Tanner, Geoff Becker, and Michael Downs for their insightful and wise feedback.

My students at the Hockaday School have taught me more than I ever could have imagined about hope, resilience, hard work, and the power to be a woman in a man's world. I hope this book makes them proud. You ladies inspire me every single day.

Thank you also to the History Department at the Hockaday School for being by my side throughout this process.

The Delta Gamma sorority is a place where I was able to find my power, and figure out who I am in this world. I will always be grateful for what my time in the sorority taught me.

Thank you also to the University of Southern California and Chapman University for giving me both an education and the resources to make good on that education.

None of this would have been possible without the creativity, support, love, and brilliance of Jessica Anya Blau. I believe I have a friend for life in you.

My grandparents are not around to read these pages, but I'd still like to thank them all for letting me know how loved I was. I'd especially like to thank my grandparents Jack and Gerry Davis, who never once doubted that I'd be the best "snoop" in the world.

Last, though certainly not least, I'd like to thank my husband, Ben Walder, who first suggested that I write this book. Instead of being intimidated by me, he is impressed. Instead of feeling diminished by my powers, he is emblazoned by them. He stood by my side and picked up the slack when I was absent in mind, body, and spirit while working on these pages. I will always be indebted to him for giving me the emotional space to embark on this intense and rewarding task.

Kent Barker Photography

TRACY WALDER is a former staff operations officer (SOO) at the CIA's counterterrorism center and a special agent at the FBI's Los Angeles field office specializing in Chinese counterintelligence operations. She now teaches global terrorism at the all-girls Ursuline Academy of Dallas and is an adjunct professor of domestic terrorism and criminal justice at Texas Christian University in Fort Worth. She is on the board of directors for Girl Security, a nonprofit, nonpartisan group that brings national security curriculum to girls in high school throughout the United States.